Sir Ken Robinson PhD is an internationally recognized leader in the development of creativity, innovation and human potential. He advises governments, corporations, education systems and some of the world's leading cultural organizations. The videos of his famous talks to the prestigious TED Conference have been watched by an estimated 300 million people in over 150 countries.

Lou Aronica is the author of two novels and co-author of several works of non-fiction, including *The Culture Code* (with Clotaire Rapaille) and *The Element*.

KEN ROBINSON
WITH LOU ARONICA

You, Your Child and School

Navigate Your Way to the Best Education

PENGUIN BOOKS

PENGUIN BOOKS

UK | USA | Canada | Ireland | Australia
India | New Zealand | South Africa

Penguin Books is part of the Penguin Random House group of companies
whose addresses can be found at global.penguinrandomhouse.com.

Printed and bound in Great Britain by Clays Ltd, Elcograf S.p.A.

A CIP catalogue record for this book is available from the British Library

ISBN: 978-0-141-98862-7

www.greenpenguin.co.uk

MIX
Paper from
responsible sources
FSC® C018179

Penguin Random House is committed to a
sustainable future for our business, our readers
and our planet. This book is made from Forest
Stewardship Council® certified paper.

To James and Kate with love

Acknowledgments

There's an old myth that the only question on an ancient Chinese Imperial Examination Paper was, "What do you know?" The candidate who gave the longest answer got the job. When I set out to write a book on education for parents, it felt a bit like that. Education covers so many issues and families are so different that it was a puzzle for a time to know what to say, short of everything I could think of. The answer, of course, was to focus on what I think matters most, and to admit that no discussion of these issues can be entirely free of personal values. Most of what I say here is rooted in research and professional experience and is as objective as I can make it. Some is naturally inflected by my own view of things. I trust it'll be clear which is which and why both are important.

Because education is such a sprawling field, and no one knows everything, I'm intensely grateful to all sorts of people whose advice I sought and who often put me right on matters of fact and steered me back onto solid ground when I was heading into a mire. As is the custom, I can't mention everyone, or I'd never be done, but I do have to mention the following, who gave me expert advice on specific issues: Lily Eskelsen Garcia, Laura Gross, Bob Morrison, Andy Hargreaves, David Price, Peter Gamwell, Hadley Ferguson, Richard Gerver, Pasi Sahlberg, Kate Robinson, Anthony Dunn, Jerry Mintz, Elliot Washor, James Robinson, Cynthia Campoy-Brophy, Mitchell Bass, Michelle Kinder, and Heather Bryant.

I owe special thanks to my writing partner, Lou Aronica, for being an expert sounding board as the book took shape and for taking on much of the initial research, interviews, and case studies, which form the bedrock of the book. Thanks are due as always to our literary agent Peter Miller, for his tireless enthusiasm for my work and his peerless expertise in promoting it. Thanks to Jodi Rose for managing my schedule and keeping people at bay when I most needed time to write. You wouldn't have this book in your hand at all if it weren't for the expert guidance of Kathryn Court, our outstanding publisher at Penguin Random House, and her terrific assistant, Victoria Savanh. Above all, I thank my wife and lifelong professional partner, Terry, for her constant belief and unrivaled support in all I do. Thank you. As always.

Contents

CHAPTER ONE

Get Your Bearings

If you're a parent of school-age children this book is for you. My aim is to help you get them the education they need to live productive, fulfilled lives. I've worked in education all my professional life. Along the way I've had countless conversations with parents about school. I'm a parent too and know firsthand that being a parent is a challenge as well as a pleasure. It gets more complicated when your children start school. Until then, you've been mainly responsible for their development and well-being. Now you entrust a major chunk of their waking hours to others, giving them enormous influence over your children's lives during their most formative years.

Seeing them go to school on that first day brings a suite of emotions. You hope they'll be excited about learning, make good friends, and be happy and inspired at school. At the same time, you probably feel a good deal of trepidation. School brings a whole new set of relationships. How will your children respond to their teachers? Will the school see what's special about them? What about the other parents and children? Will your child rise above the new social hurdles or trip over them? As your child heads into school for that first day, it's no wonder you feel a catch in your throat. You think things will never be the same. You're right.

Emma Robinson (no relation) is a teacher in England. She's also a parent and knows how it feels to leave your child at school on that very first day. She wrote a poem called "Dear Teacher," which has since been shared by thousands of other parents. Here's an extract:

> I know you're rather busy
> First day back, there's just no time
> A whole new class of little ones
> And this one here is mine.
>
> I'm sure you have things covered
> And have done this lots before
> But my boy is very little
> He hasn't long turned four.
>
> In his uniform this morning
> He looked so tall and steady
> But now beside your great big school
> I'm not quite sure he's ready.
>
> It seems like just a blink ago
> I first held him in my arms
> It's been my job to love, to teach
> To keep him safe from harm.
>
> I know as I give him one more kiss
> And watch him walk away,

That he'll never again be wholly mine
As he was before today.[1]

Parents have always worried about handing their children over, but these days they have even more on their minds about school. Many are exasperated about what's happening in education. They worry that there's far too much testing and stress at school. They feel that the curriculum has become too narrow because of cuts in important programs in the arts, sports, and outdoor activities. They're concerned that their children are not treated as individuals and that schools are failing to cultivate their curiosity, creativity, and personal talents. They're anxious about how many young people are being diagnosed with learning problems and being medicated to keep them focused. They worry about potential bullying and harassment. If they have children in high school, they worry about the rising costs of college and whether their children will be able to find a job whether they go to college or not. More than that, they often feel powerless as parents to do anything about it.

Anger and Anxiety

Recently, I asked people on Twitter and Facebook about their biggest concerns in educating their children. In less than an hour, hundreds of people from all over the world had posted responses. Bec, a young mother in the United States, spoke for many when she said that children's "strengths are not valued and their weaknesses are magnified. Their grades are more important than their sense of self." Kimmie, another mom, asked, "Will my children discover their true potential and be guided to a career that they love and are passionate about." Conchita wrote, "I have all sorts of worries about my two daughters. I feel the current system will not let them shine and my ten-year-old may not get what she needs to overcome her learning difficulties and anxiety."

Jon is worried that children "are gradually being taught to not enjoy learning: that it's somehow an arduous rite of passage we're all forced to go through with no solid reasoning. It's a constant battle to keep that spark of curiosity and delight about learning alive when the system packages it and sets narratives about education the way it does." Karin said, "Education is broken. There's too much pressure, too many tests, too many demands, too much assembly line. How can we reboot? How can we prepare our kids for a radically different life from the one the current system prepares them for?"

Carol was concerned that the "one-size-fits-all approach, orchestrated by individuals that have no business dictating educational policy, is producing students who have no ability to think for themselves and an absolute fear of failure." Another mother's top concern was whether schools "are teaching kids to be creative problem solvers. Testing doesn't teach kids to be versatile thinkers." Tracey points to a deep worry for many parents: "I'm most concerned with the fact that policy makers seem to have little regard for parent voices. The culture around parent voices is dismissive at best and those who make decisions about kids haven't a clue what actually goes on in classrooms." These are all legitimate anxieties, and if you share them, you're right to be worried.

Education is sometimes thought of as a preparation for what happens when your child leaves school—getting a good job or going on to higher education. There's a sense in which that's true, but childhood is not a rehearsal. Your children are living their lives now with their own feelings, thoughts, and relationships. Education has to engage with them in the here and now, just as you do as a parent. Who your children become and what they go on to do in the future has everything to do with the experiences they have in the present. If your children have a narrow education, they may not discover the talents and interests that could enrich their lives in the present and inspire their futures beyond school.

How Can This Book Help?

So how can this book help you? I hope it will be useful in three ways. The first is by looking at the sort of education your children need these days and how it relates to your roles as a parent. Parents often think their children need the same sort of education they had themselves. It depends on what sort of education they did have, but in general that's probably not true. The world is changing so quickly now that education has to change too. The second is by looking at the challenges you face in helping them get that education. Some of those challenges have to do with public policies for education and some more generally with the times we live in. The third is by looking at your options and power as a parent to overcome these challenges. Let me enter some caveats right away.

To begin with, this is not a manual on how to be a good parent. I wouldn't have the nerve. I'm sure this comes as a relief, because seemingly everyone else does. From Dr. Spock to the Tiger Moms, you already face a fire hose of advice on how to raise your children. Apart from the unsought advice of friends, relatives, and probably your children too about how to be a better parent, there are more than four million mom blogs on the Internet, and the online bookstores list more than 150,000 books in their parenting categories. I don't want to add to the clamor.

My wife and I have two grown children and many relatives and friends with children of their own. We've been through many of the challenges we discuss in this book. So has my writing partner, Lou Aronica, who has a large family of his own. We know that the pressures on parents never ease up. You're going to be worrying about your children and trying to help them navigate through their lives forever. Parenting is a lifetime assignment. It can be hard work at times, and the hours are dreadful. Consider this book to be a respite from some of that pressure. We're not living in some lofty alternate reality where everyone is having a better time than you. I do want to suggest some principles of parenting that are relevant to education and are widely supported by research and experience. In doing that, let me assure you that I'm here on the ground with you, and the advice I'm offering comes from the perspective of those who have missed the mark on more than one occasion.

This is not a good-schools guide either. I'm often asked about specific schools or systems and whether I'd recommend them. All schools are different. There are great and poor public schools, and great and poor charter, private, and alternative schools too. My answer is always to go and see the place for yourself and get a sense of whether it would work for you and your child. To do that, you do need some sense of what counts as a good school, and that's what we will be looking at.

I'm not suggesting a one-size-fits-all solution. On the contrary, no two children are the same and yours are no different, as it were. Your parenting choices and priorities are naturally affected by your own background and circumstances. If you're a single parent living in a poor neighborhood, your choices are different from someone with paid help living in a wealthy suburb. You may be in a position to choose the school you want for your child. Most parents are not. So you just have to play the hand you are dealt, right? Actually, no. You do have choices and we'll be looking at what they are.

Overall, my aim is to offer some advice on what counts as a good education and what you can do as a parent to make sure your children get one. That includes how to support them through the current education system, or outside it if you choose. These are some of the options available to all parents.

- You can enroll your child at the local school and leave the school to it.
- You can become active in your child's education by building relationships with his or her teachers and through the support you provide at home.
- You can become more involved in the general life of the school.
- You can influence school policy making through the local school board.
- You can campaign for change with other parents.
- You can look for another school.
- You can homeschool or unschool your child.
- You can use online learning opportunities.

If you do have a choice of schools, which one should you choose and why? If you don't, what should you expect from the school you have, and what can you do if it falls short? Deciding which way to go depends on several themes, which we'll look at in the chapters that follow. The first theme is your roles as a parent in general and how they relate to education. The second theme is the overall development of your children from birth to early adulthood. It's important to have a sense of this so you know the sorts of experiences you and the school should offer your child and why. The third theme is the importance of recognizing the talents, interests, and character of your own child. The fourth theme is why the education your children need now may be different from when you were at school. The fifth theme is why so many schools are not yet providing that sort of education and what you can do as a parent to change that.

Learning, Education, and School

Before we get into this, let me distinguish three terms, which will keep coming up: *learning*, *education*, and *school*.

- *Learning* is acquiring new skills and understanding.
- *Education* is an organized program of learning.
- *School* is a community of learners.

Children love to learn; they don't always enjoy education and some have big problems with school. Why is that?

Learning is natural for children. Babies learn at a prodigious pace. Take language. In their first twenty-four months or so, they go from being inarticulate bundles of cries and gurgles to being able to speak. It's a remarkable achievement and nobody, including you, "teaches" your child how to do it. You don't because you couldn't. Learning to speak is far too complicated. How do babies learn to speak? They have a natural capacity for it and they love to learn. How do they do it? By listening and by copying you and the others around them. You encourage them with your smiles and delight, and they encourage you with theirs. They learn to speak because they want to and they can. As they go through life, they'll pick up all sorts of other skills and knowledge just for the love of learning: because they want to and they can.

Education is a more organized approach to learning. It can be formal or informal, self-directed or organized by someone else. It might be at home, online, at work, or somewhere else. Peter Gray is a research professor of psychology at Boston College and author of *Free to Learn*. Children, he says, "are beautifully designed, by nature, to direct their own education. For most of human history, children educated themselves through observing, exploring, questioning, playing and participating. These educative instincts still work beautifully for children who are provided with conditions that allow them to flourish."[2]

A *school* is any community of people who come together to learn with and from each other. I was asked recently if I thought schools are still a good idea. I do, and the reason is that most of what we learn in our lives we learn with and from other people. Learning is as much a social as an individual process. The real question is what sort of schools help children learn best? Many young people are turned off education not because they don't want to learn but because the rituals and routines of conventional schooling get in the way.

For most of us, our main experience of formal education is grade school. What images does "school" bring to mind? If you think "high school," you may picture long corridors and lockers, classrooms full of desks with blackboards or whiteboards at the front, a hall with a stage, a gym, science labs, maybe a music room or art studio, and a sports field somewhere. What about what goes on there? You may think of separate subjects (some more important than others), fixed schedules, bells and buzzers, students streaming between rooms in age groups, assignments, tests, and after-school programs. What about preschool or elementary school? Whatever your own feelings about school, the fact is that if you passed out somewhere and woke up in one, you'd probably work out quickly where you were. Since the introduction of mass education in the nineteenth century, schools have become recognizable places that work in typical ways. Many of the rituals of schools are taken for granted largely because school has been like this for a long time. Not all schools are like this, and schools don't have to be this way at all. The fact that so many are is a matter of habit, not necessity. We'll be looking at different ways of doing school and at how the best schools create conditions in which young people enjoy learning and want to achieve at their highest levels. It's important that they do enjoy education, for them and for you.

What's It All For?

Starting as toddlers, most children in the United States spend around fourteen years in school, forty weeks a year, five days a week for an average of eight hours a day, counting homework. It adds up to around twenty-two thousand hours of schooling, not counting college. That's about the same amount of time that all the motorists in Switzerland spent last year in traffic jams. The Swiss are a patient people, but even so, that's a lot of time. This doesn't include the time you spend getting your children ready for school in the morning, dropping them off, picking them up, helping with homework, going to meetings and events, and all the hours you spend yourself in traffic jams as a result. What do you hope for from this huge investment of time and energy? Why are you educating your children in the first place? What do you expect that they and you will get from it?

In my experience, most parents want their children to learn about the world around them, develop their natural talents and interests, and acquire the skills and knowledge they'll need to become good citizens and make a decent living. These are reasonable expectations. We had them when our own children were going through school, and our parents did when we were young.

Whatever you want, what sort of education do you think they need? If you think a conventional academic education supported by perfect test scores is best, you may well be wrong. Even if you don't think that, many policy makers do and that's a problem. In my view they're wrong too.

All Change

One of the reasons you have to think differently about education these days is that the world your children are living in is so different from the one that you and your parents grew up in. We'll go into this in later chapters, but these are some of the headlines.

Families are changing. These days, only 60 percent of children in the United States live in families where their biological parents are married. The other 40 percent live in a variety of situations: with a single mother, with a single father, with grandparents, with parents of the same sex, in a blended family, or none of the above. There are similar trends in many other countries. By the way, in case you're wondering if you're a parent, let me clarify. Given these vast social changes, for our purposes, being a parent means fulfilling particular roles rather than being a specific blood relative. You may be the child's biological parent, maybe not. Whatever your situation, if you have a primary responsibility for the home care and well-being of a child, you are a parent.

Children are changing. Physically, young people are maturing younger than ever before, especially girls. They are facing huge social pressures from popular culture and social media. They are experiencing high levels of stress and anxiety, much of it related to pressures at school. They are becoming less healthy and more sedentary. For example, childhood obesity has more than doubled in the past thirty years and more than quadrupled in adolescents.

Work is changing. Digital technologies are disrupting many traditional job markets and creating whole new ones. It is almost impossible to predict what sorts of jobs today's students will be doing in five, ten, or fifteen years, assuming they have a job at all.

The whole world is changing. Let's face it, there are tumultuous changes sweeping the entire planet on every front: cultural, political, social, and environmental. Education has to take account of this if it's to help your children make their way, let alone flourish, in a world that's changing faster than ever.

Evidently, governments understand some of this and are hard at work in committee rooms and voting chambers trying to control what goes on in schools. Along the way, education has become a major political issue, and you and your children are in the crosshairs.

What's the Problem?

For over thirty years, governments everywhere have been pouring resources into attempts to reform education and raise standards in schools. Their motives are mainly economic. As digital technologies in particular have transformed international trade and employment, policy makers have recognized that high standards in education systems are vital to national prosperity and competitiveness. They're not wrong about that. The problems for you and your children lie in the strategies they've adopted to "improve" education. In many countries, there are four main ones: *STEM disciplines, testing and competition, academicism,* and *diversity and choice.* In some countries, notably the United States, there is a fifth: *profit.* At first glance, some of these reform strategies may seem to make sense. In practice, they've often backfired with worrying consequences for many young people and their families.

STEM Disciplines

As a parent, you want your children to do well in school, to get a good job that suits their talents and helps them become financially secure. Governments want something similar for the country, but they're not thinking about your child in particular; they're thinking about the workforce as a whole and of larger issues like gross national product. Consequently, they've put a particular emphasis on the STEM disciplines (science, technology, engineering, and mathematics) in schools in the evident belief that these alone are most important for economic growth and competitiveness. Their argument is that modern economies are largely driven by innovation in these disciplines, and there are good jobs to be had in them by those with the right qualifications.

The STEM disciplines are important in education, both in themselves and for economic reasons. But thriving economies are not created by scientists, engineers, and mathematicians alone. They depend on the talents of entrepreneurs, investors, and philanthropists; they also flourish through the work of designers, writers, artists, musicians, dancers, and performers. Apple is one of the most successful companies in the world. Its success has not been driven only by software engineers and coders, vital as they are, but by people in multiple disciplines: storytelling, music, film, marketing, sales, and many more.

Preoccupation with the STEM disciplines has led to reduced provision for arts and humanities programs in schools, which are just as important to the balanced development of your children and to the vitality of our communities and economies. It sends a misleading message to your children that if they're not at home in the STEM disciplines the world doesn't need them, when it really does.

In 2011, the Farkas Duffett Research Group (FDR) conducted a national survey of 1,000 third- to twelfth-grade public school teachers in the United States.[3] The aim was to gather information about teacher behavior and classroom practice. The survey asked teachers to provide details on what was happening in their classrooms and schools: how they were spending class time, how state testing was affecting their work, and which areas of the curriculum were getting more attention and which were getting less. According to most teachers, schools were narrowing the curriculum, shifting instructional time and resources toward math and language arts and away from art, music, foreign language, and social studies. All students appeared to be affected. The survey suggested that the curriculum was narrowing most in elementary schools.

Bob Morrison is the founder of Quadrant Research and a leading authority in the United States on the impact of public policies on provision for the arts in schools. He says that one of the things we're seeing across the board as a result of the intense focus on preparing students for tests is a decline in both field trips and assembly programs in the arts. When asked why, school administrators overwhelmingly cite too little time as the reason.[4]

Most of the teachers believed that a broad curriculum is essential for a good education. Most believed the state tests in math and language arts were driving the narrowing of the curriculum and that the testing regimen had caused deep changes in day-to-day teaching and in school culture. According to teachers, the focus on math and language arts at the expense of other disciplines has had other effects. Nine out of ten teachers said that when a discipline is included in the state's testing system, it's taken much more seriously in schools. Two out of three said it was easier to get money for technology and materials for disciplines that are tested.

Many educators and advocates of more balanced approaches

to education are campaigning to expand STEM to include A for the arts: STEAM. I'm delighted that they are. Schools should also make room for the humanities: so, SHTEAM? And what about physical education? You see the problem. The real answer is to have a properly conceived, acronym-free approach to children's education, and that's what we should all be pressing for.

Testing and Competition

Policy makers of all stripes emphasize the need to raise standards in schools. It's hard to argue with that ambition. Why would they lower them? The chosen method is usually the mass administration of standardized tests, often in the form of multiple-choice questionnaires. The answers are easily processed by optical scanners and generate streams of data, which can be readily compiled into comparative charts and league tables. Consistent with the focus on STEM disciplines, these tests are mainly in mathematics, science, and literacy.

High-stakes testing was meant to stimulate higher standards in education. Instead, it's become a dreary culture that's demoralizing students and teachers alike. In the 1980s, high school students in the United States could expect to take a few tests each year. I don't mean the occasional pop quiz; I mean tests that had consequences for whether they graduated from one grade to the next or from high school at all, or whether they went to college and which one. Now they can expect a seemingly endless series of tests, year in, year out, starting in elementary school (and sometimes even in kindergarten), with mounting pressures on them and you too. They're called high-stakes tests for a reason. Your child's test results are used to compile school league tables, which can affect how much teachers are paid, how well schools are funded, and if they are funded at all.

Anya Kamenetz is an American author and journalist with a special interest in education. She is also a parent. She confirms the enormous stakes in the annual standardized tests in public schools. The near universally despised bubble tests, she notes, "are now being used to decide the fates of not only individual students but also their teachers, schools, districts, and entire state education systems, even though these tests have little validity when applied this way." Because they determine eligibility for grade promotion and graduation, "this shuts out large numbers of minorities, the poor, English language learners, and the learning disabled. They double as performance metrics for teachers, who are being denied tenure and even fired, based on their student scores. Schools that fail to meet the test score targets are sanctioned, lose their leadership, or close; districts and states must give the tests and follow the rules or else lose billions of dollars in federal education aid."[5] As she says, these are only the most obvious, direct effects of testing; the indirect effects of judging our schools with these numbers ripple out through society.

The test obsession is making many public schools, "where nine out of ten American children are enrolled, into unhappy places. Benchmark, practice, field, and diagnostic exams are raising the total number of standardized tests up to 33 per year in some districts. Physical education, art, foreign languages, and other vital subjects are going on the block in favor of more drilling in core tested subjects. . . . In poor districts, teaching to the test is even more likely to replace the other activities that students desperately need."[6]

There's increased competition for places in particular schools and colleges, and test results are usually the basis of the decisions that selectors make. Students hear ever earlier that doing well on tests is the key to successful careers and that even one slipup could be disastrous. Perform badly on that test and you won't be able to take the AP class, and if you don't take that, the elite colleges won't take you seriously, and if you don't get accepted by one of those you can forget about getting a decent, well-paying job. There are so many things wrong with that message, but it's one that young people are getting every day from school, and often from their parents too.

The testing culture has soaked up billions of taxpayer dollars with no real improvement in standards. Achievement levels in math, science, and languages have hardly changed, and neither has the international ranking of the United States in these disciplines. In the meantime, they're causing enormous stress for you, your children, and their teachers. By the way, professionals in the sciences, technology, and mathematics are also worried that the testing culture is destroying students' enjoyment and creativity in their disciplines as well.

Academicism

The main focus in education reform is on raising standards in the sorts of academic abilities that are needed to earn degrees at universities. Governments are encouraging as many people as possible to go to college on the assumption that graduates have the qualities that business needs and are more employable than people who haven't been to college.

The strategy may seem well judged, but it's not working out as planned. A college degree is no longer a guarantee of a well-paid job, partly because so many people now have them. Businesspeople aren't happy either, and they're the people the politicians are trying to please. Given how rapidly the world of work is changing, employers say they need people who are adaptable and can turn their hands to new tasks and challenges; they need people who are creative and can come up with ideas for new products, services, and systems; and they need team players who can collaborate and work together. They complain that many young people with conventional academic qualifications are not adaptable, creative, or team players. Why should they be? They've spent years in education learning that the system of constant testing rewards conformity, compliance, and competition.

This is not just an American problem. In 2016, the World Economic Forum published a report on the key skills that workers around the world will need in 2020: creativity, flexibility, collaboration, teamwork, and emotional intelligence.[7] The forum recognized that these skills have to be cultivated in education. The emphasis on academic tests has also squeezed out vocational courses, which used to be a valuable route to employment for many young people whose interests and capacities are now neglected in schools.

Diversity and Choice

There was a time when parents just sent their children to the local public school. Now you may have a choice between public, private, charter, for-profit, virtual, magnet, and alternative schools, and homeschooling and unschooling. You may also live in a district that operates a voucher scheme. Schools that offer alternatives to public education may or may not be good in themselves, but the general effect of funding has been to drain resources from the public system and to reduce choice for many parents. Take voucher schemes, for example.

Several states in the United States and some countries in Europe have experimented with voucher systems. Rather than give public money to schools based on how many students they have, the money for each student is given to the parents in the form of a voucher. In theory, you can choose which school you want your child to attend and give that school the voucher. The idea is to encourage competition between schools on the assumption that it will raise standards overall by giving parents a choice. On the surface, these schemes are attractive to parents. If you don't like the look of your local public school, you can use your voucher to send your child to a different one or to a charter or private school. In practice, voucher schemes have not worked out that way.

Schools have a limited number of spaces, and popular schools soon become oversubscribed. When they have too many applicants, popular schools usually do one of two things. They set specific selection criteria—test scores or family characteristics, for example—that lengthen the odds of your child being accepted, or they hold a lottery, which you have as much chance of winning as anyone else. If you don't, you're probably left with that local public school, which may now have less money because its funds have been depleted by the voucher scheme.

Offering parents a choice of schools may seem admirable in itself. In practice, the choice is often more apparent than real.

Profit

Public education is expensive, and the governments of most countries accept that. Some, notably in the United States and in England, don't, and they seem committed to breaking up the public system by opening it up to corporate interests. Consequently, education has become a succulent market for big business, with chains of for-profit schools, new technology platforms, thousands of apps, and countless devices, all being sold for profit on the promise of better results, higher achievement, and greater success for your children. Evidently, one motive in government policies is to shift the burden of paying for education from the public purse to private enterprise. Doing that has the same result as in other profit-driven markets: profitable ventures succeed, unprofitable ones don't. The question for you is whether you believe that quality education can be guaranteed by price and whether you're comfortable with the nature of your own child's education being calculated on a private balance sheet.

Out of the Running

As they all swirl into each other, the maelstrom of these reform strategies is causing problems for many young people and their families, and parents, individually and collectively, can have important roles in pushing back against them. For some young people, they are especially damaging.

The numbers of young people who don't complete high school are worryingly high. In the United States, roughly one in five students who start ninth grade do not graduate from high school. To put that another way, every year over one million young people leave school before they graduate; that's about one every twenty-six seconds. The number is much higher in some regions and districts. The numbers vary from year to year, but as an indication of the range, an analysis published in 2016 found that the city of Albany, Oregon, had the lowest graduation rate in the nation, with just over 50 percent of high school students graduating on time. (The highest graduation rate was in Sherman-Denison, Texas, where almost 95 percent of students graduated from high school.)[8] I'm avoiding the term *dropout* here. Calling people dropouts suggests they failed the system. With numbers like this, it's probably more accurate to say that the system failed them.

Forget the percentages for a moment and think of real people—and their families. Every individual has his or her own reasons for leaving school before graduating. Poverty can be a factor. Another may be living with one parent who works several jobs and has little time to get involved in education. It's estimated that in the United States over one-third of young people under age eighteen live with a single parent. Teen pregnancy may be another reason. Only 40 percent of teen mothers finish high school. This pattern tends to repeat: only about two-thirds of children born to teen mothers go on to graduate from high school themselves.[9]

There's a host of other possible reasons for not graduating from high school, but for many who don't, a sense of pressure and boredom is certainly among them. If children are made to sit down all day doing low-grade clerical work for a test that seems pointless, it is no wonder they get anxious or tune out. So would you. Testing is one factor, but some students don't do as well as they might because of how schools typically work. It's not only the *what* of education that turns students off, but the *how*.

Room for Change

There are many wonderful schools and many great teachers working in them. There are also huge political pressures on them, which can distort the education that even the best of them want your children to have. If you don't like all this testing and its effects on your child—and you're right not to—it may comfort you to know that most educators don't like it either. Teachers are often compelled to spend countless hours on testing and test preparation at the expense of helping your children learn things that really matter. They feel overburdened and resent that their roles as professionals are reduced to tedious clerical work for the testing companies. Like you, they know that a child's education should not be a nerve-racking steeplechase of testing and grades, haunted with a constant fear of failure. Like you, they want to see change in schools and they are essential partners in helping to make it happen.

That said, some of the established routines of schools can cause their own problems. Many of them are habits, not mandates. For example, keeping children in strict age groups for every class can create obstacles for those who are moving faster or slower in particular areas of learning. Schools that scrap practical and vocational programs in favor of exclusively academic ones can alienate students whose real talents are putting ideas into practice. When schools are judged and funded on the basis of high-stakes test results in particular disciplines, it's understandable that they cut back in other areas. It's wrong, but understandable. Change the system and the problem often goes away.

The good news is that there is room for change, and many schools are changing. Parents' voices are one of the reasons for that. Some national systems are changing too, and the disruptive effects of new technologies are another reason for that. Education can be different, and as a parent you have more power than you may know in making that happen. The first step is to be clear what you hope for in educating your children in the first place and what sort of school will provide it.

Navigating Education

Let's dispense with a few myths. For one, a good school doesn't need to have a particular look. There is no correlation between the amount of ivy on a school's walls and the quality of education that goes on inside. There are schools on boats in Bangladesh, there's one in a cave in China, and a whole program of train platform schools is operating in India. Abo Elementary School in New Mexico is built entirely underground (it was founded during the height of fear of nuclear war), high-tech high schools in California have glass walls and ultra-modern design, and Philadelphia's School of the Future looks more like a museum than a place to attend ninth grade. The Florida Virtual School doesn't have any building at all, since all the classes are online. These are all real schools even if they don't look like something out of *Good Will Hunting*.

Another myth is that independent schools are automatically better than public schools. They are not. There are good schools of all types, and poor ones too. What are some of the factors to keep in mind?

Public Schools

Just over 90 percent of school-age children (50.4 million) in the United States attend public schools. These schools are paid for by taxpayers and are free to the students. Public schools are funded through the local school district based on how many students they have. They can raise supplementary funds through the community, especially parents. How well individual schools are funded depends on the district and the community. The district decides which schools students attend, usually the nearest one to where they live, and who teaches there. Unless they can show good reasons not to, public schools have to accept the students and teachers they're allocated. They also have to conform to state and federal mandates on education, including curriculum, testing, and staff certification. Good or bad, those policies have a major effect on how public schools work and on the education your children get.

The situation varies in other countries. In many countries, most young people go to public schools, but parents can choose between public schools, and teachers can apply to work in specific schools rather than being allocated to them. Public schools are funded according to standard formulas that take into account the specific needs of the schools, their students, and their communities. In most countries, public schools are by far the most important resource for education for most young people and their families.

Charter Schools

In the United States, charter schools are independently operated public schools. Charters usually specialize in some way: in particular disciplines or teaching methods or in serving specific cultural communities. Charter schools operate on some but not all federal and state mandates, which means that they have freer rein than regular public schools in what they teach and how they are run. The first charter school opened in Minnesota in 1992. They have been encouraged in other states, ostensibly to promote more innovation in public education. In 2016, there were just under six thousand charter schools in the United States, which were attended by about 5 percent of public school students.

Any group of people—educators, parents, community leaders, educational entrepreneurs, or others—can apply to set up a charter school. They have to draw up a "charter plan," setting out the principles on which the school will be based, how it will be governed, and how they will be held accountable. In most cases, charter schools operate under an agreement between the state and the school: increased autonomy in exchange for increased accountability. If the state approves the charter, it funds it like a regular public school on a per-student basis. One difference is that the district doesn't allocate the students; the school has to attract them. That means that popular charters also get to choose their students, which means that they are often selective. A common criticism is that selection gives charters an unfair advantage when comparisons of achievement are made with public schools. In themselves, charter schools are no better than traditional public schools. Some have been very successful and others less so.[10]

Private Schools

Private schools receive no public funding and are supported by fees and through other fund-raising activities. In 2016, the average cost of private school tuition in the United States was a little less than $10,000 per student, though it's much higher in certain regions of the country.[11] While private schools are generally better funded than most public schools, through fees and endowments, they too are facing financial challenges. Few parents can afford them, and with the spread of charter schools, for-profit chains of schools, and online education, some who can are being lured to less expensive options.

Private schools range in size, scope, and philosophies in every way, from faith-based to specialties in particular disciplines or methods of learning. They also vary enormously in quality and value for the students. Some have excellent facilities and small class sizes. Many private schools do not require their teachers to be state certified and often pay them less. Whatever their other benefits, some families favor particular private schools out of a sense of tradition and for the social opportunities they offer their children.

Robert Pianta is dean of the Curry School of Education at the University of Virginia. "Most of the 'effects' of private education," he says, "are attributable to families' influences on children as they grow up, and the family resources and decisions that place these children in private schools—not the private school per se."[12] If there is an effect of private schooling, it is mainly due to the influence of peers on learning and motivation, which tends to be greater in private school classrooms. When you take into account that private schools tend to have students from more privileged backgrounds, public schools often outperform them.[13]

Proprietary Schools

There are public, charter, and independent schools that are based on particular philosophies and methodologies. They include Montessori, Waldorf, Dalton, Big Picture, KIPP, Green Dot, and others. Parents often ask if I recommend them. I do strongly support some of these approaches and discuss some of them later. If you're considering enrolling your child in a proprietary school, my advice is always the same: take a close look at their general materials and then visit the school you have in mind. Any method can be practiced well or not so well. Meet the teachers, talk to other parents and the children, and get a feel for the school, to be as sure as you can that it's a good fit for you and your child.

The Greater Good

Allow me a short diversion on the importance of public schools. In most countries, mass systems of public education were developed in the nineteenth century. They grew up in the context of the Industrial Revolution, and one of the main reasons they developed was economic. Governments knew then that a suitably educated workforce was vital for the growth of the industrial economy.[14] The shape of the industrial workforce—mainly blue collar with a smaller professional class—is one reason why most education systems are organized as they are. Some pioneers of public education had other goals in mind too. They were social and cultural.

Lily Eskelsen Garcia is president of the National Education Association. She points to the wider purposes that some philanthropists and policy makers had in mind and especially to the vision of Horace Mann, who is widely seen as the father of American public schools. He was clear-eyed in seeing public education as a public good and a democratic necessity.

In the mid-1800s this Boston lawyer sees the hodgepodge of private schools, housewife tutors (dame schools) and sees the growing immigrant populations coming. He wonders how this new country is going to coalesce with such diverse languages; customs; religions. He starts to think of a place where they would all come together. It would be a physical place in the community; it would have professional teachers; it would by law welcome all children and people that would never sit next to each other in church or socialize in any way would all have started out as children sitting next to each other learning how to read. He believed that this was the system necessary for all Americans to see themselves as Americans.[15]

One of the core purposes of a publicly funded education system is to ensure equity of opportunity for all children, irrespective of their circumstances. Like equality, equity is—or should be—a basic principle in democratic societies. Equality is about affording all people the same rights and status. Equity is about recognizing that some people need more support, or resources, than others to benefit from those rights. The ideal of public education is to provide all young people with the opportunities they need to lead fulfilled lives and to contribute to the common good. That means helping those who need it most and not only helping ourselves. As parents, we naturally want the best schools for our own children, but as Eskelsen Garcia says, there are dangers for all of us "if there isn't a basic understanding that public education is a public good to serve the community's children and to serve the public functions of democracy."[16]

Charter schools, private schools, and for-profit schools may or may not offer soundly based education. I've visited many of them, and some do and some don't. I've met many dedicated and inspirational educators in the charter and private sectors. They do have more freedom to innovate than many public schools, which are bound tightly by state and federal mandates. Some do innovate and some don't. Most other countries—including those with high-performing education systems—do not promote private schools or charters as the United States does. They invest in the strength of their public school systems. One of the arguments for charter and private schools in the United States is that they can invigorate the public sector by spreading new ideas and practices. Maybe. Certainly their critics might feel better if they worked constructively with public schools rather than drained resources from them.

Either way, for most children and their families, public schools are their only opportunity in education.[17] Many public schools work in difficult circumstances and often in the teeth of harsh political headwinds. Creating the best conditions for public schools to do their best work is the real challenge of education reform. That will only be achieved by understanding, as Horace Mann and many other pioneers of public education did, that the education of our children is too important for the health of our democracies to be gambled with. We should see it as a public good, not just a personal one and not as a source of private profit. In education as everywhere these days, equality and equity are principles that need constant and vigorous protection.

Making the Change

My previous book was called *Creative Schools: Revolutionizing Education from the Ground Up*. It's about the need for radical changes in how our children are educated, if they're to meet the real challenges of living and working in the twenty-first century. It's also about how to bring those changes about, and it gives many examples of schools that are doing that. That book has a chapter for parents. The book you're holding now is a sequel to *Creative Schools* and is addressed specifically to you.[18]

As a parent, your overall role is to give your children the best shot at having a happy, productive life. One of the most important ways of achieving that is through education. Like most parents, you're probably most concerned about whether your children's education is helping them develop as the unique individuals you know them to be. Are they acquiring knowledge and information that's important and worthwhile? Are they learning valuable skills? Are they discovering their strengths and being helped in areas they may struggle with? Are they being stretched and enjoying the challenge? Are they growing in confidence and ability? These are some of the issues we'll be looking at and offering thoughts, leads, and resources to help you address.

If you're concerned about the nature or the quality of your children's education, you have three options: you can work for changes *within the current system*, particularly in your children's own school; you can press for changes *to the system*; or you can educate your children *outside the system*. You may be only interested in the education of your own children: if so, there are practical ways to become more actively engaged in it. You may be concerned with education more broadly; if so, there are practical ways of affecting policy on a broader level in your district, statewide, and nationally. You can act on your own or with others, including other parents, teachers, and advocacy groups and campaigns, which actively embrace parents' involvement in tackling education reform from a host of perspectives.

The best starting point for all of this is to understand what you want for your own children as they grow and develop, what they need from you as they do, and how education fits into the overall picture. Some parts of that picture are changing rapidly, and some are hardly changing at all. Knowing which is which is all part of the challenge and the pleasure of being a parent in the first place.

CHAPTER TWO

Know Your Role

When you think of parents and families, what's the first image that comes to your mind? It may be of Dad arriving home from work with the kids running down the stairs to greet him and Mom walking in from the kitchen to ask how his day was. Okay, maybe not; after all, it hasn't been 1956 for a long time. But it's still possible that when you think "parent," you imagine a married couple raising their biological offspring. That's still the majority setup in many countries, but only just. The classic nuclear family is not the norm in much of the world at this point.[1] The combinations are practically limitless.

In a piece in the *New York Times*, Pulitzer Prize–winning author Natalie Angier unveiled some startlingly different models of the changing American family, starting with the Burnses. Their blended family is "a sprawling, sometimes uneasy ensemble of two sharp-eyed sons from her two previous husbands, a daughter and son from his second marriage, ex-spouses with varying degrees of involvement, the partners of ex-spouses, the bemused in-laws and a kitten named Agnes that likes to sleep on computer keyboards." If the Burnses don't seem a typical American nuclear family, how about the Schulte-Waysers:

> . . . a merry band of two married dads, six kids and two dogs? Or the Indrakrishnans, a successful immigrant couple in Atlanta whose teenage daughter divides her time between prosaic homework and the precision footwork of ancient Hindu dance; the Glusacs of Los Angeles, with their two nearly grown children and their litany of middle-class challenges that seem like minor sagas; Ana Perez and Julian Hill of Harlem, unmarried and just getting by, but with Warren Buffett–size dreams for their three young children; and the alarming number of families with incarcerated parents, a sorry byproduct of America's status as the world's leading jailer.[2]

We get it. Lou's family consists of two children from a previous marriage, a daughter he and his wife had together, and a daughter they adopted from Ethiopia. Whatever your family situation, if you are a parent the role comes with a large suite of responsibilities. So what are they?

You may have seen the famous triangle composed by the psychologist Abraham Maslow, in which he identifies human beings' hierarchy of needs. We could just circle "all of the above." At the bottom of Maslow's pyramid are the physiological needs, the basic things that keep us alive. At the very least, you're responsible for providing these for your children. If you don't agree, there's not much point reading on. Next up on the pyramid is safety, the things that keep your children from harm. If this needs explaining too, you might consider professional help. The third level is love and belonging. Here's where things might get a bit more nuanced.

Level four is esteem, helping your children feel confident,

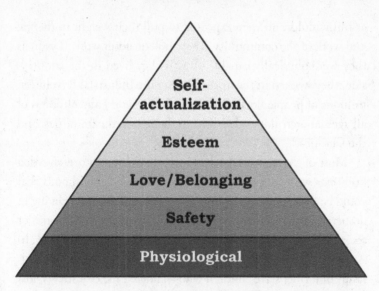

Maslow's Hierarchy of Human Needs

respected, and respectful of others. At the top of Maslow's pyramid is self-actualization. This is a curiously clinical term for a deeply human aspiration. It means finding our meaning and purpose in life and becoming the fulfilled person we all want to be. You have a role in this too for your children.

Take a moment to ask yourself if you agree that these are your roles as a parent. I do but not everyone does, and not everyone always did. There are big differences in how childhood and the roles of parents were seen in other times and still are in some cultures.

A (Very) Brief History of Childhood

Childhood as we think of it now is a relatively recent invention. It started to take shape in Europe and the United States in the late nineteenth century. Until then, young children were treated as mini adults and were expected to pull their weight in the life and work of the community. They took on adult work as soon as they were physically capable of it. If they lived in the country-side, they worked in the fields. During the Industrial Revolution millions of people flocked to the cities for work, and children of all ages labored alongside adults in the mines, the foundries, and the factories.[3]

Most of the new urban working classes lived in overcrowded buildings with little or no sanitation and in neighborhoods that could be brutal and unyielding. Countless children were living in desperate circumstances: uneducated, illiterate, with no health or social support systems and few prospects of improvement. In America, after Reconstruction in the South, they included thou-sands of former slave children who wandered the city streets, lost or orphaned.

Into this maelstrom came a mixed cast of social reformers, who created institutions, charities, and systems of social care that were aimed at relieving suffering, mitigating poverty, and saving the destitute. Many of these reformers took a special interest in the predicament of children. At the same time, educators and various other professional groups were becoming fascinated by new ideas about childhood itself.

In the late eighteenth century, the philosopher Jean Jacques Rousseau had published *Émile*, a powerful treatise on childhood and education. He pictured childhood as a time of purity and innocence that had to be cherished and protected from the cor-rupting influence of adult values. This conception of childhood resonated strongly with the Victorian social reformers and con-temporary pioneers in psychology, psychiatry, and pediatrics. Childhood came to be widely seen as a delicate period of devel-opment that needed to be guided and guarded by caring adults and professionals. It was around this time that systems of mass education began to take shape. As they did, institutionalized childhood became longer, taking in puberty, then adolescence, and eventually a previously undiscovered species: the teenager. When my father left school at age fourteen in 1928, he had no idea he was a teenager, nor did anyone else. Teenagers weren't invented until the 1950s.

The way we see our own roles as parents has a lot to do with how we think of childhood and what we think children can and can't do without our support. Our roles are also shaped by cultural values and beliefs. It's always tempting to think that how we see things in our own cultures is plain common sense. In parenting, as in most other areas of our lives, it often isn't. In Europe and North America, for example, it's taken for granted that boys and girls should have the same opportunities and be treated equally by their parents.[4] It doesn't always work out that way, but that's the assumption.

Parts of the Arab world have a different view. Culturally, women and girls are subservient to men and need the permission of their male guardians—father, husband, or brother—before making most decisions or engaging in particular activities. In parts of the Indian subcontinent, differences in parental attitudes toward sons and daughters can be extreme and fatal. Many expectant parents pray desperately for boys and feel punished if they have daughters. As a result, girls themselves are commonly punished, debased, and even killed by their own families, mainly for being girls.[5]

Being a Parent

Assuming that you do agree with the five roles implied by Maslow's hierarchy of needs, carrying them out as a parent is fraught with complexities.

Physiological Needs

Your first responsibility is to provide your child with the means of staying alive: food, water, and shelter. For many parents that's a constant anxiety in itself. Millions of families around the world struggle to get healthy food, clean water, or safe shelter. As populations continue to grow and climate change accelerates, securing these essentials may become more of a challenge for all of us.

The availability of these resources is one thing; affording them is another. Worldwide six hundred million children live in extreme poverty, and almost half the world, over three billion people, live on less than $2.50 a day.[6] This is not only a problem in the "developing" world. In the United States one in five children, about fourteen million, live below the poverty line, and another fourteen million live in families whose income is less than twice the poverty threshold. In 2015, more than forty-three million Americans lived in poverty, with $2.00 a day or less to spend before benefits. For them, putting food on the table is a daily struggle.

Nowadays, even better-off families can live on a financial knife's edge. As the wealth gap has widened, the once prosperous middle classes in America have been badly squeezed. If a family does have two parents, it's likely that both are working, and that one or both have two jobs. They're probably not doing that to get rich but to stay afloat financially. If there's only one breadwinner, it could well be the mother.

There are other pressures on parents in providing the raw essentials. Families are bombarded with mouthwatering images of cheap fast food and drinks. When money is tight and time is short, and it all tastes so good, it's easy to go with the flow and put it on the table. That may be understandable, but the result of eating so much cheap, processed food is a devastating health crisis across much of the developed world. So even level one on the pyramid can be a challenge for many parents.

Safety

Caring parents are naturally concerned about their children's physical safety, though as we've seen, cultural beliefs can lead them in the opposite direction. The instinct to protect the young runs deep through most of nature. There are exceptions. Tony Barthel is a mammal curator at the Smithsonian's National Zoo in Washington, D.C. He notes that dogs, cats, bears, reptiles, (and spiders, obviously) have all been implicated in killing and eating their young. It can seem unnatural, says Barthel, but there are reasons that have to do with resources.

Mammals can only nurse their infants if they're well nourished themselves. A mother bear, lioness, or wild dog that can't find enough to eat may eat her offspring instead. Typically, she'll only do this if her infant is sick or deformed. But in the wild, when food is scarce, mothers will take what they can get: "This nourishes her," says Barthel, and "has the added benefit of removing the carcass so there's nothing rotting in her den to attract predators."[7] This may seem brutal, but human parents are capable of drastic measures at the expense of their children. Okay, it's rare to eat them, but they do abandon them.

The surge of Victorian philanthropy came about partly because so many destitute parents gave up feeding their children and left them to the streets. Tragically, millions of children around the world still live in destitution. In some parts of the world, the daily struggle for food leads some parents to abandon their children too, or put them to work as beggars or even sell them knowingly or otherwise into forced labor. It's estimated that there are twenty-five million people living in slavery, a large percentage of whom are children. They include sex slaves, domestic and foreign slaves, fisheries and industrial slaves, and children forced into service in brutal military factions.[8]

Even in the best of circumstances, some parents are capable of terrible cruelty to their children. When we hear of them, most of us are sickened precisely because harming children goes so sharply against our instincts to protect them. And yet corporal punishment of children used to be routine in Western cultures, and still is in some. Until recently, parents in most countries including the United States were not only free but actively encouraged to discipline their children physically. "Spare the rod and spoil the child," they were told. Paddling, caning, and spanking were once common in American and European schools, and in some parts of the United States they still are.[9]

Even so, parents generally accept their responsibility for keeping their children safe from physical harm. As in all your roles, the trick is to find the right balance. Children need to feel safe, but they need to grow strong and independent too. Being overprotective as a parent has its own dangers. Safety is important; so too is enabling your child to become resilient and self-sufficient. It's another tightrope for caring parents to tread.

Love and Belonging

Helping your children feel loved and a sense of belonging is your job too. There are as many forms of love as there are families, and how you define and express love is subject to a lot of interpretation. Ancient philosophers distinguished four types of love: *eros*, romantic and sexual love; *agape*, universal love including love of nature and people in general; *philia*, friendship and goodwill to particular people; and *storge*, familial love and especially the love of parents for their children.[10]

Like other forms of love, parental love is not a fixed resource that you ration like food and water: so much for this child, so much for that. Having two children doesn't halve your love: it multiplies it. I grew up in Liverpool, England, in the 1950s and 1960s as one of seven children: six boys and one girl. It amazes me how my parents coped with so little money, few luxuries, and the constant specter of unemployment in a city ravaged by World War II. Whatever problems they were dealing with personally, and there were many,[11] they created an atmosphere of love and belonging for all of us at home. They didn't treat us all the same because we were all different. They did treat us equally and showed us every day that we all mattered to each other as a family.

Wherever there are siblings there is sibling rivalry, and we were no different. We vied for attention and formed temporary coalitions with each other to curry favor. Doubtless, it was exasperating at times for our parents, but we knew how far to push them and when to back off. At least, I think so. As a parent, you play a major part in shaping your children's emotional development and, as a result, in shaping their self-image and confidence. But it's not only you.

Esteem

How your children live their lives has much to do with how they value themselves and others. Self-esteem colors our sense of purpose, ambitions, and value and what we become in our lives. As children grow through puberty into adolescence they can be tormented by doubts about their appearance, relationships, talents, and potential. Confidence at any age can be fragile, but it's especially tender for the young.

Incidentally, there's much more, and sometimes much less, to cultivating your children's self-esteem than giving them endless praise. That approach can rebound badly and often does. Self-esteem doesn't come from being constantly hosed in uncritical praise. In their determination to make their children feel good about themselves, some parents compliment everything they do as a miraculous first for humanity. Every poem, painting, hit of the ball is greeted with "good job," "that's amazing," high fives, and squeals of delight. Appropriate praise and positive reinforcement from parents and teachers has a place in encouraging children to do well, but the currency rapidly inflates and can become worthless if it's not tempered with constructive criticism and a sense of proportion.

Children usually know when they've worked hard to do something well and if they're proud of it. If there are no standards or apparent room for improvement, self-esteem can meld into self-indulgence. It is important to cultivate children's self-esteem. It's just as important not to overdo it. It means taking an active role in their moral education, setting boundaries, and helping them learn how to make decisions.

Parents can affect their children's self-esteem in every way, and it's rarely a matter of direct cause and effect. Some children model themselves on their parents and aim to be just like them. They may be inspired to follow you into the same line of work or to emulate you in other ways. They may just feel proud of you as parents. Equally, they may decide that the last thing they want to do is walk in your footsteps and do a U-turn in work and lifestyle.

As they get older they are open to all sorts of influences from outside the home, which affect how they see and feel about themselves. In their preteens and teens, these influences may weigh more heavily on them than their families. At times it seems that everyone *but* you has some pull on your children. You can't control this, and trying too hard is likely to backfire. Even so, responsible parents know they have to monitor and support their children's emotional health even when the competition is fierce.

Self-Actualization

In my books *The Element* and *Finding Your Element*, I define the Element as the place where talent meets passion. Some people have a natural aptitude for mathematics, or the piano, or dance, or physics, or soccer. You name it. Being in your Element is partly to do with discovering what you're naturally good at. But being in your Element is more than being good at something. Plenty of people are good at things they don't enjoy. To be in your Element, you have to love it. When you do, you never work again. What may seem like hard work to others is a deep pleasure for you. Any activity you can think of can be one or the other, depending on who's doing it. Helping your children find their Element is part of them finding a sense of direction and purpose in their lives or, as Maslow puts it, becoming self-actualized. We all create our own lives. Helping your children develop what is inside them is the best guarantee of them creating a rewarding life in the world around them. It is for this reason too that a one-size-fits-all approach to education is wrong for you and your child.

It's difficult for any of us to "self-actualize" if our other needs are not being met; and it's especially here that your roles as a parent and those of education should line up. Education is an essential path to self-actualization, and making good decisions for and with your children about their education will go a long way toward helping them become the people they can be.

Real Life

Okay, that's the theory. In practice, it inevitably gets messy. Parenting is not a science, and if it's an art form, it's a rough-edged one. The patterns of love and belonging in families are complex and nuanced. Mothers and daughters, fathers and sons, daughters and fathers, and mothers and sons have different relationships with each other, and the plot can thicken at any moment. I know that firsthand. You need to treat your children fairly but not the same. You need to customize your relationship with each child. They respond to you as they do because of who they are and where they figure in the family: eldest, youngest, or somewhere in the middle. The same approach might have vastly different results depending on the child. It could yield gloriously happy results with one and create high drama with another.

Forget the kids for a moment. You have a life too. As a parent, you face pressures from every direction. You're probably juggling work life, parental life, marital life, and social life. Then, of course, most of us still parent in tandem. Even with all of the changes in family configurations, there's usually another parent in the mix—at least somewhere in the greater metropolitan area. If you're one of two (or more) parents, your relationships with your children are tied up in your relationships with each other and in theirs with both of you. How you and your co-parent relate to your children can deeply affect your relationships with each other, hopefully drawing you closer but potentially driving you apart.

Perhaps you're also watching what's happening in the lives of other parents via social media and wondering if and how you measure up. If so, you're probably feeling a grown-up version of the peer pressure you try to insulate your children against. A blogger called Foggy Mommy addressed parental peer pressure head on:

> I blame Pinterest for a lot of it. Like Martha Stewart's magazine, looking at all the cute and crafty ideas for everything from birthday party decorations to desserts to Elf on the Shelf setups has the (unintended?) consequence of feeling that you need to aspire to do them; and that if you don't, well, you're just not as crafty or smart or involved as the moms who do. I love looking at that stuff, I admit it. But I do feel inadequate afterwards, because I know I don't even have it in me to attempt any of it. It just exacerbates my mom guilt. And it's not just about making things. It's also about what family activities you do, what traditions you have, what social expectations exist for us as parents. And a lot of that is fueled by social media.[12]

These parental peer pressures have given rise to the model of the "super parent," who aims "to be a perfect parent, but they also want to be a great spouse, an excellent employee—all the while with a clean house, fit body, with a smile on their face."[13] Some parents feel like failures every time something goes wrong with their child. The bar has been set so high by an unaffiliated collective of parents no closer to attaining this ideal than the rest of us that feeling inadequate is nearly guaranteed. That said, it's important to understand the kind of parent you are and aim to be. I don't mean how good are you at being a parent; I mean how you go about your role as a parent. How you do that is shaped by your own personality and by your own experiences in being parented. All of these factors will blend into your personal parenting style. What does that mean?

Finding Your Parenting Style

In the early 1960s, psychologist Diana Baumrind undertook an extensive survey on the back of which she suggested three basic styles of parenting. Thirty years later, Eleanor Maccoby and John Martin built on her work and suggested a fourth. The four styles are authoritarian, authoritative, permissive, and uninvolved.

Authoritarian parents present a set of rules that their children have to follow, without offering either wiggle room or much explanation about why the rules exist. Breaking them often leads to harsh punishment. Authoritarian parents expect their children to follow their dictates without question. Research suggests that the children of authoritarian parents tend to be good at what they set out to do; they also tend to be unhappy and have problems socializing.

Authoritative parents have rules for their children as well, but they are more willing to explain the reasons behind them and to discuss and adapt them as circumstances dictate. When a child breaks a rule, it is seen as a teachable moment and a time for explanation rather than punishment. Authoritative parents expect their children to follow the guidelines they set for them but accept that these guidelines are a work in progress. The children of authoritative parents tend to be the happiest and most social, while standing a good chance at success at what they pursue.

Permissive parents tend to be very lenient on their children, often treating them as equals or friends. They lay out few rules and present their kids with few expectations. They prioritize nurturing and minimize consequences. The children of permissive parents often end up having problems with authority outside the home and tend not to do as well at school as others.

Uninvolved parents abstain from parenting as much as they can. They make sure that their kids have food and shelter, but they offer very little in terms of nurturing or guidance. For reasons that are probably obvious, the children of uninvolved parents tend to have issues with self-control, self-esteem, and happiness.[14]

At the far end of the spectrum are the so-called *helicopter parents*. The term was coined to describe parents who are obsessively protective of their children: supervising them continuously, always at their side to make sure they never fall down or get hurt, completing their homework assignments for them, and rushing to the school to complain at the first sign of any action by teachers or other students that might upset their self-esteem. Chris Meno, a psychologist at Indiana University, says, "When children aren't given the space to struggle through things on their own, they don't learn to problem-solve very well. They don't learn to be confident in their own abilities, and it can affect their self-esteem. The other problem with never having to struggle is that you never experience failure and can develop an overwhelming fear of failure and of disappointing others. Both the low self-confidence and the fear of failure can lead to depression or anxiety."[15]

It would be easy to look at this list and say, "Obviously, I need to be an authoritative parent." Certainly, the children of authoritative parents seem to have the best shot at a happy, successful life. There are a couple of things to keep in mind. One is that we're not all cut out for this sort of parenting. Maybe your own upbringing, your background, or circumstances make this unrealistic. Maybe your child has special needs that make authoritative parenting more of a challenge. Few of us are all of one thing all of the time, and neither are our children.

The favors you do, the latitude you offer, and the time you

spend with each child are not necessarily the same, and these relationships are going to change over time. Your children need you for different things at different points in their lives, and your approach needs to be flexible enough for you to be what they need when they need it. You don't get to use the same script over and over again; you're going to need to consider your approach to parenting afresh every time out. There are times when laying down the rules and insisting they're followed without question is the best course: for example, where young children and safety are concerned or where the explanation might cause unnecessary anxiety in your child.

I'd have a hard time advocating uninvolved or helicopter parenting, so we'll leave those out for now. Your natural parenting style is probably some combination of the other three. If you try too hard to go against your natural style as parent, there's a good chance that neither you nor your children will be the better for it. You also need to be aware of the parenting style of your co-parent(s) and how your child is affected by them too.

Finding Your Way

Being a parent can be the most enriching experience of your life. Even so, it's wise to accept that it can be a heartache and a headache too. It can be a constant struggle to get your children to behave as you think they should and take the path you think best: not only in their infancy but through the turbulence of toddlerhood and the turmoil of adolescence. You can love, encourage, and support them; set boundaries, chastise, admonish, and hope for the best. But as a parent you face all sorts of factors over which you have no direct control but which are relevant to your role.

For better or for worse, you will have an indelible influence on them, but you can't control their souls or what they will do in the world. All you can hope to do is create the best conditions and opportunities for your children to grow. That's your role. Knowing your role is only half the equation; the other half is knowing your child.

CHAPTER THREE

Know Your Child

You know your child is different. You'd never mistake your own child for another one who lives down the street. We'll avoid snowflake analogies here, but the plain fact is that no child is the same as any other on the planet, or even in the same house. If you have two or more children, you know they weren't born as blank pages. They each have their own innate character, talents, and one-off personalities and are genetically destined to live their lives in different ways. Of course, some children look alike but their characters are unmistakably their own. What does that mean for how you educate them?

Who Are These People?

You've probably heard the "nature versus nurture" debate before. Are children shaped mainly by their genetic inheritance or by their cultural experiences? If you're a biological parent, you've made a major contribution to your child's genetic nature. She may have your eyes, your hair, and your intolerance for spicy food; your partner's nose, height, and tendency to sneeze in bright sunlight. She may also have your fascination with 1960s rock bands and your partner's aversion to mystery novels featuring cats. That's probably the nurture side at play. So which matters most for who your child is and may become?

The "naturists," so to speak, argue that our innate capacities and dispositions dictate the course of our lives: that our destiny is DNA. The "nurturists" (why not?) counter that we become who we are because of the environment in which we develop and what life throws at us. This debate has raged for years and I'm pleased to report that it seems to have ended in a tie. A recent landmark study tracked over fourteen million sets of twins in thirty-nine countries and examined more than seventeen thousand traits. It concluded that our genes contribute about 49 percent to whom we turn out to be, while our environment contributes about 51 percent.[1]

If that's so, give or take a percentage point, we shouldn't be talking about nature *versus* nurture but about the relationship *between* nature and nurture—and that relationship has major implications for education. What's unique about your child matters, and we'll come to that later. Before we do, let's talk about what all children have in common, because that matters too.

Born to Learn

Every newborn baby is a seething bundle of possibilities. When you look at a baby in the crib, what do you see? You may see a picture of innocence and dependency. Babies do seem helpless and in many ways they are, but they're evolving at a breathtaking pace. What you're really looking at is "the greatest mind that has ever existed, the most powerful learning machine in the universe."

The tiny fingers and mouth are exploration devices that probe the alien world around them with more precision than any Mars rover. The crumpled ears take a buzz of incomprehensible noise and flawlessly turn it into meaningful language. The wide eyes that sometimes seem to peer into your very soul actually do just that, deciphering your deepest feelings. The downy head surrounds a brain that is forming millions of new connections every day. That, at least, is what thirty years of scientific research have told us.[2]

From the moment they're born to the day they get their first paycheck, your children go through a miraculous metamorphosis. Providing they have the right nutrition, rest, and exercise, they change *physically* in size, strength, and appearance. They evolve *emotionally* as their brains and neural systems become more sophisticated. They develop *cognitively* as their knowledge and understanding of the world increases. They grow *socially* in their ability to relate to other people. And, hopefully, they develop *spiritually*, as they find meaning, purpose, and compassion in their lives.

It's one thing to distinguish these processes but it's misleading to separate them. Your children's development isn't organized in separate compartments. Their physical development affects their cognitive development, which is wrapped up in their social experiences, all of which interleaves with their feelings and emotions about themselves and the world around them. In the first months of life, babies cry uncontrollably when they feel uncomfortable or insecure, but their self-control increases as they become more experienced and coordinated. As toddlers they have more motor control over themselves and their environment (though they're called "toddlers" for a reason): they walk, they talk, and they perfect the art of pounding their fists on the floor and screaming if they don't get their way.

As school-age children, they hone their motor skills and have more mastery over their physical environments. Then puberty hits, their bodies and brain chemistry shoot off into previously uncharted territory, and you start treading softly past their bedroom doors. Hormones continue to flood adolescents' bodies, bringing overwhelming feelings about themselves and their relations with others. The mature ability to control emotions is related to the multiplying connections in the brain, especially in the prefrontal cortex, and in most young people, that takes until their mid- to late twenties. Finally, adulthood arrives, hopefully with a relative sense of equilibrium and control, at least until it's time for hip replacements.

Harvey Karp is a world-renowned pediatrician and the bestselling author of *The Happiest Toddler on the Block*. He makes a fascinating analogy between the early development of children and the historical evolution of our species. Between your children's first and fourth birthdays, he says, their rapid maturation resembles a superfast rerun of ancient human evolution. The landmark achievements that took our ancestors eons to master spring forth in our children over the space of just three years:

- Walking upright
- Skillful use of the hands and fingers
- Talking
- Juggling ideas (comparing/contrasting)
- Beginning to read[3]

Although some people still don't like to hear it, our nearest genetic relatives are chimpanzees. We share with them over 98 percent of the same genetic material, but that 2 percent sliver makes all the difference in what we can do and become in our lives.

Your children are born with immense capacities, and they continue to develop long after those of other species have plateaued. In their first two years, humans and chimpanzees seem to progress neck and neck. Just one year later, the human infant has outpaced the chimp in almost every way. The higher apes are intelligent, but even adult chimpanzees have only some of the mental abilities of a three- to four-year-old child. They can learn basic sign language and they have intricate social systems, but they can't produce speech as we do and they have no comparable capacities for higher-order reasoning and creativity.

Human beings have more sophisticated forms of intelligence than any other creatures on Earth. We're unique in our use of symbols to think and communicate, including language, mathematics, the sciences and the arts, and the myriad varieties of insight and innovation that flow from them. We have unparalleled powers of decision making, control of emotions, compassion, logic and reason, creativity, and critical judgment, all of which can increase as children grow and mature. What accounts for this huge developmental gap?

One factor is that we have longer childhoods than most species. For some, childhood is over in a virtual blink of the eye. The baby chimpanzee will grow up twice as fast as his human cousin. While your three-year-old is still stumbling around the bedroom and checking his toes, the infants of many other species are striking out on their own and taking care of business. One reason for that may be that our developing brains burn so much energy that there isn't enough left for the rest of our bodies to mature any faster.[4] The human brain is about three times the volume of those of other apes. An adult human brain weighs about three pounds, which is enormous in proportion to our bodies. Our large brains use about one-quarter of the nutrients that we eat and about a fifth of the oxygen we breathe.

Even more important is the size of the cerebral cortex, the crinkled outer layer of the brain, which is much denser in humans than in chimpanzees. The brain of a human baby has about 100 billion neurons and an infinite number of possible connections. As the baby grows and learns, these neurons connect in countless combinations through long fibers called axons. This complex web of connections facilitates your child's burgeoning mental powers. And then there's all that myelin.

Myelin is a white fatty substance that coats the axons and speeds up the electrical impulses that pass along them. It takes much longer to form in humans than in chimpanzees. It's hardly present at all in the newborn human brain; it develops slowly during childhood and continues throughout adolescence and into early adulthood. In chimpanzees, it is already well under way at birth and stops developing before puberty. The slower rate at which myelin forms in human brains may be important in forming the billions of neural connections, which are essential to the higher-order cognitive powers that are the hallmark of human intelligence.[5]

It's Child's Play

For children there are few things more serious than play. There is a direct correlation between active, novel play and increased brain activity and development, which facilitates creative and analytical thinking, problem-solving skills, the ability to collaborate and cooperate with others. We'll come back to the many benefits of "real play" in the next chapter. As we'll see in Chapter Four, they relate to the numerous ways in which physical exercise and being outdoors are essential to the healthy development of your children. Our long childhood allows us to learn language in a richer and more holistic way, to use play to gain critical social skills, and to learn from mistakes and failures.[6] We have more intricate social and cultural systems as a result. The prolonged development of the human brain also provides more opportunities for children's abilities to be shaped by their cultural experiences as they grow up.

All in all, we've traded our enormous intellectual potential for years of uneasy relationships with gravity and the inability to get our own milk from the fridge. It turns out to be a good deal. We may be slow to start, but then we accelerate past other species like a dragster. So next time your four-year-old is running rampant through a restaurant while you're trying to finish a plate of pasta, and it seems he'll never grow up, remind yourself that this long development process should eventually pay off.

The Long and Winding Road

We all know of precocious children who run ahead of the pack in some ways and of others who lag behind. But in general, children's development follows similar patterns. Scientists and scholars have tried to identify its various stages. One of the best known is Jean Piaget, who argued that there are four stages: *sensorimotor* (birth to age 2), *preoperational* (2 to 7), *concrete operational* (7 to 11), and *formal operational* (11 and up).

In the sensorimotor stage, children discover the relationship between their bodies and the world around them. They learn about object permanence, the understanding that something continues to exist even if it is not visible. During the preoperational stage, they begin to think of things symbolically and to make metaphorical connections between them. In the concrete operational stage, children begin to reason and to work things out in their minds rather than exclusively by doing. During the formal operational stage, they learn to use abstract concepts and begin to reason.[7] You can expect your children to go through some version of these stages at relatively predictable times, simply because they are children.[8] That's one of the effects of nature. What about nurture? If nurture has a slight edge over nature (about 2 percent, apparently), what gives it that edge?

Culture and Opportunity

Whatever their natural capacities, the environment children grow up in has a deep influence on how they develop: on what becomes of their natures.

Shamdeo was discovered in a forest in India in 1972. He was about four years old. He was found playing with wolf cubs and had sharpened teeth, long, hooked fingernails, and a refined talent for hunting chickens. He had no language and none of the social traits that we would normally associate with four-year-old boys. The authorities moved him to a facility where he eventually stopped eating raw meat, but he never learned to speak and gained only the bare rudiments of sign language.

Oxana Malaya was eight years old when she was found in a dog kennel in 1991 in Ukraine. Her alcoholic parents had left her outside one night when she was two, and Oxana wound up living with the dogs. When she was found, she walked on all fours, barked and snarled, and only remembered the words *yes* and *no*. She ultimately learned some form of communication and now works with farm animals in the hospital where she lives.

John Ssebunya's story has a happier ending than the first two, though it had an awful beginning. When he was three, John saw his father murder his mother, and the Ugandan child ran away into the jungle. There, he lived with monkeys for three years, during which he learned to climb trees and search for food. Perhaps because he wasn't in the wild as long as the others, John ultimately learned to readapt to human life. His verbal skills are limited, but he has developed a beautiful singing voice, which he used with the Pearl of Africa children's choir.[9]

Shamdeo, Oxana, and John are three examples of so-called feral children who grew up in isolation from other human beings. Over a hundred cases of such children have been reported; undoubtedly there are many more that have not been. These are extreme stories, but they shine a clear light on the effects of culture on all of us.

These effects are not always so easy to detect. Moving to a neighborhood with a tribal commitment to the local soccer team might not have as much impact on you as growing up with wolves, but it's only a matter of degree. Your children are not growing up in a cultural vacuum, and countless factors can influence their development, from your sister's decision to dump her fourth husband, to how often you have a family game night, to whether you're raised in a faith community (and which one), to whether you live in a gang-ridden urban sprawl or a vegan commune in the high desert. Some factors can be more influential than others. Let's look at two that are often attributed to nature but are also closely wrapped up in nurture.

Money Matters

Family income can have drastic effects on the achievements of children and young people, not only on what they can buy and do but on how they feel about their lives and prospects.

There are many causes of poverty. A company might go bankrupt and cause a financial crisis for its former employees. A recession can pitch an affluent family into a morass of unexpected debt.

Divorce or health issues can deprive a family of the main bread-winner. A family may have parents with low levels of education themselves. They may be unemployed or unemployable, through crime or indigence or both. The problems of low income can be compounded by other social problems: the family may live in a blighted neighborhood that suffers from other forms of depriva-tion or high rates of crime. Depending on the circumstances, pov-erty can be catastrophic for children.

Children in extreme poverty are six times as likely to be neglected or abused and are more likely to live in neighbor-hoods with risks to their physical safety. Children who live in poverty in their early years suffer more than children who experience it later. Young children who live in poverty for years on end tend to suffer most. Because of poor nutrition, children who grow up in poverty are twice as likely to be in poor health and have problems of physical development as those in families with good incomes. They may have lower birth weights and stunted growth. They're more prone to learning disabilities, spend fewer years in school, and have lower rates of high school completion. They may have emo-tional and behavioral problems and are three times as likely to experience teenage pregnancies.[10]

Poverty is not the children's fault. Even so, this cycle can become self-perpetuating. Children from poor backgrounds are more likely to have low levels of education and few qualifica-tions, to have lower earnings as adults, and to go on to rear their children in poorer environments as a result.[11] None of this is inevitable and most of us can think of exceptions to the trend, but the evidence is strong that family income can be a major factor in how children develop and what they achieve. It's just one example of the complex dance between nature and nurture. Another is evolving definitions of gender.

Will Boys Be Boys?

The question all expectant parents wonder about is whether they're having a girl or a boy. When the baby's born, it's one of the first questions that family and friends ask, and the legal question that the doctor or midwife has to answer. It may seem an easy call, but often enough it isn't. We tend to think of male and female as distinct categories with a sharp line between them. In practice, the line can be very blurred. There's a difference between sex, gender, and sexual orientation. Sex is about anatomy; gender is about identity; sexual orientation is about affinity. All three are related and more complicated than they seem. Let's look at sex first.

The intuitive way to check a baby's sex is to look at its genitals, but anatomically, sexual identity is more than you can see from the outside. There are at least four physical dimensions of sexuality: external organs, internal organs, chromosomes, and hormones. I don't need to tell you how external genitals of males and females are usually different. At least, I hope not. There are *internal organs* that normally differentiate them too. Girls usually have wombs and ovaries; boys have testicles. A female typically has XX *chromosomes*, and a male has XY. But they don't always. Some babies have the external genitals of a girl but no ovaries or womb. Externally, some babies look like boys but have female genes and female internal organs. Some have ambiguous genital structures and are classified as intersex, neither boys nor girls in the commonly understood sense. There are up to eight variations that blur the lines between male and female.[12]

Hormones matter too. In the early stages of pregnancy, the amount of testosterone in the mother's womb determines whether the same tissues in the fetus will form into a penis and scrotum, or labia and a vagina. As children grow, variations in hormonal levels affect both their physical and emotional development. Some baby girls have female genes but produce male hormones; some boys have male genes and produce female hormones. Because of all of this variety, Facebook has dropped the requirement for users to say whether they are either male or female. They can now choose among fifty-two possible options.

For the time being, at least doctors still have to describe newborns as either male or female. If the external genitalia are ambiguous, the decision is often based on whichever they and the family believe the child will grow up to identify with best. This can be a tortured choice. A child may have male genitalia and be raised as a boy but be female hormonally and in terms of self-identity.

Gender is more complicated than a person's physical sex. It is "the complex interrelationship between an individual's sex (gender biology), one's internal sense of self as male, female, both, or neither (gender identity) as well as one's outward presentations and behaviors (gender expression) related to that perception, including their gender role."[13] Together, the intersection of these three dimensions produces one's authentic sense of gender, both in how people experience their own gender and in how others perceive it. When the gender a person is assigned at birth is different from what they identify with later, they commonly suffer acute distress, a condition known as *gender dysphoria*. They face the constant torment of feeling and acting like a girl but being forced to behave and be treated as a boy, or vice versa. Variations in sexual identity, gender, and sexual orientation often provoke bullying and teasing in schools, especially during adolescence.

Another potential source of tension is how gender roles and stereotypes are reinforced in the home. Take the tendency to associate pink with girls and blue with boys. Up to age two most children, regardless of gender, seem to prefer blue. By age two, girls begin to show a preference for pink. This may be due to cultural influences: girls are often dressed in pink and given pink toys to play with.[14] Children also learn about behavior from the adults that surround them. In homes where gender stereotypes are rigidly defined, children who feel conflicted about their sexual identity may feel cornered into roles that jar with their natural sensibilities.

Your children are genetically similar to all other children, but they are also unique individuals. So what about your child in particular, and what can you do to nurture their particular talents and sensibilities?

Identify Your Child's Genius

When our son James was seven years old, my wife and I knew his school wasn't right for him and we started to look at others that might be a better fit. At the first one we visited, the head teacher spent fifteen minutes telling us how great the school was and then took James off to another room so that he could "assess" him. We assumed that this would take some time. It didn't. Ten minutes later, they were back. "Well," said the head teacher, "he's no genius, but we'd be happy to take him." Without conferring, we decided that he wouldn't have that chance.

It seemed outrageous that anyone, even an experienced head teacher, could make that judgment in less than ten minutes. What conception of ability, let alone genius, was he working with? How could he have discovered enough about James's interests, talents, strengths, and weaknesses in a brief chat and, presumably, a couple of standard tests? The fact that he felt confident to make that judgment on such scant evidence was enough for us to have no confidence in it—or him.

We also disagreed with his idea of genius. Whether our child or yours is a genius in the common sense of the term is not the issue here. There are mounting social pressures to prove as early as possible that your children have remarkable talents. The argument goes that if your kid hasn't established herself as a prodigy of some sort by age two, you could just about forget getting her into a good school and you might as well start preparing yourself for her minimum-wage career. That's preposterous and if you're feeling this pressure, please do everything you can to avoid laying it on your children. Not every child is going to invent a revolutionary technology, make a medical breakthrough, be a chess grand master, or write a song that lives forever. I'm using the term *genius* here in a more fundamental sense that goes beyond the iconic examples of Stephen Hawking, Maya Angelou, Steve Jobs, or Mozart.

Thomas Armstrong is executive director of the American Institute for Learning and Human Development. In *Awakening Genius in the Classroom*, he uses the term to mean "giving birth to one's joy."[15] *Genius* derives from Greek and Latin words that mean "to be born" or "to come into being." It is related to *genesis* and *genial*, which mean, among other things, "festive," "conducive to growth," "enlivening," and "jovial." This conception of *genius* resonates with my own long-held view that all children have great natural talents, and they all have them differently.

One of the deep problems in education, which should concern you as a parent, is the limited idea of intelligence that permeates school culture. Achievement in education is still largely based on a narrow conception of academic ability and the tendency to confuse that with intelligence in general. Academic ability involves particular sorts of verbal and mathematical reasoning, which is one reason why children in school spend so much time sitting down writing and calculating. Academic ability is important, but it's not the whole of intelligence. If it were, human culture would be far less interesting.

When education operates on a narrow idea of ability, all sorts of other abilities can go undiscovered. Your child may have many talents and interests that are not recognized in school, and you, your child, and the school may all conclude that he's not very smart, when the real problem is how narrowly "smart" is being defined. Once we recognize that all our kids are intelligent in a variety of ways, we can see that they have many different paths to fulfillment, not just one.

In at least three ways, human resources are like the Earth's natural resources.

Diversity

People's talents and interests are stunningly diverse, which is why human accomplishments are so breathtakingly multifarious. Think of the boundless variety of occupations, skills, knowledge, and achievements in the arts, sciences, technology, sports, architecture, crafts, business, politics, health care, agriculture, social care, and on and on. Harvard psychologist Howard Gardner identifies eight forms of intelligence:

- *Spatial:* The ability to conceptualize and manipulate large-scale spatial arrays (e.g., airplane pilot, sailor) or more local forms of space (e.g., architect, chess player)
- *Bodily-Kinesthetic:* The ability to use one's whole body, or parts of the body (like the hands or the mouth) to solve problems or create products (e.g., dancer)
- *Musical:* Sensitivity to rhythm, pitch, meter, tone, melody, and timbre. May entail the ability to sing, play musical instruments, or compose music (e.g., musical conductor)
- *Linguistic:* Sensitivity to the meaning of words, the order among words, and the sound, rhythms, inflections, and meter of words (e.g., poet)

- *Logical-Mathematical:* The capacity to conceptualize the logical relations among actions or symbols (e.g., mathematicians, scientists)
- *Interpersonal:* The ability to interact effectively with others. Sensitivity to others' moods, feelings, temperaments, and motivations (e.g., negotiator)
- *Intrapersonal:* Sensitivity to one's own feelings, goals, and anxieties, and the capacity to plan and act in light of one's own traits
- *Naturalistic:* The ability to make consequential distinctions in the world of nature, as, for example, between one plant and another, or one cloud formation and another (e.g., taxonomist)[16]

Psychologist Robert Sternberg argues that intelligence has three main components: *analytical*, the ability to make judgments and comparisons between things; *creative*, the ability to come up with new ideas or deal with unfamiliar situations; and *practical*, the ability to work within your environment and manage the world around you.[17] There are other theories, and they vary in the forms of intelligence they identify and how they distinguish them. They all acknowledge that there is no single form of intelligence, that we are intelligent in different ways and use our intelligences in combinations that are unique to us as individuals.

Discovery

Like the Earth's natural resources, human talents are often buried beneath the surface and need to be uncovered before we can use them. If you live where only one language is spoken, how would you know how many languages you could speak, given the opportunity? If you have never picked up a violin, or a microscope, a tenon saw, or a racquet, how would you know if you have a talent or passion for music, biology, carpentry, or tennis? Our children are always sending signals about who they are becoming. In the *Element* books, there are many examples of people who were drawn early in their lives to different sorts of activities. Sometimes their real talents were hiding in plain sight, even though their families and schools alike ignored them at the time. They include children who played endlessly with Lego then went on to become accomplished architects, obsessive doodlers who became celebrated cartoonists, "hyperactive" toddlers who became professional dancers or gymnasts, and quiet readers who became studious academics.

Development

There's a difference between capacities and abilities. Capacities are what we are born with; abilities are what they become when we discover and refine them. Plenty of people can't read or write, not because they have no capacity to do so but because they haven't learned how. Whatever your talents, without practice, encouragement, and determination, how would you know how good you could become at them?

It doesn't follow that children who realize their gifts will always be happy, but those who do are more likely to lead lives that reward them and benefit others. This will be especially so if you help your children discover the pleasure that comes from doing well in something they really care about. Providing the right sort of education is one of the surest ways of doing that.

The school should provide a varied and balanced program that consciously cultivates your child's physical, emotional, cognitive, social, and spiritual development. The school doesn't have sole responsibility for these areas of development. In the early years especially, the main responsibility is with you, your family, and the community, of which the school may well be a part. You should see the school as a partner. As your children grow, the balance of opportunities should change to keep pace with their developing capabilities as learners and with their evolving interests as individuals. Good schools always fulfilled these roles. These days, your children face some particular challenges that also bear on your roles as a parent and what you should expect from education.

CHAPTER FOUR

Raise Them Strong

> I see no hope for the future of our people if they are dependent
> on the frivolous youth of today. All youth are reckless beyond
> words. When I was a boy, we were taught to be discreet and
> respectful of elders. The present youth are impatient of all
> restraint.
>
> *Hesiod, Greek poet, 700 BC*

Every generation jars with the ones before them. Young people routinely rail against adults; adults typically despair at how the moral fiber of young people has decayed since they were young themselves. Hesiod is in a long line of irritable elders. As Samuel Johnson noted 250 years ago, "Every old man complains of the growing depravity of the world and of the petulance and insolence of the rising generation."

Some of your children's growing pains are as old as humanity. You'll find them in the epic poems of antiquity, the plays of Shakespeare, and every coming-of-age movie you've ever seen. That much is natural. Young people's struggles for maturity are also shaped by their circumstances: by nurture. The child laborers of industrialism, the infants of slavery, the privileged progeny of wealth, and the young conscripts of war have all had to play the hand they were dealt. Some of the challenges your own children face are peculiar to our times. These challenges bear on your roles as a parent and on what you should expect from their schools.

Under Pressure

If you think back to your own school days, you probably remember feeling stressed over an important test, a difficult class, or a big game or performance. The anxiety you felt from time to time was probably less troubling than the chronic stress that many students now feel all the time. More than eight out of ten teenagers in the United States experience extreme or moderate stress during the school year, and one in four experiences extreme stress.[1] Large numbers experience stress-related headaches, loss of sleep, anger, and irritability. Over a third of teenagers expect to become more stressed in the year ahead. Sometimes the issue is deeper than stress. According to the American Academy of Pediatrics, one in five children in the United States have a diagnosable mental disorder, and only one in five of them are getting the treatment they need.[2]

If you don't feel that young people today are especially stressed, you're not alone. A recent survey shows a wide gap between how stressed young people feel and how stressed their parents think they are. Almost half of the teenagers studied felt seriously stressed; only a third of their parents noticed. Fewer than one in twenty parents thought their kids were extremely stressed, but almost one in three teenagers said they were. More than 40 percent of teens say they experience headaches; only 13 percent of parents realize it. Half of all teenagers have trouble sleeping; just over a tenth of parents know about it. About 40 percent of teens have anxieties about eating; only 8 percent of parents notice.[3]

Why are young people so stressed these days? In study after study, high school students list as their greatest stressors worries about their academic performance, the relentless pressures of testing, concerns about getting into a good college, and parental pressure to excel at school and distinguish themselves as extraordinary. Another is all the other demands on their time, which have amped up considerably in the past decade or so: increased levels of homework, prep classes, and organized programs after school. Many complain about feeling overscheduled without any realistic option for lightening their load, intense competition from their peers, and the challenges of navigating the social waters within their school. It adds up to nearly every waking hour being assigned, plotted, and planned with little to no time for just "being a kid." Two in every three high school students point to trouble managing their time and commitments at home and school as a key cause of their soaring levels of stress.

Then there are the stressors that come from family dysfunction—parents fighting, complaints about money, sibling cruelty, and trying to live up to the accomplishments of an older sibling. All children face at least some of these issues at some point in their lives. A combination of several can be the difference between manageable stress and the kind of stress that has profound negative effects on daily life. These pressures are wrapped up in other trends.

Digital Culture

In less than a generation, digital technologies have revolutionized how we live, work, learn, and play. In the 1960s, when the

Beatles and the Rolling Stones were touring the planet and the war in Vietnam was raging, no one had heard of the Internet, there were no websites, and no one had a mobile phone. I recently watched a documentary about the rock festival at Woodstock in 1969; I wasn't there, so this was the next best thing. Thousands of people were lying around, listening to music (well, some of them), talking, or dancing. Not one of them was staring at a handheld device (at least not the sort we're talking about), texting, taking selfies, or surfing the Internet. There were no such things. But they were coming.

In the 1950s, only a few well-heeled organizations in Europe and the United States were using computers. They were not computers as we know them now. People didn't have them in their homes, much less in their pockets. They were truck-size, slow-acting, expensive contraptions, full of valves and coiled wires, that only government agencies and some large businesses could afford or were interested in. But the technology was accelerating. In the mid-1960s, the U.S. government commissioned research into improving communications between academic and military facilities using networks of computers. By the 1980s a prototype network called ARPANET was doing just that.

Meanwhile, computers were getting smaller, faster, and cheaper. Investment in networks was growing too. In 1989, Tim Berners-Lee, an English computer scientist working in Switzerland, developed the protocols for the World Wide Web, and in the early 1990s the Internet began to take shape. In the last thirty years, it has evolved into the most dynamic, ubiquitous system of communication humanity has ever known. As I write this, half the world's population—over 3.5 billion people—is connected to the Internet. Every year, the number is ballooning as the technology continues to get smaller, faster, and cheaper.

Digital culture is changing us. The Internet is like a vast and vibrant digital cortex, enveloping humanity with trillions of connections that are affecting how we think and behave and what we may become. It's only just beginning. In the early days of domestic computers, we used desktops and laptops for computer things and our mobile telephones to, well, make telephone calls. Ten years ago, digital culture made a step change. In 2007 Apple launched the first iPhone, and things have not been the same since.[4] Billions of people now find it impossible to function without their smartphones. We use them to communicate, shop, take photographs, play games, listen to music, get news, store memories, and otherwise pass the time. They are embedded so deeply in our lives that it's easy to forget they weren't around just ten years ago.

Facebook now has two billion active users worldwide. Every day, one billion of them log on, mostly through mobile devices, and share more than five billion pieces of content, including 300 million images, and the Like and Share buttons are seen across more than ten million websites.[5] Every second, five new profiles are created. Every minute half a million comments are posted, 300,000 statuses are updated, and 150,000 photos are uploaded. This is a new world, and your children are at the heart of it.

There are countless benefits in all of this connectivity. Digital networks are wonderful resources for work, leisure, creativity, and collaboration, and they have massive potential for learning, education, and school. There are some big problems too. One is the torrent of information that gorges from the Internet night and day through countless blogs, websites, archives, promotions, campaigns, and personal pages, on every conceivable topic and from every possible point of view. Before the Internet, published material mainly flowed from producers to consumers. A small number of people created it, and the rest of us received it. Now that anyone can "publish" whatever they want to, it's difficult to know what's true or false, real or fake. Searching the Internet can be like panning for gold; you need to be careful where you look, cast a critical eye on what you find, and have some way of verifying it.

Digital culture can be a black hole for our time and attention. Young people spend hours every day in front of screens. Before you become too self-righteous, it's likely that you do too. Adults typically spend up to nine hours a day on digital devices, at least as much time as their children: some of it working, some of it idly bouncing from one hyperlink to another through aimless curiosity or lured by the expert baiting of advertisers. That's not counting the time playing video games, which are now a multibillion-dollar industry.[6]

Digital culture is not only changing how we spend our time, it's transforming our relationships.

Social Media

How many real friends did you have at school? I mean friends you could trust and talk with about more or less anything. I had about four. There were other people I got on with well enough but only a few genuine friends. Was it like that for you? If so, you followed a well-trodden path before social media. For most of human history, the main way to have a relationship with people was to be in their physical presence. About two thousand years ago, writing systems introduced other options for staying in touch. After that, nothing much changed until the telephone was invented about 120 years ago. I know people even now who don't like to talk on the phone because they can't "read" the person at the other end. Social media are a new twist on the spiral.

In some ways, keeping up through social media with people you know already is no different from old-style correspondence, except that it can happen in real time with images, music, and videos as well. When your online circle of "friends" includes lots of people you don't know otherwise, the very idea of friendship begins to morph. Social media friendships can be no more than episodic exchanges with a disparate network of relative strangers: a reflex thumbs-up/thumbs-down or like/dislike. Every post is like a mini opinion poll of your social cachet. Successful posts are liked; unsuccessful posts are not. The only thing worse is no response at all. You can develop good relationships online with people you don't know otherwise, but the curious conventions of social media can affect young people's confidence in regular relationships.

I've always thought that "social media" is an ironic title. At best they are asocial and at worst antisocial. I'm not alone in thinking this. There's some evidence that social media sites can make people feel more alone. A recent study suggests that the more time young adults spend on social media, the more likely they are to feel cut off from the rest of society. More than two hours a day on social media doubled the chances of feeling isolated. The number of times they visit social media sites is one factor; another is how much time they spend on them.

Professor Brian Primack, from the University of Pittsburgh School of Medicine, who led the study, said: "This is an important issue to study because mental health problems and social isolation are at epidemic levels among young adults. . . . We are inherently social creatures, but modern life tends to compartmentalize us instead of bringing us together." In his view, this study suggests that "social media may not be the solution people were hoping for."[7]

Social media are also a channel for old-fashioned meanness,

except now people can be mean from the privacy of their own devices and anonymously if they choose. Then there are the trolls, the cyberbullies, and the predators for whom the Internet is an easy, anonymous route to intimidation, abuse, and worse.

Being a teenager has always involved issues of social status, insecurity, first romances, and volatile friendships. Even so, before social media, you might have seen a friend or two after school, but school was mostly out of your life until the next morning. With social media your network is with you around the clock. That's great if you forgot the science assignment or need to talk to someone about a new movie, but it's not so good if you're in the throes of high drama with your peers or being pushed to go to an event that you want to avoid. I'm getting stressed just thinking about it.

Brain Development

Technology these days is not just another factor in children's lives; it's changing how they think and feel. Jim Taylor is a professor of psychology at the University of San Francisco. There's some evidence, he says, that frequent exposure to technology "is actually wiring the brain in ways very different than in previous generations." For example, frequent use of video games and other screen media may "improve visual-spatial capabilities, increase attentional ability, reaction times, and the capacity to identify details among clutter . . . rather than making children stupid, it may just be making them different."[8] There's a good reason why children and adults love video games: they're wildly entertaining and playing them can have real benefits for your child.

Others find the extensive use of technology by children to be more disturbing. "Children's developing sensory, motor, and attachment systems have biologically not evolved to accommodate this sedentary, yet frenzied and chaotic nature of today's technology," said pediatric occupational therapist Cris Rowan, CEO of Zone'in Programs. "The impact of rapidly advancing technology on the developing child has seen an increase of physical, psychological and behavior disorders that the health and education systems are just beginning to detect, much less understand."[9]

Health

For the first time in modern history, children may live shorter lives than their parents. Child obesity and diabetes are now national epidemics in both Canada and the United States. In the United States, childhood obesity has more than doubled in the past thirty years and more than quadrupled in adolescents. Obese kids are likely to become obese adults, which leads to increased risk for heart disease, diabetes, stroke, and more.[10] The causes are manifold but have much to do with diet and especially the ubiquity of fast food with high levels of fats and sugars, the lower cost of poorer-quality food, and food insecurity. Poor physical health is also related to the highly sedentary lifestyles that come from overuse of digital technologies. All of these may also be contributing to rising diagnoses of ADHD, autism, coordination disorders, developmental delays, unintelligible speech, learning difficulties, sensory processing disorder, anxiety, depression, and sleep disorders.[11]

Drugs

Many countries are enveloped in an epidemic of opiate addiction and abuses of prescription drugs and alcohol. The rate and scale of addiction are proving catastrophic in many communities and are creating intolerable anxiety for many parents and families. Even at their best, families can be a maelstrom of status struggles and turf wars. It can get much tougher for parents if a child gets into trouble with drugs at school, on the street, or with the law. According to the National Institute on Drug Abuse, when a family member takes drugs, that person becomes unreliable and distracted and may commit additional crimes to get drugs, lose a job, stay out all night, and do other things the person would never do if drugs weren't in the picture.[12] Love may be unconditional but it's not uncritical. For parents, there are times when knowing how to love your children is as important as loving them in the first place. It's another way that being a parent can be as testing as it is rewarding.

Pornography

The Internet began as a facility for scientific research. It's now one of the most prolific sources of pornography ever devised. I'm not here to guide you on the definition of pornography. As a British judge once famously said, it's very hard to define but we know it when we see it. It's not my role either to guide you on the moral status of pornography, but widespread and easy access to pornography is generating deep concerns about its effects on young people's attitudes toward each other, their own sexuality, and intimacy and relationships.

The Great Indoors

When you were a child, how much time did you spend outdoors, playing on your own or with friends without adult supervision? What about your own children? How much time do they spend doing that now? Probably much less.

I've been advising an international initiative, funded by Unilever, on the importance of children's play titled Dirt Is Good. In March 2016, Dirt Is Good launched a campaign called Free the Kids. The goal was to encourage parents to talk about the barriers to allowing their children to go outdoors to play in the real world. The project team conducted a survey of twelve thousand parents around the world. They found that on average children now spend less, often much less, than one hour a day outdoors playing. That's less than half the time outdoors each day that international law requires for maximum-security prisoners. We wondered what such prisoners would say about that, so we shot a film inside the Wabash Valley maximum-security prison in Indiana.[13]

There, prisoners talk about how much they cherish the two hours of outdoor time they get every day. "You have time to feel the sun on your face," says one. "It's everything to me." They are asked about how they'd feel if that time were cut to an hour. "It's going to build more anger," one responds. Another says, "It would be torture." The interviewer tells them that children have on average only one hour outdoors every day. The inmates react emotionally to how wrong this seems to them. "Climb a tree, break a leg . . . that's part of life," one says, while another just adds, "Learn to be a kid." These convicted criminals are touched deeply by the fact that the average child just doesn't get to play outside any longer. Our children tend to spend significantly less time outdoors than people who society deems need to be behind bars. I know our kids can make us crazy sometimes, but shouldn't their conditions be better than *The Shawshank Redemption*?

There are several reasons why kids don't play outdoors anymore. One is that there's so much entertainment *inside*. When I was growing up, playing outdoors was the only viable option. The television didn't have much to offer. Now, when you can be an alien hunter, mercenary, or football superstar without leaving the living room, I imagine it's tougher to convince yourself to kick a ball with some friends, especially if they're inside by themselves doing some variation on what you're doing by yourself.

Home entertainment isn't the only reason that young people spend so much time indoors. Take something as simple as walking to school. In 1969, 48 percent of children age five to fourteen walked or biked to school. By 2009, it was only 13 percent. Part of this is because people tend to live farther from their children's schools now than they did in the 1960s, but even among the group who live within one mile of school, the percentages have dropped by over 50 percentage points, from 89 percent to 35 percent.[14] The top reason that parents give for not letting their children outdoors to play or walk to school on their own is fear for their safety.

It's understandable that parents feel this way given the proliferation of terrible news conveyed by twenty-four-hour networks. Of course, there are regions in the world where children are exposed to all sorts of traumas. There are probably neighborhoods in your own city where children on their own may be in danger. As I said in Chapter Two, the safety of our children is essential, but the idea that things out there are increasingly dangerous for all kids everywhere is a fiction. Crime against children is down significantly, particularly for assault, bullying, and sexual victimization.[15] This is true even in low-income neighborhoods, where crime rates tend to be higher.

What Can You Do?

After food and safety, the social and emotional health of our children is of paramount importance. I mentioned earlier that often parents seem unaware of how stressed their children are. There can be good reasons for that. One is that parents are so stressed and busy themselves, sometimes from dealing with their children. Then there are all the other demands on parents from work, relationships, and trying to have a life. On top of that, Dr. Lisa Firestone believes that parents' lack of awareness of their children's mental states often comes from the best intentions. "As parents in today's culture," she says, "we find ourselves encouraged to center our daily lives on our kids. Yet as we focus our attention on carpools, homework, and play dates, we run the risk of becoming dangerously distracted from what's most important: how our children feel."[16]

Continuous stress can have long-term ramifications for your children, setting them up for adulthoods filled with anxiety and chronic illness. "If stress is constant and unrelieved, the body has little time to relax and recover," says educational consultant Victoria Tennant. And it takes a physical toll: "The stress button keeps getting pushed, continually releasing stress hormones when we don't need them, putting the body into overdrive." Scientists call this state hyperarousal: blood pressure rises, breathing and heart rates speed up, blood vessels constrict, and muscles tense up. "This can all result in stress disorders such as high blood pressure, headaches, reduced eyesight, stomach aches and other digestive problems, facial, neck and back pain."[17]

Signs

How can you tell if your children are stressed out and what can you do if they are?

Melissa Cohen is a licensed clinical social worker and certified coach in New York City. She breaks the signs of stress into four categories:

- *Physical:* headaches, nausea, trouble sleeping, fatigue
- *Emotional:* impatience, restlessness, irritability, pessimism
- *Cognitive:* lack of concentration, decline in memory, increased worrying, greater expression of anxiety
- *Behavioral:* change in eating habits, increased isolation, nail biting, failure to complete everyday responsibilities[18]

Every child is going to show some of these signs at various times. If yours is exhibiting several of these signs at once, it may be time for a conversation and further action. The American Psychological Association has similar advice:[19]

- *Watch for negative changes in behavior:* Does your child seem more irritable or moody? Is she answering your questions with fewer and fewer syllables or maybe being outright hostile? This could be a sign.
- *Understand that "feeling sick" may be caused by stress:* Stress could very well be the underlying cause behind his more frequent trips to the school nurse or complaints about headaches.
- *Be aware of how your child or teen interacts with others:* Your child may seem the same to you at home, which may explain why you haven't noticed how stressed she is, but she may be behaving very differently with others. Checking in occasionally with teachers, parents of her friends, and even the friends themselves can be informative.
- *Listen and translate:* Not everyone can see signs of stress in themselves, and this is especially true with young people. Your child therefore may express

feelings of stress in other ways, such as calling himself stupid or regularly saying that he's annoyed.
- *Seek support:* If you suspect that your child may be feeling high levels of stress, it may be useful to seek the help of a mental health professional.

What else can you do to stop these pressures from building up and to mitigate them if they do? There are many strategies. Here are some guiding principles to underpin all of them. By the way, these are sound principles for parenting in any circumstances.

Let Them Sleep

There's mounting evidence that regular, deep sleep is essential to our health and well-being and that young children and teenagers especially need plenty of it. The pressures of social media, schoolwork, and early mornings mean that many young people are not getting enough sleep or sleep of the right quality and are experiencing the physical and psychological consequences of sleep deprivation.

Given that almost every living creature has to sleep, it's remarkable that until fairly recently scientists and doctors weren't sure why. Matthew Walker is a professor of neuroscience and psychology at the University of California, Berkeley; director of its Sleep and Neuroimaging Laboratory; and author of *Why We Sleep: Unlocking the Power of Sleep and Dreams*. Imagine the birth of your first child, he says. The doctor enters the room and says, "Congratulations. It's a healthy baby and everything looks good. There's just one thing: from this moment forth and for the rest of your child's entire life, he will repeatedly and routinely lapse into a state of coma. While his body lies still, his mind will often be filled with stunning bizarre hallucinations. The state will consume one-third of his life, and I have absolutely no idea why he will do it or what it is for. Good luck!" It sounds bizarre, but until recently that was broadly the situation: neither scientists nor doctors could fully explain or agree why we sleep.

We now know that sleep is more than a refreshing recovery from feeling tired. It's essential in every way to our mental and physical health and emotional well-being. It is vital to our ability to learn, remember, and make logical decisions and choices. During sleep, the brain flushes out toxins that have accumulated during the day, while neural networks are busy processing the day's experiences, some of which fade as others pass from short-term to long-term memory. Sleep is essential to your emotional health. "Benevolently servicing our psychological health," as Walker puts it, "sleep recalibrates our emotional brain circuits, allowing us to navigate next-day social and psychological challenges with coolheaded composure." Dreaming is not a fruitless kaleidoscope of meaningless imagery. It provides a unique suite of benefits including "a consoling neurochemical bath that modifies painful memories and a virtual reality space in which the brain melds past and present knowledge, inspiring creativity."[20]

The benefits of sleep are not confined to the head on the pillow. Sleep refreshes the whole body and all the intricate neural and organic systems within it. Sleep "restocks the armory of our immune system, helping fight malignancy, preventing infection and warding off all manner of sickness. Sleep reforms the body's metabolic state by fine-tuning the balance of insulin and circulating glucose." If all this isn't enough for one night, sleep regulates the appetite and helps to control body weight. It maintains the vitality of the microbiome within the gut, on which our nutritional health depends. Sleep is also intimately tied "to the fitness of our cardiovascular system, lowering blood pressure while keeping our heart in fine condition." Unlike the once-bewildered doctor in the delivery room, we no longer have to ask what sleep is good for, says Walker: "We are now forced to wonder whether there are any biological functions that do not benefit from a good night's sleep. The results of thousands of studies insist that no, there aren't."[21]

It's all the more worrying, then, that so many children and their parents get far less sleep than their minds and bodies need. In 2014, the National Sleep Foundation (NSF) published a major survey of young people's sleeping patterns. The NSF found that one in three six- to eleven-year-olds sleep for less than nine hours a night, much less than they need at that age. There are similar deficits across all age groups. The main reasons for this sleep deficit include staying up to watch TV, playing video games, doing homework, preparing for tests, and connecting on social media. How much sleep should your children have? On the next page there are internationally agreed-upon guidelines, as published by the NSF.

While you're checking how much sleep your children are having, take a look at how much you need. The chances are that you're sleep deprived too. The incidence and the problems of sleep deprivation run well into adult life.

Arianna Huffington is the founder of the *Huffington Post* and an internationally acclaimed journalist, author, and social activist. In her groundbreaking book, *The Sleep Revolution: Transforming Your Life One Night at a Time*, she confirms that the sleep crisis is global. In a survey in 2011, one in three people in the United Kingdom said that on average they'd had less than seven hours of sleep a night in the previous six months. By 2014, that number had rocketed up to two in three. In 2013, more

Age	Recommended	May be appropriate	Not recommended
Newborns *0–3 months*	14 to 17 hours	11 to 13 hours 18 to 19 hours	Less than 11 hours More than 19 hours
Infants *4–11 months*	12 to 15 hours	10 to 11 hours 16 to 18 hours	Less than 10 hours More than 18 hours
Toddlers *1–2 years*	11 to 14 hours	9 to 10 hours 15 to 16 hours	Less than 9 hours More than 16 hours
Preschoolers *3–5 years*	10 to 13 hours	8 to 9 hours 14 hours	Less than 8 hours More than 14 hours
School-age children *6–13 years*	9 to 11 hours	7 to 8 hours 12 hours	Less than 7 hours More than 12 hours
Teenagers *14–17 years*	8 to 10 hours	7 hours 11 hours	Less than 7 hours More than 11 hours
Young adults *18–25 years*	7 to 9 hours	6 hours 10 to 11 hours	Less than 6 hours More than 11 hours
Adults *26–64 years*	7 to 9 hours	6 hours 10 hours	Less than 6 hours More than 10 hours
Older adults *≥65 years*	7 to 8 hours	5 to 6 hours 9 hours	Less than 5 hours More than 9 hours

than one-third of Germans and two-thirds of Japanese said they do not get enough sleep on weeknights: "In fact the Japanese have a term, *inemuri*, which roughly translates as to be asleep while present—that is to be so exhausted that you fall asleep in the middle of a meeting. This has been praised as a sign of dedication and hard work but it is actually another symptom of the sleep crisis we are finally confronting."[22]

One of the best steps you can take for your children's health and well-being is to make sure they have not just the amount but also the quality of sleep they need. While you're at it, you should do yourself the same favor.[23]

Get Them Up

It's important to get our children on their feet and moving. Your children aren't detached heads that float through your living room on occasion. They have bodies for a reason. It's generally recommended that young people (indeed all of us, however old we are) should have about one hour of moderate to vigorous physical activity every day. They typically have much less. In 2016, the World Health Organization published a special report on ending childhood obesity. It estimated that around the world, four out of five adolescents age eleven to seventeen have far too little physical activity for their own health and well-being. It seems that girls are slightly less active than boys. In many parts of the world, young people have less than twenty minutes of moderate to vigorous activity, and some have almost none at all outside school.[24]

John J. Ratey is an associate clinical professor of psychiatry at Harvard Medical School and a leading figure in the growing movement to reconnect mind and body, especially in education. In 2008, he published *Spark: The Revolutionary New Science of Exercise and the Brain*. As Ratey puts it, "In today's technology-driven, plasma-screened-in world, it's easy to forget that we are born movers—animals, in fact—because we've engineered movement right out of our lives."[25] We are embodied creatures, and the mind-body thing really is a package deal. Too many people neglect or misunderstand this relationship and seem to assume that their body is just a way of getting around and that the shape we're in has little to do with how we think and feel. In reality, the relationship is critical and inseparable.

We all know that exercise makes us feel better, but most of us have no idea why. We assume it's because we're burning off stress or reducing muscle tension or boosting endorphins, and we leave it at that. "But the real reason we feel so good when we get our blood pumping is that it makes the brain function at its best, and in my view, this benefit of physical activity is far more important—and fascinating—than what it does for the body. Building muscles and conditioning the heart and lungs are essentially side effects. I often tell my patients that the point of exercise is to build and condition the brain." Neuroscientists are now studying the impact of exercise within brain cells—at the genetic level. Even there, says Ratey, "in the roots of our biology, they've found signs of the body's influence on the mind. It turns out that moving our muscles produces proteins that travel through the bloodstream and into the brain, where they play pivotal roles in the mechanisms of our highest thought processes."[26]

As we saw earlier, the brain responds to activity like muscles do: it grows with use and atrophies with inactivity. As we apply and exercise our minds, the neurons in the brain connect to one another in dense networks. Ratey's point is that physical exercise, as well as mental exertion, also causes those networks "to grow and bloom with new buds, thus enhancing brain function at a fundamental level."

Physical activity has invigorating effects on the brain in the best of circumstances. It has special value in mitigating stress and depression. High levels of cortisol can impair or damage many aspects of physical health. According to Ratey, toxic levels of stress or depression can also erode the connections between nerve cells and even shrink certain areas of the brain: "Conversely, exercise unleashes a cascade of neurochemicals and growth factors that can reverse this process, physically bolstering the brain's infrastructure."[27] For all these reasons and more, it's essential to recognize your children's whole beings—mind and body—and to encourage them to cultivate the life-enhancing synergies within them.

Let Them Play

Perhaps the simplest advice I can offer parents concerned about preparing their children for the world is this: let them play more. I don't mean they should spend more time with Little League or the school basketball club, as valuable as that can be. I'm talking about inventing games on the spot with their friends, turning a pile of twigs into a faerie wood, or hiking along a stream to explore the wildlife there. Play is the work of a child, and children must have time, space, and permission to engage in a variety of play in order to maximize the developmental benefits that play offers.

I mentioned in Chapter Three that the young of all species love to play, but that human children play for much longer than any others. Our children are built to move, run, touch, get dirty, collaborate, and, most importantly, play together. Sadly, they seem to do that much less now than previous generations did. The way they spend their time is changing, and they give much less of it to unstructured play and running free outdoors than you or your parents did. When children do play, they're doing it differently. Play is increasingly an indoor or urban experience rather than something that happens outside and in nature. With more calls on their time from a growing number of sources, children across the globe have fewer opportunities for free, self-directed outdoor play than ever before. They also spend less time playing outside partly because of parental fears for their safety and for lack of available spaces. When children do play outside, they are often oversupervised by adults, which affects whether they feel any benefit from playing or even perceive it as free play at all.

Unilever's Dirt Is Good (DiG) campaign came from a growing concern among many parents and educators that children's lives are out of balance and that this "play deficit" is having a profound impact on what it means to be young. The campaign is rooted in the belief that children benefit enormously from enjoying unstructured, active, and imaginative play, as children always have done. The aim is to encourage conditions in homes, schools, and communities where all children can experience real play every day.

What Is Play?

Play is a primary way that children learn to understand and experience the world around them. Play is not any particular activity: it is a frame of mind, in which all sorts of activities are done. The Dirt Is Good campaign came to use the term *real play* as a way of distinguishing essential developmental play from the other, often more dominant forms. Real play is unsupervised and self-initiated. It is hands-on, multisensory activity, which connects children to the external world around them and to their inner world of ideas and imagination. It involves a range of senses—smelling, touching, listening, and being physically active. It includes activities such as playing with sand, painting, climbing trees, chasing games, role play, juggling, and hiding games.

We contrast real play with two other common forms of play. The first is the supervised, structured play organized for children by adults. The second is screen-based games. Both have value in themselves but they don't offer the opportunities for active, physical, imaginative, and social play that can have such positive benefits in children's social, emotional, cognitive, and physical development. The International Advisory Board for DiG lists six characteristics of real play.

- *Play is intrinsically motivated:* The goal of play is the playing itself. It is done for the satisfaction of the activity. The means are more important than the ends.

- *Play is a state of mind:* Real play is freely chosen. If children are forced to play, they may not feel in a state of "play" at all and see it as another obligation. Like you, children can see the same activity as either play or work, depending on whether they've been assigned it by an adult.
- *Play is pleasurable:* The experience of play itself is more compelling than the outcome of the activity.
- *Play is nonliteral:* When playing, children tend to engage in make-believe that bends reality to accommodate their interests and imagination.
- *Play is actively engaging:* Real play activities engage children fully—physically, psychologically, or both. If children are passive or indifferent to an activity, they're unlikely to be in a full "state of play."
- *Play has no external rules:* The rules and structure of play come from the child. They include roles, relationships, entry to and from the game, and what counts as acceptable behavior within the game.

Why Does Play Matter?

Evidence from numerous studies suggests that the kind of imaginative, self-directed play where children create their own games and rules significantly enhances their development in all the ways that are essential for a happy childhood and for becoming independent adults.

There are powerful links between play and the *physical development* of healthy bodies. Growing children need the stimulation that comes from vigorous physical activity, good nutrition, and a safe environment in which to explore their abilities. Children naturally enjoy the immediate rewards that come from physical movement. Video games facilitate the development of some fine motor skills. Children don't master advanced motor control and new physical abilities by simulating them onscreen. They do it through practice and by "doing and repeating."

Active play has powerful effects on children's *cognitive development*. In the early years, as we've seen, the brain is immensely plastic. As children grow, the connections between various regions of the brain become denser and more clustered. The more pathways that are developed, the stronger the patterns and behaviors become, making it more likely that they'll be retained into adulthood. During early adolescence, neural pruning takes away pathways that are less used. Play helps children form and maintain vital new neural connections in the brain while also strengthening existing pathways. The implication is that if children are not engaging regularly in a wide range of different play styles during childhood, they may not achieve the full range of cognitive and emotional capabilities as adults.

Real play facilitates children's *emotional development*. Through play they explore and express their personal feelings and ideas and learn how others feel and respond. Play also has essential roles in children's *social development*. Through play, children learn about life—and themselves. The skills they acquire teach self-control, give-and-take, and the ability to get on with other people in reaching common goals. They learn about teamwork, communication, and problem solving, all of which are at the center of real play.

Alison Gopnik is a professor of psychology and affiliate professor of philosophy at the University of California, Berkeley. "One of the things we've learned," she says, "is that when children engage in pretend play, have imaginary friends, or explore alternative worlds, they are learning what people are like, how people think, and the kinds of things people can do. This helps children learn to understand themselves and other people. We also have evidence that this kind of understanding leads to social adjustment in school and social competence in life."[28]

Through shared play, children learn resilience and an ability to manage the stresses and uncertainties of life as they move toward adulthood. In all of these ways, adequate, active play in childhood isn't just important; it's essential to becoming a happy and successful person in later life too. Why, then, don't children play like this as much as previous generations did? There are several reasons.

What's the Problem?

While the evidence is strong that play has huge benefits in children's lives, the value of play—like that of sleep—is still not widely understood or prioritized in homes, schools, or public policy. The evidence of that is in the steady fall in the amount of time devoted to play in schools and in the lack of safe spaces given over to play by community planners.

One reason is that young people themselves often prefer to stay indoors, seduced by the attractions of screens and video games. While these forms of play can have significant benefits, their dominance in the play mix is worrying. Another is that children often have such busy, overscheduled lives. Many are under intense pressures from school and from home, and their lives are increasingly managed and structured. By structuring their children's free time or allowing them to play mainly educational and skill-based games onscreen, some parents believe they're doing their best to prepare their children for an uncertain future. Their desire to help them compete in education and in the workplace has often come at the expense of real play.

Some parents think play is trivial and unproductive. Others agree that real play is important, but it just slips off the activities list. To illustrate how play loses out to other activities, the Dirt Is Good Advisory Board created a simple visual guide. It suggests that real play should not be an occasional activity but something that can and should happen anywhere, anytime. Real play should become a mind-set rather than something to be ticked off a parent's daily to-do list.

In some ways, play is like sleep. Each is essential for your children's overall well-being and development. By the way, time spent playing outdoors helps your children sleep longer and better. It makes for earlier and easier bedtimes and less likelihood of waking up too soon. So you get to sleep longer too.

Get Them Out

Young people need to spend time out in the world. Screens can (and maybe even should) be a part of your children's lives, but they need much more. It's rapidly getting to the point where the world beyond their computers is becoming a fanciful construct: something to observe rather than something to interact with. Even so, children and teachers have a genuine appetite to get out of the classroom and into the wider world that surrounds them. One example is the runaway success of Outdoor Classroom Day.

On Outdoor Classroom Day, schools from every part of the globe take children outdoors to play and learn. Teachers report that children's behavior improves, and individuals who feel inhibited by the curriculum thrive in the outdoor environment.

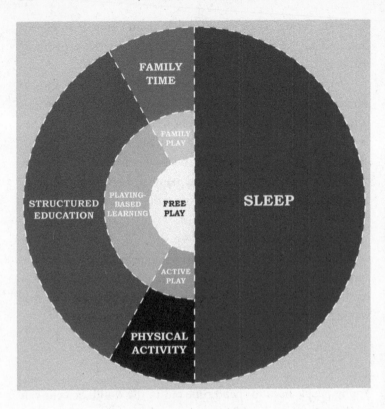

In 2017, over one million children in eighty-one countries took part. As well as a worldwide celebration, Outdoor Classroom Day is a catalyst to inspire more time outdoors *every* day, both at school and at home. Because of this, the campaign has been recognized as a key change maker, winning Best Global Education Project at the 2017 Global Good awards. Learning beyond the classroom is valuable in itself. It's especially valuable when young people connect with the natural world. Sadly these days, too few of them do.

Richard Louv is the author of *Last Child in the Woods*. "A kid today," he says, "can likely tell you about the Amazon rain forest—but not about the last time he or she explored the woods in solitude, or lay in a field listening to the wind and watching the clouds move." A growing body of research confirms what I hope we all know through common sense anyway: that our mental, physical, and spiritual health is positively affected by our association with nature. As Louv notes, "thoughtful exposure of youngsters to nature can be a powerful form of therapy for attention-deficit disorders and other maladies. Just as children need good nutrition and adequate sleep, they may very well need contact with nature."[29]

Given how much some parents program their children's activities, they may consider wandering through the woods to be a trivial experience. After all, you aren't going to learn Chinese or ace the SATs by communing with nature. But even that may not be true. A recent study showed that cognitive function improved among participants who were allowed to walk through a quiet park during a break.[30]

Some innovators are using the very technology that has people glued to their screens to get them up and about. The company Hybrid Play has created an app that attaches to playground equipment and incorporates kids' movement on that equipment into action in a video game. An app from the company Biba allows children to play with a robot companion while running around the park. "After a career of putting people on their butts for hundreds of hours playing games," said Greg Zeschuk, who heads Biba, "I'm trying to pay back the world by making games that make kids go outside."[31]

Augmented reality is helping to turn the entire world into a computer interface. This isn't nearly as terrifying as it may sound. Lou had firsthand experience with this when he was out stargazing with his seventeen-year-old daughter, who is an aspiring astrophysicist. Abigail pointed her cell phone at the night sky and used an augmented-reality app called Sky Guide to identify planets, stars, constellations, and even orbiting satellites. They were out in nature, but the app allowed them to have a richer experience than they might have had otherwise.

Let Them Fall

Children need to learn how the world works and how to make their way in it. There are few ways for them to do that from the comfort of their homes. You may think that your children may not be safe doing these things. It's true that they can get hurt while out playing on their own, and I'm not suggesting you send them to play in a busy intersection or on the edge of a cliff. But they could hurt themselves tripping up the stairs while absorbed in their smartphones. And the benefits of taking that "risk" are less than those to be gained by going outside.

Gever Tulley is the founder of Tinkering School, where kids take apart appliances and use power tools, among other risky endeavors. In his book *50 Dangerous Things (You Should Let Your Children Do)*, he advocates the value of exposing our children to measured risk. Among the fifty things are driving in nails, diving in a Dumpster, and squashing pennies on a railroad track. If the thought of letting your children do any of these things makes you cringe, Tulley has a response. Of course we must protect children from danger, he says, but when protection becomes overprotection, "we fail as a society because children don't learn how to judge risk for themselves. So we must help them understand the difference between that which is unknown (or unfamiliar) and that which is truly dangerous." How do we build competence in children? We do it "by giving children opportunities to distinguish that which is truly dangerous from that which merely contains an element of risk; we introduce them to risk through measured, supervised exposure; we teach them how to explore safely, and set them on a path to exploring on their own."[32]

Virtual reality is a remarkable thing and will only become more remarkable in the coming years. But it does not and should not replace the benefits of being outside in the natural world, exploring and experiencing new things, even if they may be a little dangerous from time to time.

Let Them Fly

Safety is important, but so too is enabling your child to become resilient and self-sufficient. If young people are exposed to certain manageable levels of risk, they learn how to deal with adversity; they learn how to get up after scraping their knees. If they're allowed to see the world as a place of opportunity, they're much more likely to develop the creativity and ingenuity they need to thrive.

Angela Duckworth is a professor of psychology at the University of Pennsylvania. She has made a special study of the need for children to develop perseverance and self-control, or "grit." She describes grit as a passion and perseverance for very long-term goals: "Grit is having stamina. Grit is sticking with your future, day in, day out, not just for the week, not just for the month, but for years, and working really hard to make that future a reality. Grit is living life like it's a marathon, not a sprint." Her research suggests that success and fulfillment in any field often depends more on grit than talent. Grit is largely independent of talent. People with great talent often lack it and fail to make the most of their natural abilities; those with less ability may achieve more because of greater determination and perseverance to achieve at their highest levels. Commitment and persistence are vital factors in life, but they have to be honed by experience: by the disappointments of failure as well as by the rewards of success.[33]

Plus Ça Change

Kurt Hahn was born in Berlin in the late nineteenth century. In the early twentieth century, he became a globally influential educator whose work was inspired by a conviction that the young people of the time (these were your great-grandparents, by the way) were then heading down a fateful path. He identified what he dubbed the "Six Declines of Modern Youth," all of which were the result of the technological innovations and resulting lifestyles of the day:

- Decline of Fitness due to modern methods of loco-motion.
- Decline of Initiative and Enterprise due to the wide-spread disease of spectatoritis.
- Decline of Memory and Imagination due to the confused restlessness of modern life.
- Decline of Skill and Care due to the weakened tradition of craftsmanship.
- Decline of Self-discipline due to the ever-present availability of stimulants and tranquilizers.
- Decline of Compassion due to the unseemly haste with which modern life is conducted, or what William Temple called spiritual death.[34]

This is a bleak perspective, and some of Hahn's predictions of our decline may have been premature since we've managed to survive (and in many cases do much more than that) many decades since he made them. At the same time, he was hitting issues that are still with us now. While Hahn did suggest that youth were in decline, he believed there was a path out of this decline. He suggested "Four Antidotes to the Declines of Modern Youth":

- *Fitness Training*: to compete with one's self in physical fitness to develop discipline and determination of the mind through challenging the body
- *Expeditions*: via sea or land, to engage in long, challenging endurance tasks
- *Practical Projects:* involving crafts and manual skills
- *Rescue Service*: surf lifesaving, firefighting, first aid[35]

Hahn went on to found an international organization of schools now called Round Square, and the wider United World College movement, and he was a catalyst in founding the Duke of Edinburgh's Award. He was also involved in the foundation of Outward Bound, an international program that teaches young people teamwork, tenacity, and self-reliance through a series of physical challenges. Hahn believed that the aim of education is "to impel people into value-forming experiences, to ensure the survival of these qualities: an enterprising curiosity, an indefatigable spirit, tenacity in pursuit, readiness for sensible self-denial, and above all, compassion."[36] In other words, he believed that the way to keep the youngest generation thriving was to engage them in many of the activities we've been discussing.

Time and Tide

I mention Hahn's work (and could cite many others too) to emphasize that although many of the challenges you and your children face have a contemporary turn, the solutions are as old as time. Ultimately, our job as parents is to create an environment where our children can be as strong, resourceful, and fulfilled as they can be. Our children are capable of accomplishing so much, but only if we help them become independent of us. You need to be clear about your roles, understand who your children are as individuals, help them find their own spark of "genius," and help them hone their bodies and their spirits. To do all of that you also need to play an active role in how they're educated.

CHAPTER FIVE

Understand What School Is For

Children love to learn; they don't always enjoy being educated, and some have big problems with school. So what kind of education should your children have, and how can you tell if their school is providing it? The best starting point is not a list of subjects to be studied and tests to be taken. Ask first what you want your child to know, understand, and be able to do, and then look at what he or she needs to learn and how.

Living in Two Worlds

The relationship between nature and nurture shows that your children live not in one world but two. You live in two worlds too. They are the world around you and the world within you. The world around you exists whether or not you exist: it was there before you were born and it will be there after you've gone. It is the physical world of nature and the material environment and the social world of other people, history, and culture. Education must help young people understand that world: how it works and how they can make their way in it. The world within you exists only because you exist. It came into being when you did, and it will end when you do (according to your beliefs). It's the world of your own consciousness: your feelings, ideas, private imaginings, hopes, and anxieties. Education should help your children understand their inner world too: how they feel, think, and see themselves and the talents, interests, and characteristics that make them who they are.

Education should pay equal attention to both of these worlds, both in what your children learn and in how they're taught. How we think about the world around us is deeply affected by our feelings and attitudes; how we feel is shaped by our knowledge and experience of the world around us. To engage your children in both worlds, education should offer them a rich curriculum and a wide range of learning experiences through which to explore it. So what is education for? In my view it is this:

> *To enable students to understand the world around them and the talents within them so that they can become fulfilled individuals and active, compassionate citizens.*

Within these broad aims of education there are four main purposes, each of which should matter equally to you as a parent.

Economic Development

I imagine that one of the reasons you educate your children is so they'll eventually be able to find a good job and make a living. I'm sure that's not the only reason, but it is a perfectly good one. What kind of jobs do you hope your children will find? Irrespective of their particular interests, you may hope, as many parents do, that they'll go into "secure," well-paying professions like the law, finance, or medicine. Alternatively, you may not mind what work they do as long as they're happy doing it. Or you may cross your fingers and hope for both. Whatever you want, if you think a traditional academic education is the best way to prepare them for their future lives in work, you may well be wrong. The world of work is changing rapidly, and those changes seem likely to accelerate like a Tesla in the years ahead; so too will the challenges that your children face.

Until relatively recently, if you did well at school, went to university, and got a degree, you were virtually guaranteed a secure job for life. That's not true anymore. One reason is that the job market has changed so dramatically. In the last thirty years, new technologies, globalization, and offshoring have transformed the world of work. In the 1970s, many high school graduates in the United States went straight into manual or blue-collar jobs in manufacturing. About one in four employees in the United States worked in manufacturing then. Now it's about one in ten. The decline in manufacturing jobs began in the 1980s, and since then nearly seven million such jobs—over a third—have disappeared, a drop from nineteen million jobs to twelve million. Many communities have been devastated as a result, and whatever politicians may say, most of those lost jobs are not coming back.[1]

As jobs in manufacturing have shrunk, others have grown in the "knowledge economies"—education, marketing, design, technology, advertising, and the media—and in the service sectors, including hospitality, travel, sales, and health care. Nowadays, few employees wear overalls, and many more go to work in suits (okay, jeans). In response, governments have urged more and more young people to go to college and get degrees, and they have. In the 1950s in the U.S., about one in seven high school graduates went to college. Now it's more like two out of three. That strategy has not always worked out as planned for you, them, or the country.

There are more than 1.2 billion young people in the world between ages fifteen and twenty-four. They make up about a sixth of the world's total population.[2] Just over seventy million of them (that's one in eight, or 13 percent) are unemployed. That's about twice the rate of adult unemployment. A surprising number of them are college graduates. Many graduates who have found work are in jobs for which their degree is unnecessary. They are underemployed. Why is this? One reason is that there are now so many college graduates looking for work. The value of degrees has fallen as more and more people have them. Put simply, the currency has inflated.

The situation is worse for young people with no qualifications. But college degrees are not the only qualifications that have value. One of the tragic ironies of youth unemployment is that there are millions of unfilled jobs, partly because so many people don't have the necessary skills to do them. The emphasis on academic work and the pressures of testing have led to a massive decline in vocational programs in schools. In the 1980s, many schools offered a range of "shop" and practical programs. Now they seldom do. Such programs came to be seen as second rate in the race to raise academic standards. There was a time when high school students routinely took shop class, home economics, carpentry, and other applied classes. For many of them, these classes were where they came alive, as others did in chemistry labs or in the art studio.

"This bias against vocational education is dysfunctional," says Mark Phillips, professor emeritus of secondary education at

San Francisco State University. "It is destructive to our children. They should have the opportunity to be trained in whatever skills their natural gifts and preferences lead them to, rather than more or less condemning them to jobs they'll find meaningless. To keep a young person with an affinity for hair design or one of the trades from developing the skills to pursue this calling is destructive."[3]

What does the future look like? As always, it's hard to say, but it's probable that robotics and artificial intelligence are about to trigger another reversal in the job market. Manufacturing jobs will almost certainly continue to disappear. Millions of service jobs may evaporate too, as many roles that we think can only be done by human beings are replaced by "intelligent" machines, which will do them more efficiently, more cheaply, and without complaint. As before, new sorts of jobs may well spring up in unexpected places. We don't know what they will be, but the field will be open, for a while at least, for human beings to do whatever it is that human beings do best. Either way, there is a continuing earthquake in the job market, and we're not doing our children any favors if we deny them access to the talents and competencies they're going to need to make their living in this fast-changing new landscape. We'll come back to what you can do about this as a parent in the coming chapters.

Social Development

A second purpose of education is social development. As a parent, you have a big role in your children's social and emotional development, but there's only so much you can do yourself. Schools need to be places where relationships matter in the everyday culture of living and learning together. The social purposes of education matter for several reasons. One is that learning is inherently social. How children learn to speak is just one example. They learn by listening to the people around them. In general, much of what we learn is with and from other people. Through group work, students can learn to cooperate with others in solving problems and meeting common goals, to draw on each other's strengths and mitigate weaknesses, and to share and develop ideas. They can learn to negotiate, to resolve conflicts, and to support agreed-upon solutions. The best schools know this and actively encourage social learning through group activities, collaborative projects, and community programs. Sadly, not all schools do. In many classrooms, children still learn alone; they work *in* groups but not *as* groups. They sit at their desks with their arms around their work so others can't copy and aren't accused of cheating. The tendency to treat learning as a solo activity is reinforced by the competitive culture of constant testing.

There is a second reason for emphasizing the social roles of education. As we saw earlier, for some young people, the effect of social media is to make them awkward in face-to-face relationships. By encouraging them to learn, play, and work together, schools can ease these problems. This is not just about getting on well in school. There is a strong economic case for social learning, but the benefits are even wider. There are now seven and a half billion people on Earth, and we may be nine billion by the end of the century. Outside schools, we live in highly complicated communities, with well over half of us in sprawling cities. Some are megacities of over twenty million people. The ability to work with others is what holds our communities together. It is essential to meeting the needs of everyday life and vital in dealing with the larger challenges we collectively face.

Cultural Development

Educating young people about the world around them means learning about their own and other people's cultures. This is one reason why the humanities—history, geography, sociology, and religious studies—and the arts have such an important place in education. "Culture" is often used to mean the arts in particular and especially the "high arts": opera, ballet, contemporary dance, serious literature, theater, and cinema. I'm a passionate advocate of the arts in education. But here, I mean "culture" in the more general sense of a community's overall way of life: the values, beliefs, and forms of behavior that make it what it is.

Although learning is natural, much of what children learn is cultural. Just as they learn to speak from the people around them, they also absorb the culture, the general way of life, of the communities they are part of. One of the roles of education is to enrich their understanding of their own culture—of the people, events, and circumstances that have shaped it—and why those who are part of it think and believe as they do.

A second role is to enable them to appreciate cultural diversity: to understand how cultures vary between communities and how they affect each other. In *Creative Schools*, I quoted a wonderful observation I found on the Internet about what it is to be British these days. "Being British," it said, "means driving home in a German car, picking up an Indian curry or Greek kebab, then sitting at home on Swedish furniture, drinking Irish Guinness or Belgian lager, watching American programs on a Japanese TV." And the most British thing of all? "Suspicion of anything foreign."

Few people live these days in one isolated cultural group. More than ever, young people live in a complex web of cultures. I live in Los Angeles. Like most great cities, it is an intricate patchwork of thousands of neighborhoods, housing millions of people from hundreds of ethnic and social backgrounds. The Los Angeles Unified School District (LAUSD) is the second largest in the United States with more than seven hundred thousand students. Collectively, they speak ninety-two languages and, for more than two-thirds of them, English is their second language. At home they may be part of a particular cultural community. At school they are part of an intricate mosaic of cultures. That is how it is for all of us. Being British— or French, German, American, Nigerian, Polynesian, or whatever—illustrates just how interwoven our cultural identities are becoming.

Some of the biggest challenges we face on Earth are cultural. The diversity of cultures is a wonderful illustration of the abundance of human creativity. But cultural differences can and do breed hostility. Human history is an often lurid chronicle of cultures clashing and conquering each other, sometimes for loot, sometimes for ground, and sometimes just because. Some of the most catastrophic conflicts are fueled by different beliefs— between Christians and Muslims, Sunni and Shia, Catholic and Protestant, Hutu and Tutsi, and the rest. As the world becomes more populated and connected, living with our differences may be existentially important for our species as a whole.

Personal Development

None of the other purposes of education can be met if we forget that it is about the hearts and minds of people, not data points and league tables. Think of your children, those unique individuals you care for and treasure that no one knows quite like you do. To benefit them as it should, education has to intrigue and enliven them from the inside out.

I said earlier that while children love to learn, they do not always like to be educated, and some have big problems with school, where they often become restless and bored. That's more likely if the work they do strikes them as pointless. I'm not suggesting that they should only study what interests them already and that we should avoid tempting them with things that don't. It's often said that education should start where the child is, but not leave him or her there. That is true. Education is about extending children's horizons, developing their skills, and deepening their understanding.

Great schools work hard to create the conditions in which students want to learn. They know that a rich curriculum and imaginative teaching can fascinate the most listless students in topics they might otherwise not be interested in at all. They know too that whatever the topic, education should tune in to your child's strengths and weaknesses as a learner. In other words, education should be personalized.

Education should help your children handle their inner worlds of thoughts and feelings. Processing feelings and perceptions about the world around us is part of what being alive in the world is about. It goes on constantly, whether we are awake or asleep, whether we think about it or not. This is true in the best of circumstances. There are times when the relationship between the inner and outer worlds can become tortuous. Puberty and adolescence can be especially difficult to handle. These personal issues can be exacerbated or eased by how your children are educated.

There is a third way in which education must be personal. Although learning is social, all learners are individuals. Part of your role as a parent is to press for the kind of education that enables your children to learn about the unique world within them and to make their own way in the world around them.

There's no one in the world exactly like your child. Many people go through their lives without knowing what their real talents are, or wondering if they have any at all. That is one reason why so many adults do not enjoy the work they do or the lives they lead. Others do. They have lives or careers that feel exactly right for them and fill them with a sense of purpose and meaning. They are in their Element.

Before we go on, let me give an example of how these various purposes of education can flow together in the lives of individuals, especially when the programs they take are designed to take account of their lives.

ArtworxLA—The Story of Jonathan

The arts are often low down on the list of priorities in schools, not least because of the pressures of testing. Provision for the arts is especially poor in poor areas, even though it's been shown time and again that high-quality arts programs can be a lifeline for young people in poverty.

ArtworxLA is one of the most effective organizations in the United States in combating the high school "dropout" crisis. Based in downtown Los Angeles, it uses long-term, sequential arts programs to reengage young people in education who have pulled out of conventional schools. It offers them a "ladder" of increasingly advanced arts learning that includes classroom workshops and student exhibitions, after-school residencies, scholarships to college and nonprofit arts programs, internships and job shadowing at creative companies, and one-on-one mentorship. These intensive experiences in the arts give young people who are at the highest risk of leaving school without a diploma compelling reasons to stay in education. Professional teaching artists help them to discover their own artistic creative talents, to rekindle their interest in learning, and to explore practical opportunities for further education and careers. One example of the impact of artworxLA is Jonathan.

In 2012, Jonathan, who was already struggling in the eighth grade, was expelled from school because of a serious fight and anger management issues. He also had insomnia. In his own words: "I came from a really, really troubled background. I was that kid that nobody paid attention to. I was that kid that was always like, you know, he's probably going to go today and probably gonna kill someone in the future. I was that kid that everybody told, 'You're not gonna make it in life.' . . . I was that person starving for someone to help me out."

To give him a second chance, Jonathan was enrolled at the Hollywood Media Arts Academy (HMAA), which was launched jointly by artworxLA and the Los Angeles County Office of Education. HMAA was the first institution of its kind in the region to provide focused arts education and support with "core academics" to alternative high school students and one of twenty-five school sites that collaborate in artworxLA's weekly workshop program. Jonathan completed art projects at HMAA in a variety of media-based programs, including sessions at prominent L.A. cultural organizations.[4] He was encouraged by his teacher to draw, even when he didn't want to, and it made a huge difference. "I started getting pumped about going to school, actually asking myself in the morning: 'I wonder what I am going to make today?'" Jonathan went to the academy with no hope of graduating. In the first year, he had a near-perfect attendance record with no incidents. He found that drawing was an effective way to manage his anger and stress. He began to carry a thick, black sketchbook with him wherever he went, with page after page of intricate drawings—a frightened clown, an ink drawing of a young woman, a sketch in big block letters spelling out *hope*. "It has helped me a lot," he said. "You need to have patience for drawing. It's just like you need to have patience for everything."

Jonathan often rode the bus across town to a park with a racetrack and a beautiful vantage point to sketch the area and the people. "The people are so nice there. They're actually friendly. It's not like my neighborhood. At the park, everyone is always greeting each other and asking questions about what I'm up to . . . they try to have conversations. I can tell they're trying to connect."

With the support of HMAA staff and by climbing the artworxLA program ladder, Jonathan has become deeply invested in visual arts and music production.[5] He also found a job through artworxLA working at a silk-screen printing shop. In 2016, he collaborated with students from around the nation at Otis College's Summer of Art, a rigorous four-week summer program, and worked on illustration techniques while exploring new areas of art making and toy design.

Jonathan says simply that artworxLA saved his life. He's been transformed from an angry, incarcerated teen to a high school graduate, interning at a TV commercial production company and applying to college. Most of all, he found great fulfillment in making art. "Before artworxLA, I was always negative, always down on life. Now, I want to challenge myself. I want to try. I feel like I'm where I need to be." The benefits for Jonathan have been economic, social, cultural, and personal. Not one or the other, but all of these, because properly conceived, a balanced and dynamic education confers all of them through each other.

Some argue that schools should be kept away from social and personal issues altogether and just focus on teaching cognitive skills and cultural knowledge and leave the rest to parents, churches, social workers, counselors, and police. For all the reasons we discussed, this approach is not feasible even if it were desirable, which it isn't.

Learning to Live

I said earlier that if you think a conventional academic education is necessarily best for your child, you are probably wrong. The word *academic* looms large in education. High schools commonly emphasize core academics above other programs. Politicians make speeches about the need to raise core academic standards. Students are ranked mainly on the basis of academic ability, and the admissions policies of many colleges only count grades in the core academics in calculating students' grade point average (GPA). What are core academics? Typically, they are mathematics, languages, science, and social sciences.[6] The arts, physical education, vocational education, and other practical programs are usually much lower down the list of priorities.

Colleges may want additional credits in the arts and a foreign language, but they're not included in the GPA. Some high school students think they can improve their GPA by taking electives, such as a physical education class. Not so, says a leading advisory service for students and parents: "While a good grade in a non-academic class might give you a confidence boost . . . scoring well in an elective class probably won't help when it comes to college entry. Take fun classes to break up the schedule, but don't count on them to pave your way into college."[7] One way or another, core academics are at the top of the food chain all the way through education policy. What's wrong with that? What is an academic education anyway?

Academic work draws on two sorts of ability, which are closely connected. One is understanding theoretical and abstract ideas; the other is handling and memorizing certain sorts of information. Mainly, these are what philosophers call propositional knowledge, or knowledge of facts; for example, that there are fifty states in the

United States, or that the capital of France is Paris. Propositional knowledge is sometimes referred to as "knowing *that*."

Both aspects of academic ability—abstract thinking and propositional knowledge—depend on a facility with words and numbers, which is why students spend so much time writing and calculating (and why the "pencil and paper" testing culture is the way it is). These abilities are very important, and education should certainly develop your child's capacities for them. They are invaluable skills in themselves and the foundation for learning in many other disciplines. They are necessary, but they are not sufficient for the education your child needs. As I argued in Chapter Three, there is much more to your children's intelligence than academic ability, and given the four purposes we have outlined, education should consist of more than academic work.

Knowing *that* is part of the bedrock of education. Acquiring factual knowledge about the natural world and about the cultures of the human world is at the heart of all four purposes of education. So too is learning about the theories and ideas that shape our understanding of them. But there is more to knowledge than facts and more to thought than theory. There is knowing *how*, which is about applying ideas and getting things done. Living in the world takes more than a facility with words and numbers; it involves working with people and materials and coping with practical circumstances. From growing food to building cars to making music, our ways of life are created from people applying ideas and making things happen. To be of real value to your child, education has to be practical as well as academic: it has to connect knowing *that* with knowing *how*.

There is another form of knowledge. It's about understanding how things feel to us as individuals, and if others feel the same way or differently. This sort of understanding is sometimes called "knowing *this*." It's about understanding ourselves and our relationships with others. Knowing *this* is the daily stuff of conversation and of our private ruminations. And it is at the heart of the arts: the current of experience that flows through painting, sculpture, animation, music, movies, poetry, dance, theater, and novels. All three forms of understanding—knowing *that*, knowing *how*, and knowing *this*—are fundamental to a balanced education.

Being Competent

Competence is the ability to do something well. In *Creative Schools*, I suggested that there are eight competencies. The competencies relate to the four purposes of education and develop all three ways of knowing. These competencies don't come online at distinct stages of students' time in school. They should evolve from the beginning of education and be practiced throughout with increasing confidence and sophistication.

Curiosity

Children are immensely curious. The first priority in education is to keep their curiosity alive. When children want to learn, they enjoy education, welcome its challenges, and value its rewards. We talked earlier about the plasticity of your child's developing brain. The more curious children are as they grow, the more they will learn, and the more subtle their abilities and sensibilities will become. How do parents and teachers keep children curious? By intriguing them with questions that interest them. By giving them tasks that challenge them. By engaging them in projects that inspire them. Cultivating curiosity is vital from the earliest days of childhood, but education is not only about childhood and adolescence. Learning should be a lifelong adventure of understanding. Kindling your children's curiosity in their most formative years is a gift that will sustain them in a lifetime of learning.

Creativity

In most respects, human beings are like the rest of life on Earth. But in some we are unique. One is that we have immense powers of imagination and creativity. Imagination is the ability to bring to mind things that are not present to our senses. Imagination is related to creativity but is not the same thing. You could lie in bed all day being imaginative and not do anything. Being creative involves getting something done. I define creativity as the process of having original ideas that have value.[8] It is putting your imagination to work, and it can flourish in every field of human activity. As the challenges that face young people become more complex, it's essential that education help them develop their powers of creative thought and action.

Criticism

Critical thinking is about examining ideas and information using reason and evidence. It involves taking account of various points of view and the values that underlie them and making relevant comparisons.[9] Critical thinking is becoming even more important as the Internet inundates young people with information and opinions from every direction. The more saturated they become, the more they need to think critically about what they see and hear and to weigh it for bias, truth, or nonsense. Critical thinking should be at the heart of every discipline in education and a cultivated habit outside it too.

Communication

We are social beings, and learning to communicate ideas clearly and coherently is essential in our relationships. Fluency in reading, writing, and mathematics are accepted imperatives in

education, and so they should be; it's just as important to cultivate clear and confident speech. Communication is not only
about words and numbers. Some thoughts can't be properly
expressed in these ways at all. We think in sounds and images,
in movement and gesture too, which gives rise to our capacities
for music, visual arts, dance, and theater in all their variations.
The ability to communicate thoughts and feelings in all these
ways is fundamental to personal well-being and to social confidence and connection.

Collaboration

Collaboration is working together toward common outcomes. A
lot of the effort to raise standards in schools is rooted in competition. Of course, there's a place for competition. Being driven
by the challenge of others has always been a spur to higher
performance. I'm not against competition, but collaboration is
just as important in raising achievement, for active citizenship,
and for the health and strength of our communities. Collaboration does not come about by telling people they should do it; it
comes about by practicing it.

Compassion

Compassion is the practice of empathy. It begins by recognizing
what others are feeling and how we would feel in the same circumstances. Many of the problems that young people face are
rooted in a lack of compassion. Bullying, violence, emotional
abuse, social exclusion, and prejudices based on ethnicity, culture,
or sexuality are all fueled by failures of empathy. Cultivating compassion is a moral and a practical imperative. It is also a spiritual
one. Practicing compassion is the best expression of our common
humanity and a deep source of happiness in ourselves and others.

Composure

Many young people experience anxiety and depression in school. Schools can mitigate the effects by changing their cultures in all the ways we have discussed. They can also give students the time and techniques to explore their inner worlds through the daily practice of mindfulness and meditation. The purpose is to help young people to know more about themselves and their motivations and to be more capable of dealing with their inner worlds of feeling.

Citizenship

Democratic societies depend on people being active citizens who are aware of their rights and responsibilities, informed about how social and political systems work, concerned about the welfare of others, articulate in their opinions and arguments, and responsible for their own actions. Schools have vital roles in cultivating that sense of citizenship. They won't fulfill them by running academic courses on civics but by being the sorts of places that practice these principles in how they operate every day. It's essential that schools do not just talk about citizenship but exemplify it in how they work.

Young people who feel confident in these eight areas will be equipped to engage in the economic, cultural, social, and personal challenges that they will inevitably face in their lives. As a parent, you can use these four purposes and eight competencies as a template for judging whether your child's school—or your homeschooling program—is providing the kind of education they really need and to press for improvements where necessary.

The Meaning of Happiness

Before we move on, let's pause on one outcome of education, which many parents put at the top of the list for their children: happiness. I said in Chapter One that my aim is to help you and your children get the education they need to lead happy and productive lives. In most surveys of parents' hopes for their children, happiness comes at or near the top. What is happiness, and what if anything can you do to help your children have it? A few years ago, Lou and I published a book called *Finding Your Element*, which aimed, among other things, to discuss that question. Here's a quick summary of the relevant parts.[10]

It's sometimes assumed that happiness means being in a constantly cheerful mood. It really doesn't. Martin Seligman is one of the founding figures of the positive psychology movement. Seligman says that happiness can be analyzed into three different elements: positive emotions, engagement, and meaning. Positive emotions are what we feel. Engagement is about flow: "being one with the music, time stopping, and the loss of self-consciousness during an absorbing activity."[11] The third element of happiness is meaning, or "belonging to and serving something that you believe is bigger than the self."[12] If you feel that what you're doing matters to you or to the people around you, you're more likely to enjoy doing it. Happiness, then, is a state of fulfillment as well as pleasure. It's possible to be happy in one part of your life and not in others. For this and other reasons, Seligman went on to conclude that happiness is better seen as part of a larger concept of well-being. The Gallup organization conducted research into well-being in 150 countries, from Afghanistan to Zimbabwe. The research gives a glimpse into attitudes to well-being across a broad swath of the world's population.[13] It concludes that well-being is best understood in relation to five broad areas of life.

- *Career well-being:* how you occupy your time or simply liking what you do every day
- *Social well-being:* having strong relationships and love in your life
- *Financial well-being:* effectively managing your economic life
- *Physical well-being:* having good health and energy to get things done on a daily basis
- *Community well-being:* your sense of engagement with the area where you live

Tom Rath concludes, "If we're struggling in any one of these domains, as most of us are, it damages our well-being and wears on our daily life. . . . We're not getting the most out of our lives unless we're living effectively in all five."[14] At a fundamental level, says Rath, we all need something to do and look forward to when we wake up every day. What you spend your time doing each day shapes your identity, whether you're a student, parent, volunteer, or retiree or you have a more conventional job. We spend most of our waking hours during the week doing something that we consider a career, occupation, vocation, or job.

When people first meet, they ask each other, "What do you do?" If your answer to that question is something you find fulfilling and meaningful, you're likely thriving in career well-being. "If your career well-being is low, it's easy to see how it can cause deterioration in other areas over time."[15] For many people, career well-being is intimately connected with relationships with others and engaging with the wider community. While happiness is an internal state, it is often enhanced by looking beyond yourself and engaging with the needs of others.

Sonja Lyubomirsky is a professor of psychology at the University of California, Riverside. In her best-selling book, *The*

How of Happiness, she argues that three main factors affect your personal happiness: your *circumstances*, your biological *disposition*, and your *behavior*. Of all those three, your *circumstances*—health, wealth, status, and so on—contribute only about 10 percent. A well-known study demonstrated that "the richest Americans, those earning more than $10 million annually, reported levels of personal happiness only slightly greater than the office staffs and blue-collar workers they employ."[16] People who live in poverty often report levels of happiness that differ little or not at all from those who live in affluent surroundings. Happiness and well-being are based on many more factors than our material circumstances alone. A more significant factor is our individual biological inheritance, or *disposition*.

To some degree, our capacity for happiness has to do with nature as much as nurture. We each have a set point around which we fluctuate but to which we tend to return. Studies of identical and fraternal twins suggest that we're all born with a particular happiness set point that originates from our biological parents: "This is a baseline or potential for happiness to which we are bound to return even after major setbacks or triumphs."[17] Some people are naturally buoyant and cheerful, and others seem naturally long-suffering. Often their outlook has little to do with the events they're actually facing. How much does your disposition influence your levels of personal happiness and well-being? It may account for up to 50 percent of how happy you are at any given time.

If your biology plays such a large part in your happiness and your circumstances have a relatively small role, what can you do to become happier? The good news is, quite a lot. You have more power than you might imagine to increase your own levels of happiness and well-being. According to Lyubomirsky and others, 40 percent of what affects your actual levels of happiness is your own *behavior*: what you choose to do and how you choose to think and feel. The key to happiness lies not in changing your genetic makeup, which you can't, or your circumstances, which may or may not be possible, but in your "daily intentional activities."

French Buddhist monk Matthieu Ricard is an accomplished writer and the subject of a study on happiness conducted at the University of Wisconsin–Madison, and he has been dubbed in media circles as "the happiest man in the world." In *Happiness: A Guide to Developing Life's Most Important Skill*, he says that he's "come to understand that although some people are naturally happier than others, their happiness is still vulnerable and incomplete, and that achieving durable happiness as a way of being is a skill. It requires sustained effort in training the mind and developing a set of human qualities, such as inner peace, mindfulness, and altruistic love."[18]

What does all this mean for your children's well-being and for your roles as a parent and for their school? The answers are implicit in what we've discussed so far. For your children as for you:

- Well-being is more than a fleeting sense of pleasure. It comes in part from helping them finding their talents, interests, and purpose: their Element.
- Well-being comes from helping them look outward as well as inward: from mindfulness and service to others more than self-absorption.
- Well-being is as much about effort as circumstances. It takes intention, experience, and resilience.

Well-being is not a material state; it's a spiritual one. I don't mean that in a religious sense but in the sense of being in high or low spirits: of feeling fulfilled by having a sense of purpose and meaning in your life. The eight competencies I've outlined are not ends in themselves or boxes to be checked. They are the means to your children becoming fulfilled individuals and engaged citizens in a world with few fixed points but some constant truths. In the end, neither you nor their school can make your children learn. What you can do is create conditions in which they will want to learn, with a clear idea of what and how they should learn and why. On that basis, you can look at whether the education they're receiving is fit for that purpose, and consider how to enhance it if it is or improve it if it isn't.

CHAPTER SIX

Choose the Right School

A school is a community of learners. What makes a good school? It should create the best conditions for your children to learn and develop in all the ways we've discussed: cognitive, affective, social, and spiritual. It should bring out the best in them as individuals and help develop the competencies they need to make their way in the world. What sort of community should it be?

The Elements of Excellence

Whatever the school, what does the best education look like, and how will you know when you see it? There are several elements, all of which have a bearing on the quality and value of education:

- *Curriculum:* the content that students are meant to learn
- *Teaching:* helping them to do that

- *Assessment:* understanding how they are getting on
- *Schedule:* the organization of learning time and resources
- *Environment:* the physical setting where the learning is done
- *Culture:* the values and behavior that the school promotes

The quality of education is in how these elements work together. A great curriculum is not enough if the assessment system only values part of it. A wonderful environment is not enough if the quality of teaching is poor. What makes a school great is having the balance and the dynamics right. How rich is the curriculum? How well do the teachers personalize their approach to each child? How much discretion and creativity does the school allow its teachers? How well does the school relate with parents and the community at large? For now, let's look at the elements separately.

Curriculum

Does the School Have a Broad, Balanced, and Dynamic Curriculum?

The curriculum is the content of education: what students are meant to know, understand, and be able to do. There is the *formal* curriculum, which is what students are required to cover. There is the *informal* curriculum, which is what they can choose to cover, including optional programs and after-school activities. There is the *whole* curriculum, which is all of the above—the complete range of experiences the school offers.

There is also what is sometimes called the *hidden* curriculum, which is another way of talking about the culture of the school, and that's as important as anything that's written in the brochure—if there is one. Students learn more in school than what's on the syllabus, and so do their parents. They take in what the school thinks is important and what isn't. They get that by what's on the curriculum and what is not, what's mandatory and what's optional. They get it in how their work is assessed. Do they get useful comments and feedback or just a letter grade? They pick up on the values of the school and on what counts as acceptable behavior.

You should look at the balance of the whole curriculum and at which parts are compulsory, which are optional, and why. A balanced curriculum should include equal provision for the following:

Language Arts

Language is one of the foundations of human intelligence. No one teaches your children how to speak. You encourage and mentor them, but you don't formally instruct them in how to do it. They absorb speech from the people they grow up with. Reading and writing are different. In ordinary circumstances, everyone learns to speak; not everyone learns to read and write. Doing so involves learning a different set of codes altogether.

In most written languages, reading and writing involve associating vocal sounds with visual marks (letters), and groups of letters (words) with specific meanings. It involves understanding the conventions by which patterns of words (sentences) make sense or not. There are fine physical skills in learning to write; there are also complex intellectual skills in learning how to encode your own thoughts in writing and to decode other people's thoughts by reading what they've written. Language education involves learning all these skills. It should include developing a love of literature in all its forms. It should involve developing the skills of what is sometimes called *oracy*—being able to speak clearly and confidently and to listen with patience and attention to others. Although most people can speak, they don't always do it concisely or well. One of the roles of language education is to help them do so more effectively for different purposes and in different settings.

Mathematics

A good way to start an argument at a conference of mathematicians is to ask for a definition of mathematics. To the layperson it may seem obvious; to the specialist with a close understanding of its many forms and complexities, not so much. For our purposes, and risking the wrath of the conference, mathematics is the ability to understand and work with numbers. Its foundations in education are in arithmetic, including addition, subtraction, multiplication, and division. It may go on to encompass the practical application of mathematical concepts and tools through geometry, algebra, trigonometry, and calculus. Like literacy, mathematics is the gateway to learning in many other disciplines and involves essential skills for social and economic independence. The ability to apply mathematics at some level is essential in many fields, including computer sciences and programming, economics, and almost all trades and crafts. Regardless of what our smart devices can now do for us, it's very difficult to get by in our world without a solid foundation in numeracy. More than that, mathematics is a beautiful discipline in its own right, populated with exquisite ideas and some of the highest achievements of human thought and culture. The math conference would certainly agree about that.

Science

We live in two worlds: the world around us and the world within us. Science is the systematic study of the world around us through analysis, observation, and experiment. Scientists aim to produce theories and explanations, which can be verified by evidence. The natural sciences—physics, biology, and chemistry—look at the nature and dynamics of the physical world and aim to fathom the laws that govern them. In doing so, natural scientists aim to produce knowledge that can be validated by anyone who repeats their observations. The human sciences—including psychology, sociology, and anthropology—aim to investigate human life using some of the same techniques, although the altogether messier nature of human behavior inevitably takes its toll on the "objective" status of their findings. Scientists of all sorts depend on logical analysis, but logic is only one of their resources. Scientific discoveries in any field sometimes come from unexpected leaps of intuition and imagination. Science education is important for all young people because it provides an essential grounding in gathering evidence and in the skills of logical analysis. It provides access to the rich store of scientific knowledge of the world around us. It promotes an understanding of how science has shaped the world and of the often breathtakingly creative ideas and achievements that have driven these changes.

The Arts

The arts are about the *qualities* of human experience. Through music, dance, visual arts, drama, literature, and the rest, we give form to our feelings and perceptions of the worlds within and around us. At the heart of the arts is the artifact. Musicians make music, painters make images, dancers make dances, and writers produce books, plays, novels, and poems that capture the qualities of their personal insights and experience. The arts can inspire us at many levels: through their inherent beauty and form, by the ideas and sensibilities they embody, and by the cultural values and traditions they represent. The pulse of culture beats most strongly in the visual, verbal, and performing arts. Arts education should include learning to practice the arts and to understand and appreciate them. I argued in Chapter Two that intelligence is multifaceted. Music, dance, theater, visual arts, and verbal arts, in all their varieties, illustrate this tremendous diversity and provide practical ways of cultivating it in your children. Through the arts young people can formulate ideas and feelings in a wide variety of modes and media. They can explore their own cultural values and identity. They can engage with the values and traditions of other cultures.

The Humanities

The humanities are concerned with the study of human life and culture. They include history, languages, religious education, geography, social studies, and philosophy. The humanities have essential roles in deepening young people's understanding of the world around them: its diversity and its complexity. The humanities enlarge young people's understanding of what they share with other human beings, including those in other times and cultures, and help them develop a critical awareness of the societies and times in which they live. The humanities overlap in several ways with the sciences and the arts. Like the arts, they are concerned with understanding the nature of human experience. Like the sciences, they typically use the tools of academic inquiry and analysis. The humanities include what are sometimes called the liberal arts. In ancient times, the liberal arts (from the Latin *liber*, meaning "free") were the disciplines that cultivated the qualities of judgment and understanding that are necessary to the vitality of free and democratic societies. Studying the humanities and liberal arts cultivates the qualities and understanding that we all need to sustain complex and civilized ways of life.

Physical Education

Your children's cognitive, emotional, social, and physical well-being are all intimately related. Physical education contributes directly to their physical vitality and to their overall development as they grow and learn. Physical education can also enhance learning in all areas of education by quickening young people's concentration and mental agility. Physical education and sport are inextricably bound up in the cultural traditions and practices of our communities. Games and sports can evoke powerful feelings of excitement both in relation to the games themselves and in the sense of belonging they can generate. The range of physical activities and games provides young people with many opportunities for different forms of physical achievement. Dance and gymnastics, for example, are powerful forms of creativity and aesthetic appreciation. Team games develop individual skills, a close sense of collaboration, and ways of sharing success and failure in controlled, safe environments. In all these ways, physical education has essential roles in a balanced approach to the education of all of our children.

Life Skills

Life is not an academic exercise. Education should help your children to deal confidently with some of the many practical tasks and challenges they'll face as they make their way in the world. Some schools offer practical programs in financial literacy, health and nutrition, cooking and household management. The best of them are not taught as theoretical courses but through practical experiences, starting in elementary school, where young children have a ready appetite for learning through play, for keeping shop, and generally for taking care of business.[1]

Although we can talk separately about these different areas of education, the power of learning is in how they can work together. That has everything to do with how they're taught. In that respect, there is nothing more important to your children's education than their teachers.

A Dynamic Approach to Learning

Do the Teachers Adapt Their Approaches to Different Students and Material?

Most teachers care deeply about their profession and about the children they teach. That doesn't mean that every teacher is going to be right for your child. The right teacher can inspire your child to learn and achieve more than you thought possible; the wrong teacher can make learning feel like a chore. Methods of teaching and learning should be appropriate for your child's various types and phases of development. Newborn and infant children have enormous latent capacities. The extent to which these are encouraged in the first years of life has a crucial bearing on the development of the brain. Children brought up in bilingual or multilingual households, for example, normally become competent in all the languages they use. The same applies in other areas of development, including music.

Teenagers and adults often find it harder to learn an instrument or a second language. Teachers should give your children individualized support and feedback to develop their strengths and help them where they struggle. You should look for a balance between the following areas.

Theory and Practice

Is There a Proper Balance between Desk Study and Practical Work?

One of the evergreen images of schools is that classrooms have to look a particular way: the teacher's desk at the front facing neat rows of desks and chairs and students looking straight ahead. It used to be the case, and still is in some schools, that students spend most of the day at their desks with only brief breaks for some sort of physical exercise or to switch classes. There are important health reasons for not doing this, as we saw. There are equally powerful educational reasons.

In Chapter Five, I argued that academic ability is very important but that there's more to intelligence than academic ability alone, and general education has to recognize that. I made a distinction between knowing *that*, knowing *how*, and knowing *this*. Cultivating these different forms of understanding involves different sorts of activity and different approaches to teaching.

The brain is wonderfully pliable, especially in the early years. Some experiences have such a powerful impact on us that they instantly form long-lasting memories. Less vivid, everyday experiences may live for a time in our short-term memory, but unless we dwell on them or they're repeated, we remember them vaguely, if at all. Learning new ideas, facts, or skills is the same.

To commit them to long-term memory in ways that we can use, we have to practice them so they become part of the fabric of our minds.

To retain propositional knowledge (knowing *that*) takes concentration and effort. Nobody can do that for you. I sometimes hear criticisms of rote learning in education, as if it's necessarily a bad thing. It isn't. If your children are learning a new language, or the laws of chemistry, or the details of specific historical events, or the principles of arithmetic, in ways they can readily use, they'll need to commit them to their long-term memory. When they do, their brains will be subtly changed by the effort. Teachers should help them enjoy the process and make it feel worthwhile. They can be stimulated by practical activities and by working with others, but the effort of memorization is inevitably personal. It may take a lot of concentration, repetition, and reflection. That's the only way that some material can be learned. The problem with the evergreen image of the classroom is the assumption that this is the best way to learn everything. It isn't.

Knowing *how* to do something can only be learned by doing it. Learning to play an instrument, make a design, create objects from physical materials, master a sport, or practice a craft all depend on a synergy of cognitive and physical skills. In every activity that involves practical expertise as well as theoretical knowledge—from ballet to surgery to engineering—good practitioners eventually acquire "muscle memory," which comes from the repetition and refinement of practical techniques. Education should also involve your children in a wide range of practical activities: working with materials and with other people on the application of ideas, in just the ways that life itself constantly demands.

Knowing *this* is about understanding the qualities of our

experiences. Learning to understand their own feelings, making sense of their experiences, and being positive in their relationships are essential to your children's happiness and well-being. They don't learn these things through the abstract study of emotions. They learn them through experience and by practicing the disciplines that have feelings, values, and relationships at their core. In schools, they include the visual, performing, and verbal arts and the reflective techniques of meditation and mindfulness.

The four purposes of education and the eight competencies I outlined earlier can only be fulfilled through a broad curriculum and by approaches to teaching and learning that include but go well beyond the conventions of the traditional academic classroom.

Get Moving

Do Students Have Enough Physical Activity?

I argued earlier for the equal importance of the arts alongside other major areas of learning. Most schools make some provision for the arts: usually visual arts, music, and literature. Theater and dance are usually given shorter shrift, when they're given any shrift at all. There's good evidence that less provision is made for the arts overall in schools in low-income areas and in many charter schools, which often have a specialist curriculum focus or selected student population.[2] As we've seen, many schools have also reduced provision for physical education to make more time for math, reading, and science programs. The assumption is that the only way to raise standards in these areas is to focus on them at the expense of others. This is a mistake, for all sorts of reasons.

Math and Dance

In 2006 I gave a talk at the TED conference titled "Do Schools Kill Creativity?"[3] In that talk, I said that schools tend to educate people from the neck up and that this imbalance has poor consequences for children's overall development. Dance is a test case. In most school systems it's at the bottom of the food chain, if it's there at all. Many people think of dance as a marginal activity in schools: discretionary at best, but certainly not necessary like mathematics, science, or technology. A few years ago, I was interviewed by the BBC and, at one point, the interviewer said, "In the talk you gave at TED you said that dance is as important as mathematics. You can't be serious." I said, "I am serious. Of course dance is as important as mathematics." I know that many people have a hard time with this idea, so let me elaborate.

For several years, I've been a patron of the London School of Contemporary Dance. In 2016, I was invited to give the annual lecture in honor of the founding principal, Robert Cohan. The invitation arrived just after my BBC interview, and I decided to call my talk "Why Dance Is as Important as Maths in Education."[4] In anticipation of the lecture, I tweeted the title. I had a lot of positive responses and some incredulous ones. One tweet said, "Isn't that going to be one of the shortest lectures ever?" Another said flatly, "Ken, dance is not as important as math." Okay, I thought it was. Some were ironic: "Fortunately the skills of reading calendars aren't as important as nailing a decent rumba." Another person tweeted, "So what? Telephones are more important than bananas. Ants are not as important as toilet ducks. Paper clips are more important than elbows." At least that was a creative response. Clearly he thought I was comparing things that are incomparable and being ridiculous in doing so.

Some responses were more pertinent: "Is that so? Important for what and to whom? By the way I'm a math teacher."

An aphorism that is attributed to the philosopher Friedrich Nietzsche goes like this: "Those who were seen dancing were thought insane by those who could not hear the music." When skeptics doubt the place of dance in education or say foolish things like reading a calendar is more important than nailing a rumba, I have to assume they can't hear the music. Let me turn it up a little.

I'm not arguing against mathematics, of course not. Mathematics is an indispensable part of the great creative adventure of the human mind. It's also intimately involved with the dynamics of dance. This is not an argument against math; it's an argument for equity in educating the whole child. Important for what and to whom? I'm talking about the equal importance of dance with the other arts, languages, mathematics, sciences, and the humanities in the general education of every child. Who says so? I do, for one, and so do many others in various cultures and traditions.

Dance education is not a new field. There is a long history of expert practitioners and advocates of dance in education that stretches back before the emergence of mass schooling and far into antiquity. Since time immemorial, people have understood the importance of dance as an essential part of life and education. The fact that it's neglected in systems of mass education doesn't negate the compelling evidence of its value. Scholars in various disciplines have researched and written about dance in its many forms and have contributed to a growing body of evidence about its power to enrich lives and transform education.

In *Dance Education around the World: Perspectives on Dance, Young People and Change*, Charlotte Svendler Nielsen and Stephanie Burridge bring together some recent studies of the value of dance in all kinds of settings: from Finland to South Africa, from Ghana to Taiwan, from New Zealand to America.[5] The low status of dance in schools is derived in part from the high status of conventional academic work, which associates intelligence mainly with verbal and mathematical reasoning. These studies explore how a deeper understanding of dance challenges conventional conceptions of intelligence and achievement. They show the transformative power of dance for people of all ages and backgrounds even in the harshest circumstances: in peace, in war, in abundance, and in deprivation. They show that dance can help restore joy and stability in troubled lives and ease the tensions in schools that are disrupted by violence and bullying.

What is dance? It is the physical expression through movement and rhythm of relationships, feelings, and ideas. Nobody invented dance. It is deep in the heart of every culture throughout history. We are embodied creatures and dance is part of the pulse of humanity. It embraces multiple genres, styles, and traditions and is constantly evolving. Its roles range from recreational to sacred and cover every form of social purpose. Dance is everywhere and for everyone. Why should it be in schools? The reasons are *personal*, *social*, *economic*, and *cultural*. Here are some brief examples.

There are countless forms of dance and numerous professional companies that practice them. Many offer programs for schools. One of them is Dancing Classrooms, a nonprofit company based in New York City, which brings ballroom dancing into elementary and middle schools. It works with some of the most challenging schools and districts in the country, including schools in New York, Los Angeles, and Detroit. Through dance, the company aims to improve social relationships especially between genders, and to enrich the culture of the schools as a whole through cultivating collaboration, respect, and compassion. The program was founded in 1994 by the dancer Pierre Dulaine and now offers each school twenty sessions over ten weeks, culminating in a regional showcase. It has inarguable benefits for the students and their schools.[6]

Toni Walker is the former principal of Lehigh Elementary School in Lee County, Florida. In praising the program generally, she tells of its *personal* benefits for individual students, including one who was particularly troubled. "When this young lady first came to Lehigh the file on her was probably two inches thick. She came from an inner-city background. She was very street smart and very angry. She felt she needed to prove herself and make sure everyone knew she was strong and would fight." When the school started the program, she didn't want to take part, but participation wasn't optional. She had to join in and soon she found she had a natural ability. "In the next lesson, she had a little bit of a different attitude and we didn't have to fight with her to dance. She just got in line." By the third and fourth lessons, Toni says, she was transformed: "She carries herself differently; she speaks differently; she is kind; she is respectful; she has not had one referral, not one. Her mother can't believe what she sees. It's amazing. Amazing. The program is far greater than people understand."[7]

Dance education has important benefits for students' *social* relationships, particularly between genders and age groups. Many forms of dance, including ballroom, are inherently social. They involve moving together in synchrony and empathy with direct physical contact. In an evaluation of Dancing Classrooms in New York City, 95 percent of teachers said that as a result of dancing together there was a demonstrable improvement in students' abilities to cooperate and collaborate. In a survey in Los Angeles, 66 percent of school principals said that after being in the program their students showed an increased acceptance of others, and 81 percent of students said they treated others with more respect.

Dance has important *cultural* benefits. St. Mark the Evangelist is an elementary school in New York City. Principal Antwan Allen took part personally in the sessions with his eighth-grade students. To begin with, it was to make up the numbers: "There were too many girls in our eighth grade and not enough boys, so I joined the first class to help them out and have loved it ever since." Part of the value of him dancing, he says, is the example it sets for the boys. It also shows all the students that he's more than an authority figure; he's "someone who can understand the world through their eyes." He sees the program as an important element of the school's culture and demonstrates that through his own participation. As he says, we make time for things that we think are important: "If I can make an hour for a meeting I can make an hour to dance with my students. I just put it in my calendar—twice a week for one hour I'm dancing with my eighth grade. I treat that no differently than I would treat an observation with one of my teachers or meeting with a parent because it's all important and all part of building the culture of the school."[8]

These personal, social, and cultural benefits of dance are important in themselves, and there are economic benefits too. As well as dance being a field of employment for those with the specialist talents and determination it takes, it also promotes many of the personal qualities and sensibilities that employers increasingly recognize as essential in a collaborative, adaptable workforce. You may agree but still think that math will be more useful for young people when they leave school than being able to dance. We looked earlier at the need for education to address the cognitive, emotional, physical, social, and spiritual development of your children. Different disciplines contribute in different ways to their overall development, including math and dance. When they grow up, young people will draw on all they've learned in school. Some will deepen their interests in specific fields. Some will become mathematicians. Most won't, but everyone who's studied math will find aspects of it invaluable, even if they never solve another quadratic equation or find a regular use for calculus, as most of us don't. Some young people will develop a passion for dance and may go on to be dancers. Most won't, but everyone who's practiced it properly will find invaluable benefits, even if they don't pursue it purposefully after school, as most of us don't.

In case you're still worried that, valuable as it may be, time spent dancing in schools takes away from time doing math or other academic work, it does not. On the contrary. As I said, this is not an argument against math; it is one for dance. They're not mutually exclusive in education or in life. As well as being inherently important, the benefits of dance can have a direct impact on students' achievements in other areas of learning, including math, as it happens. Ironically for the skeptics, there's strong evidence that when children dance, their math results may improve as well.

Another of the schools in the Dancing Classrooms program is Emanuel Benjamin Oliver Elementary School in the Virgin Islands. The principal, Dr. Lois Habtes, was especially impressed by the improvements in reading and math scores among the fifth-grade students who took part in Dancing Classrooms: "We tested in September on reading and math, and just before they went home in December we tested again. Every single year come March we do the Virgin Islands tests. Every year with Dancing Classrooms our fifth-grade students have been our top scorers. There's no ifs, ands, or buts about the impact of Dancing Classrooms in the academic lives of our children. When I first got here, they were failing scores. Last year, our second year, they got up to 83 percent. This year our fifth grade scored 85 percent on the reading test, the highest in the school. In every test we've used with the children from kindergarten to fifth grade, the fifth grade has been way beyond the rest, because of Dancing Classrooms."[9] This is not an isolated phenomenon. It's just one example of a well-documented relationship between physical activity and educational achievement.

In Chapter Four I referenced the work of Dr. John J. Ratey, associate clinical professor of psychiatry at Harvard Medical School and a leading figure in the growing movement to reconnect mind and body in education. His 2008 book, *Spark*, was inspired by an extraordinary program of physical education in Naperville District 203 in Illinois. The district has fourteen elementary schools, five junior high schools, and two high schools. Naperville Central was concerned that too many students were underperforming in reading. The school knew of studies that showed the positive relationships between exercise and learning and organized a physical education (PE) class before school for students who took an elective reading program. They called the class Learning Readiness PE (LRPE).

LRPE is not a conventional PE program of circuit training and competitive sports. It emphasizes physical conditioning and staying active and offers various choices for doing that, including climbing walls, kayaking, ropes courses, weight training, and dance. Classes include monitored cardio workouts so that students can reach and improve their personal fitness targets. The program monitors the students' fitness and its impact on their other work in school. The program has gone on to transform the district's nineteen thousand students into perhaps the fittest in the nation. Among one class of sophomores, only 3 percent were overweight, compared to the national average of 30 percent. As Ratey notes, "What's more surprising—stunning—is that the program has also turned those students into some of the smartest in the nation."[10]

In 1999 Naperville's eighth graders were among students from around the world who took an international standards test called TIMSS (Trends in International Mathematics and Science Study), which evaluates knowledge of math and science. TIMSS has been administered every four years since 1995. The 1999 tests included 230,000 students from thirty-eight countries, 59,000 from the United States. Students from China, Japan, and Singapore routinely outperform American students in these tests. In some Asian countries nearly half of the students score in the top tier; normally, only 7 percent of U.S. students achieve that. In the 1999 tests, U.S. students ranked eighteenth in science and nineteenth in math, with districts from Jersey City and Miami scoring last in the world in both. The story was different for the students from Naperville. Almost 97 percent of Naperville's eighth graders took the test, so these students were not especially selected to take part. On the science section of the TIMSS, they finished first in the world, just ahead of Singapore, and sixth in the world in math, just behind Singapore, Korea, Taiwan, Hong Kong, and Japan.

As Dr. Ratey comments, "At a time when we're bombarded with sad news about overweight, unmotivated, and underachieving adolescents, this example offers real hope." He is properly cautious about attributing the outstanding performance of the Naperville students entirely to their unusual physical education program. As he says, there are always other factors to take into account.[11] On the other hand, "the correlation is simply too intriguing to dismiss."[12]

Why did the Naperville students ace the tests? "It's not as

if Naperville is the only wealthy suburb in the country with intelligent, educated parents. In poor districts where Naperville-style PE has taken root, such as Titusville, Pennsylvania, test scores have improved measurably. My conviction is that its focus on fitness plays a pivotal role in its students' academic achievements."[13] The strategy in these high-performing schools is exactly the opposite of the trend in most American school districts of cutting physical education and reducing other programs in favor of increasing time for math, science, and English. These measures have simply not improved achievement as so many policy makers and administrators assumed they would—and evidently still do—despite all the evidence to the contrary.

On the other hand, the evidence is mounting of the positive impact of physical well-being on young people's overall achievement—and engagement—in education. Ratey quotes a massive review in 2004 by a panel of noted researchers from kinesiology to pediatrics of more than 850 studies about the effects of physical activity on school-age children. Most of the studies measured the effects of thirty to forty-five minutes of moderate to vigorous physical activity three to five days a week: "They covered a wide range of issues, such as obesity, cardiovascular fitness, blood pressure, depression, anxiety, self-concept, bone density, and academic performance." Based on strong evidence in a number of these categories, the panel firmly recommended that students should participate in one hour (or more) of moderate to vigorous physical activity a day. Looking specifically at academic performance, the panel found strong evidence to support the conclusion of other studies, that "physical activity has a positive influence on memory, concentration, and classroom behavior."[14]

Most children in public schools in the United States have

some education in music and visual arts, patchy though it often is. Dance and theater are mostly seen as second-class citizens in schools, and opportunities in the arts in general are lowest for students in areas of high poverty.[15] Bob Morrison, the founder and director of Quadrant Research, confirms that "there are still millions of students who do not have access to any arts instruction. Many of them are in our poorer communities where the programs are arguably needed the most." Would it be okay to have millions of students without access to math or language arts? he asks. "Of course not and it should not be tolerated in the arts. There is a persistent myth that arts education is for the gifted and talented, but we know that the arts benefit everyone regardless of their vocational pathways. We don't teach math solely to create mathematicians and we don't teach language arts solely to create the next generation of novelists. The same holds true for the arts. We teach them to create well-rounded citizens who can apply the skills, knowledge, and experience from being involved in the arts to their careers and lives."

And yet those who were seen dancing were thought insane by those who could not hear the music.

Individual and Group Work

Is There a Balance between Students Working on Their Own and Together?

Sometimes the best way to master material is to take in a classroom lecture, review the material at home, and then test one's understanding through exercises. This is a largely individual approach to learning and it can be very effective. At other times, the most powerful way to find things out might very well be to learn in concert with others, and a school should offer a mix of both. Dr. Maryellen Weimer lists five essential values that group learning offers:

- *They truly learn the content:* When students work with content in a group, they are figuring things out for themselves rather than having the teacher tell them what they need to know.
- *They understand the content:* When students are trying to explain things to each other, to argue for an answer, or to justify a conclusion, that interaction clarifies their own thinking, and often it clarifies the thinking of other students.
- *They learn how to function in a group:* Productive group members come prepared, they contribute to the group interaction, they support each other, and they deliver good work on time.
- *They learn the value of group decisions:* If students take an exam individually and then do the same exam as a group, the group exam score is almost always higher because students share what they know, debate the answers, and through that process can often find their way to the right answer.
- *They learn to work with others:* Group work helps students learn how to work with people outside their circle of friends, including those who have different backgrounds and experiences.[16]

Across the Ages

Are Students Encouraged to Learn in Mixed-Age Groups?

Different children learn different things at different paces. Usually, children in school are taught in specific age groups. Mixing children of different ages together can benefit all of them. Mixed-age classes have the benefit of grouping kids by their stage of mastery rather than their chronological age, which can help those who are having a little more trouble with a particular task or idea. The younger ones can benefit from the relative sophistication of the older ones, who reinforce their own learning by helping the younger ones learn.

Lilian G. Katz is a professor emerita of early childhood education at the University of Illinois at Urbana-Champaign. She notes that although humans are not usually born in litters, we seem to insist that they be educated in them. The goal of mixed-age grouping is "to capitalize on the differences in the experience, knowledge, and abilities of the children." Mixed-age classes offer children the opportunity to nurture each other. Our young children "need real contexts in which their dispositions to be nurturing can be manifested and strengthened." They need exposure to different ways of learning: the wider the age span in a group, the wider the range of behavior and performance likely to be accepted and tolerated by the adults as well as by the children themselves. And they need more highly developed social participation. In a mixed-age group, she argues, "younger children are capable of participating and contributing to far more complex activities than they could initiate if they were by themselves."[17]

Some elementary schools are introducing mixed-age classes

that stick together from year to year with the same teacher. The potential benefits for the students are extra learning time, because the teacher doesn't need to learn about each student at the beginning of each school year; an increased focus on learning at their own pace; and a greater sense of camaraderie with their peers. In American high schools, mixed-age classes are relatively common. It's not unusual for a sophomore to take a third-year French class with a senior, for instance, or for three grades of students to be in the same elective science class. Students in mixed-age groups learn at least as well as those in single-age classrooms.

Assessment

Does the School Have an Open and Informative Approach to Assessment?

How does the school assess your children's progress? If assessment is only through standardized tests, there's a chance that any struggles your child might be having won't be identified until it is too late to do anything productive about it. What are they doing to identify the progress and achievements of your individual child? How much stock do they put in the perceptions of your child's teacher or your own observations? How important are the scores on standardized tests to how your child is perceived as a student and how he or she is challenged and assisted? Is any consideration given to your child's personal strengths and weaknesses during assessment?

Good schools use both formative assessments, which provide information and feedback for students, teachers, and parents during a course of study, and summative assessments, which report on achievement at the end of a course of study. In

Chapter Eight we'll look at some new and better ways of offering both.

Most teachers willingly offer additional assistance to students who need it, but if the school makes this difficult by pushing the teacher to get through the curriculum quickly (something that is happening increasingly in schools because of pressures at the state and federal level), such extra help might not be possible.

A Flexible Schedule

Is the School Schedule Varied and Flexible?

Most schools have a fixed schedule, which tells everyone where they have to be, when, and why. Until recently, planning the schedule for even a small school was a logistical challenge, and for a large one a guaranteed headache. Giving all students their own personal schedules seemed impossible, and the result has long been the familiar inflexibility of the typical school day. The trouble is that students learn at different paces according to what they're doing, and in practice, activities often don't fit neatly into prearranged slots of time.

There have long been sound educational reasons for having more flexible schedules in schools to take these differences into account. The good news is that digital technologies now make that possible and more and more schools are putting them to work. In some schools, every student now has a personal schedule and a personal assessment portfolio to record and support what they do. This doesn't mean they always work alone. It means they can work at their own pace and with groups of other students, irrespective of their ages, who are working on the same materials and projects.[18]

A Safe and Stimulating Environment

Is the School a Safe and Invigorating Place for the Students and the Community?

Schools often operate with limited budgets and resources, but I've been in schools in depressed areas that project vibrancy, pride, and deep compassion for everyone who walks through the halls. I've been in schools in wealthy neighborhoods that feel antiseptic and joyless. How does your school announce itself to its students? Does it feel more like a joyous place of learning or a cold institution? Are the walls adorned with student artwork and practically vibrating with activity? Your children are going to be there seven hours a day. How is the setting going to affect their mood and appetite for learning?

A Sense of Community

How Well and Effectively Does the School Engage with the Wider Community?

Finally, try to gauge the school's sense of community. How does the school engage with parents and with the neighborhood? How active is the parent-teacher organization in the school? How welcome are you to sit in on a class, help out with activities, and share your expertise or experience? Does the school interact with area businesses and community centers? Are they creating a sense of community for the children?

Eric Schaps founded the Developmental Studies Center in Oakland, California, an organization that designs school programs that merge academics, ethics, and social development. These programs have been used in more than 150,000 schools and after-school programs.[19] Schaps feels strongly that schools with a strong sense of community offer students an invaluable suite of benefits:

> Students in schools with a strong sense of community are more likely to be academically motivated; to act ethically and altruistically; to develop social and emotional competencies; and to avoid a number of problem behaviors, including drug use and violence.
>
> These benefits are often lasting. Researchers have found that the positive effects of certain community-building programs for elementary schools persist through middle and high school. During middle school, students from elementary schools that had implemented the Developmental Studies Center's Child Development Project were found to outperform middle school students from comparison elementary schools on academic outcomes (higher grade point averages and achievement test scores), teacher ratings of behavior (better academic engagement, respectful behavior, and social skills), and self-reported misbehavior (less misconduct in school and fewer delinquent acts). A study that assessed the enduring effects of the Seattle Social Development Project—another elementary school program—on former participants at age eighteen found lower rates of violent behavior, heavy drinking, and sexual activity, as well as higher academic motivation and achievement, for program participants relative to comparison group students.[20]

Alternative Education

I said in Chapter One that you can improve education within the system, you can make changes to the system, or you can educate your children outside the system. A small but growing number of parents are taking the third option. I'm a firm believer in public education and have spent my professional life advocating on behalf of it. Even so, as a parent you may find that your own children are not getting the education they need at the local school and that, try as you may, you can't make the changes there that are needed in time to benefit them. In that case, you might choose to explore the alternatives.

Jerry Mintz has been a leading voice in the alternative school movement for over thirty years. In addition to spending seventeen years as a public school teacher and a public and independent alternative school principal, he founded several alternative schools and organizations. In 1989, he formed the Alternative Education Resource Organization, and has been its director since then.[21] He suggests ten signs that it may be time to look for an alternative educational approach for your child.

1. **Does your child say he or she hates school?** If so, something may be wrong with the school. Children are natural learners. If your child says she hates school, listen to her and find out why.

2. **Does your child find it difficult to look an adult in the eye, or to interact with older or younger children?** If so, your child may have become "socialized" to interact only within their own age group rather than with a broader group of children and adults.

3. **Does your child seem fixated on designer labels and trendy clothes for school?** This is a symptom of a culture that emphasizes external rather than internal values, causing children to use shallow means of comparison and acceptance.

4. **Does your child come home from school tired and cranky?** Students can have hard days in any school, but consistent exhaustion and irritability may be signs that education is not energizing but debilitating.

5. **Does your child complain about conflicts or unfair situations in school?** This may mean that the school does not have a student-centered approach to conflict resolution and communication. Many schools rely on swift, adult-issued problem solving, depriving children of their ability to process and discuss the situation thoughtfully.

6. **Has your child lost interest in creative expression through art, music, and dance?** The neglect of the arts often devalues or extinguishes these natural talents and interests in children.

7. **Has your child stopped reading or writing—or pursuing a special interest—just for fun?** Are they investing the bare minimum in homework? The emphasis on meeting standardized test requirements can result in an increasing apathy toward other activities that were once exciting, and in a loss of creativity.

8. **Does your child procrastinate on homework until the last minute?** This is a sign that the homework is not really meeting his or her need: perhaps it's "busywork," which may be stifling their natural curiosity.

9. **Does your child come home excited about any-thing that happened in school that day?** If not, maybe nothing in school is exciting for your child. School and education should be fun, vibrant, and engaging.

10. **Has the school suggested that your child should be given a behavior-regulating drug?** Be wary of these diagnoses and keep in mind that much of the traditional school curriculum these days is be-havior control. If students are expected to sit for five or six hours a day with limited personal atten-tion and interaction, it might be time to get your child out of that situation.

None of these signs by themselves should be taken as a rea-son to panic, but if you've noticed several of them consistently, Jerry argues it may be time to explore the alternatives. What are they? There are various options, both public and private. In the U.S., for example, many public school systems have alterna-tive programs. There are two general approaches:

- Public Choice Programs: These are open to any stu-dent in the community and are sometimes called Schools Within Schools.
- Public At-Risk Programs: These are for children who've had a variety of problems coping with school. Some of them are tailored to individual needs and are very supportive; some are more like holding cen-ters and offer few benefits.

I noted earlier the growth of charter, magnet, and private schools. They include over 4,500 Montessori schools, based on the experiential approach designed by Dr. Maria Montessori, and hundreds of Waldorf schools and other so-called progressive schools, which aim in different ways to offer a proper balance between the various "elements of excellence." There are hundreds of independent alternative schools where parents and students take active responsibility for their own education. The latter are often called democratic schools, free schools, or Sudbury schools. Mintz is author of *School's Over: How to Have Freedom and Democracy in Education*, which I recommend as a valuable overview of the history, practice, and values of alternative, and especially democratic, education.[22]

In my foreword to that book, I emphasize that democratic schools are radically different from conventional schools. In fully democratic schools, students have executive powers in the governance of their own learning and in all the decisions that affect it, including how the school is run, the schedule, curriculum, assessment, facilities, and even the hiring of faculty. Democratic schools may seem the polar opposite of the adult-directed and custodial nature of much of conventional education. In many ways they are. They're also the embodiment of principles that school systems everywhere typically proclaim: the need to develop independent learners, to cultivate diverse talents, to produce thoughtful, compassionate, and productive citizens. This is especially evident in the work of Yaacov Hecht.

Yaacov is a visionary educator and international leader in democratic education. In 1987, in Hadera, Israel, he founded the first school in the world to call itself democratic. He has since helped to establish a network of democratic schools and convened the first International Democratic Education Conference (IDEC), which connects educators, schools, and organizations. Today, there are hundreds of democratic schools throughout the world, nearly a hundred of which are in the U.S., including Brooklyn Free School in New York, the Farm School in Summertown, Tennessee, and Youth Initiative High School in Viroqua, Wisconsin. Yaacov also cofounded Education Cities—the Art of Collaborations, an organization that fully integrates schools with the systems and resources of the cities in which they're based.[23] In his book *Democratic Education* he lays out the primary components of a democratic school. They include:

- A choice of areas of learning: the students choose what they want to learn and how
- Democratic self-management
- Evaluation focusing on the individual—without comparison to others and without tests and grades

Democratic education depends on shared respect for individuals, empathy with the needs of the group, and the commitment of the whole community to common purposes and mutual well-being. So far from being an alternative to conventional education, these values should be at the heart of every school. They are, after all, what democracy is meant to be about.

Homeschooling

A small but growing number of parents are taking direct control of their children's education through homeschooling or unschooling. Around 3 percent of all school-age children in America are now homeschooled, and this percentage is likely to grow. What are the attractions of homeschooling?

To begin with, you have intimate knowledge of your children's interests and personalities, which means that you can tailor activities exactly to them. You can be flexible in how you organize their learning. Homeschoolers often say that their school days are consistently shorter than the traditional school day. Because they organize their own times and adjust the rhythm of the day to suit the activities, they feel they get as much or more done. While some of you might think that hours teaching your children might be testing in other ways, many homeschool families report a deepening of family bonds. Homeschooled children have more opportunities to learn and act independently and to make choices about what they learn.

Because they aren't tied to a specific location, many home-schooled students can travel more than their peers and explore the world around them. They also have more opportunities for physical activity and play.

There are two common questions about the potential draw-backs of homeschooling. One is whether homeschooled children miss out on building social relationships with other young people. In practice, families often come together to homeschool, pooling resources to widen their children's social networks and their own. According to Jerry Mintz, virtually all homeschoolers are part of some kind of homeschool group. Some of these groups have coalesced into homeschool resource centers, which operate as often as four or five days a week.

Another question is whether they're at a disadvantage in gaining conventional qualifications. Families take a variety of approaches. Some try to create "school at home" with a standard curriculum. Some sign up with a curriculum designed by an umbrella school, which helps parents create their own curriculum, grade homework, and help with any necessary report forms. Not all families are interested in their children taking conventional tests or following traditional routes to college; sometimes they choose homeschooling precisely to avoid them. Those that do take conventional tests, like SATs, may do as well as non-homeschooled children, according to their abilities and application.

Homeschooling isn't for everyone. Many parents can't afford to (or don't want to) give up their jobs to focus on their children's education. Others don't feel they have the necessary skills. Some families have wonderful experiences of homeschooling, and some don't. Much depends on how well prepared parents and their children are, and how deeply they devote themselves to what's involved. Teaching, as we'll see in the next chapter, takes more than enthusiasm. The best homeschoolers know that and work hard to develop their knowledge and expertise as well as those of their children. If you're considering homeschooling your children, there are many online resources that you can turn to for support.[24]

Unschooling

"The best ever Saturday . . . the day people dream about when they are stuck in school." That's how blogger Sandra Dodd describes the average unschooling day.[25] Unschooling is a form of homeschooling that eschews formal lessons altogether. It's estimated that 10 percent of homeschoolers are unschoolers. Because children are natural learners, the assumption of the unschooling movement is that their curiosity will lead them to discover the tools they need to navigate through the world and allow them to delve deeply into the areas that truly fascinate them.

Unlike most homeschooled children, unschoolers don't receive curriculum from their parents or other adults unless they specifically seek it out by taking a music class, language program, art instruction, or any number of other offerings that might be available in nonschool environments. The parents base their approach on the interests of the child rather than on a pre-set curriculum. As Jerry Mintz notes, in some cases, curriculum "is designed retroactively, by keeping records of the activities throughout the year and at the end of the process dividing the experiences into the appropriate subject areas." Unschoolers tend to take no tests, and they usually don't comply with state graduation standards.[26]

"Children do real things all day long," Earl Stevens, coauthor of *The Unschooling Unmanual*, wrote, "and in a trusting and supportive home environment, 'doing real things' invariably brings about healthy mental development and valuable knowledge. It is natural for children to read, write, play with numbers, learn about society, find out about the past, think, wonder and do all those things that society so unsuccessfully attempts to force upon them in the context of schooling."[27] Stevens mentioned that his own son showed an early interest in reading and language, so much so that he felt no temptation to intervene in the experience in any way. English became his son's favorite "subject," even though he never spent a moment inside an English class.

Professor Peter Gray conducted a survey among unschooled adults to see how they succeeded in the world. The overwhelming majority of respondents said the advantages greatly outweighed the disadvantages and that they believed unschooling helped them become self-motivated. A common concern among the group was dealing with the opinions of others. While some felt isolated because of unschooling since most of their peers were in school, many said that their ability to interact with people of all ages (as opposed to being in a same-age classroom) was a real benefit. More than 80 percent of respondents went on to some form of higher education, with more than half graduating college or on their way to graduating college, and some getting degrees from Ivy League schools. Interestingly, while none found college academically difficult, several noted that the structure felt strange to them.[28]

Backward and Forward

In *Creative Schools*, I emphasize that personalizing education might sound revolutionary, but this revolution is not new. It has deep roots in the history of education. Many people and institutions have argued for forms of education that follow the natural rhythms of children's development, and the importance of these forms of education for bringing about fairer and more civilized societies. These advocates and practitioners have come from many cultures and perspectives. What they have in common "is a passion for forming education around how children learn and what they need to learn to form themselves."[29]

Rudolf Steiner, for example, was an Austrian philosopher and social reformer who developed a humanist approach to education that formed the foundation of the Steiner Waldorf Schools Fellowship. The Steiner approach is built around the individual needs of the *whole* child—cognitive, physical, emotional, and spiritual. The first Steiner school opened in 1919. There are now nearly three thousand of them in sixty countries.[30]

A. S. Neill founded the Summerhill School in England in 1921, creating the model for all democratic schools that followed. The school's philosophy is "to allow freedom for the individual, each child being able take responsibility for their own life, and following their own interests to develop into the person that they personally feel that they are meant to be. This leads to an inner self-confidence and real acceptance of themselves as individuals."[31]

Maria Montessori was a physician and educator. She began her career in education in San Lorenzo, Italy, in the early twentieth century, working with poor and disadvantaged children. There are now more than twenty thousand Montessori schools throughout the world, which follow Montessori's approach to teaching and learning. One of these is Park Road Montessori, a wonderful public elementary school in Charlotte, North Carolina, which I've had the pleasure of visiting. As the policy of Park Road school makes clear, Montessori's methods are based on several core principles:

> **Movement and cognition:** In the Montessori method, letters are learned by tracing sandpaper letters while uttering the sounds rather than merely by visual recognition; mathematical concepts are introduced with materials that show how the mathematical operations work; geography is learned by making maps.
>
> **Choice and control:** Montessori education allows children considerable choice and control in their activities. They're not free to misbehave or avoid parts of the curriculum, but each day they choose what to work on, who to work with, and how long to work with it. Choice enhances creativity, well-being, and problem-solving speed and ability.
>
> **Interest and curiosity:** Montessori education begins with the learners' personal interests and is structured to allow them to pursue those interests. Montessori designed specific materials and lessons to stimulate children's interests and curiosity.

Intrinsic rewards: Prizes and punishments are incentives to unnatural or forced effort. Montessori education keeps rewards intrinsic, and monitors performance with self-correcting materials, peer correction, and teacher observation. There are no grades or tests.

Collaboration: Children learn well when they collaborate and they learn to get along better with peers, which creates a more positive classroom climate for everyone. Montessori education capitalizes on peer tutoring, which benefits the tutor just as much as the one being tutored.

Context: Montessori's hands-on materials show children what their learning applies to and why different procedures work. Mathematical concepts, the study of literature, the sciences, etc., are all presented in their historical context.

These and other approaches to personalized learning are often grouped together under the general banner of "progressive education," which some critics seem to imagine is the polar opposite of "traditional education." The history of education has been an oscillation between these supposed poles. The standards movement is the latest swing. My argument here, as elsewhere, is that effective education is a balance between rigor and freedom, tradition and innovation, the individual and the group, theory and practice, the inner world and the outer world. And that balance is, after all, what we should want for all our children.

Learning and Teaching

We looked earlier at the elements of excellence in good schools. At the heart of these is the quality of teaching. A school may have a wonderful curriculum policy and a sophisticated approach to assessment, but their value depends on how well your children learn, and that has everything to do with their teachers.

CHAPTER SEVEN

Go to the Source

Who were your favorite teachers when you were at school? I can't remember all of mine, but some still stand out after all these years: some for their eccentricities, others for their inspirational teaching, some for both. In the middle years of high school, our Latin teacher was Mr. Davis, a pallid, thin-faced man in his sixties who looked like an older relative of Mr. Bean. He was disheveled in the way of many academics and impressively erudite. When he was talking, he cradled his cheek in his upturned hand, as if he were comforting himself, which he probably was. He did it when he was sitting, with his elbow propped on his desk. What intrigued me was that he carried on doing it even when he stood up and paced around the room, when it seemed a more awkward maneuver.

He often carried a short baton, like a magician's wand, which he pointed at whatever took his interest—something on the blackboard or a student he'd singled out for attention. When he asked you a question, he would stand over you and tap the stick menacingly on your desk while he waited, like a mantis, for the answer. It was a singular technique, but it concentrated the mind wonderfully. I learned a lot of Latin that way.

In my last two years of high school, we were taught English by Dr. Bailey, a quiet, dignified man of great presence and authority. He too was near the end of his career, which he'd mostly spent studying and teaching the classic texts of English literature. He could recite on demand whole screeds of Shakespeare, Milton, and the Romantic poets. In our first lesson together, he said his aim in the year ahead was to convince us that *Antony and Cleopatra* was the finest play ever written in English. He almost did. At the end of our two years together, we asked him for a list of the ten books in English that we should all read. I lost the list a long time ago, but remember that at the top of it was the King James Bible. He encouraged us to read it not for its religious content—that was a personal matter for each of us, he said—but for the unsurpassed beauty of the language in which it was couched.

Dr. Bailey impressed me in every way, not least because he was blind. His revision notes were punctured in Braille on thin rolls of paper, like ticker tape, which he drew beneath his fingertips as he spoke. I tried to imagine the hardships he'd faced in pursuing his passions in the printed world of letters, books, and archives.

The Importance of Teachers

Alistair Smith has worked with teachers throughout the world. In his book *High Performers: The Secrets of Successful Schools*, he says, "Students with the best teachers in the best schools learn at least three times more each year than students with the worst teachers in the worst schools . . . investing in the quality of teaching and teachers is a must."[1] We expect a great deal from teachers and with good reason. They expect something from you too.

The Demands on Teachers

The main role of a teacher is to help students learn. That may seem obvious, but teachers spend a lot of time doing other things. They have to plan lessons that conform to school policies and, in public schools, to the demands of local and national legislation. They have to assess students' work, which may take hours of their time after school and on weekends. They do a great deal of routine clerical work, record keeping, writing reports, and attending meetings. These days they can spend inordinate amounts of time administering standardized tests. They have to deal with behavioral problems and tensions between students. In high schools, they may work with hundreds of students every week. They may substitute for teachers who are absent, and they often take on a host of other commitments—running after-school programs, clubs, sports teams, rehearsals, or performances. They also have a life outside teaching.

All in all, teaching is a demanding profession. To be a great teacher takes knowledge, skill, and a passion for students' achievement. As with lawyers, doctors, and dentists, there are some poor teachers and some who would prefer to be doing something else, but in my experience the overwhelming majority of teachers are committed to the success of their students. That's a big responsibility, and good teachers take it on gladly and take it seriously. It's important when dealing with your children's teachers to respect their professionalism and keep in mind the pressures they face from students, school administrators, legislators, and other parents. Given all of that, what should you expect from your children's teachers, and how do their roles relate to yours as parent?

Teaching and Learning

Learning is like physical exercise. No one else can do it for you. It's a personal achievement and it takes energy and commitment to do it at all, let alone well. You can be put in a gymnasium for six hours a day, five days a week, but if you just lean against the equipment daydreaming, you won't be any more fit at the end of it. If you persuade someone else to exercise on your behalf, they may get more fit, but you won't. If you grudgingly lift some weights or do some perfunctory push-ups, you might get some benefit, but far less than if you made a proper commitment.

Your children can turn up dutifully at school and sit in class all day, but no one else can do their learning for them. They may go through the motions, take the path of least resistance, or get you or someone else to do their homework for them, but to get the most from education, they have to want to learn and then do it themselves. There is no proxy. The role of their teachers is to motivate and help them do it.

The Roles of Teachers

If I asked you for a synonym for *teach*, what would it be? A word that comes up often is *instruct*. Another is *explain*. If you were to draw a picture of "teaching," what would it look like? Often, we picture teachers standing at the front of a classroom, addressing the whole class. Sometimes they do that, sometimes not. At times, the best way to help students learn something is to explain it to them as a whole class. For example, if the topic is irregular verbs, linguistic idioms, historical dates, or other forms of propositional knowledge, a direct explanation may be the right way to teach it, and telling everyone at the same time makes good sense.

If the lesson is about specific techniques in math, science, music, art, or sport, an instructional demonstration may be just the thing. The students still have to learn it, of course, and they all have their own strengths and weaknesses in how they do so. Great teachers personalize their approach to individuals, often working with smaller groups or one-on-one to give them the right support. The need to personalize education is one reason why there's more to teaching than whole-class instruction. Another is that there's more to education than propositional knowledge.

If you look back at the aims and purposes of education and the eight competencies I suggest, you'll see that much of what we want our children to learn doesn't come through instruction alone. It comes from practice, experience, debate, reflection, relationships, challenges, and inspiration. Great teachers know this and that they have several roles, not just one. Let me highlight four of them.

Enable

I see an analogy between education and agriculture. Farmers and gardeners know that plants thrive in certain conditions and not in others. They know they don't make plants grow—they don't attach the roots and paint the leaves. The plants grow themselves. The role of gardeners is to provide the best conditions for that to happen. It's the same with education. Great teachers know they can't make children learn. Children do the learning themselves. The role of teachers is to create the best conditions for that to happen.

Expert teachers have a repertory of techniques, and direct instruction is only one of them. They adapt their approach to the needs of the moment: sometimes whole-class instruction, sometimes facilitating group activities, sometimes individual coaching. Great teaching takes judgment, flexibility, and creativity and knowing what works best here and now with these students on this day.

Engage

Great teachers keep their students involved, curious, and excited about learning. They inspire their students to achieve at their highest levels. They instill a joy for learning, for seeing class time and the work that comes with it as something to be anticipated rather than endured. They set off sparks of curiosity in the classroom, and you never know what these sparks will ignite.

Sarah M. Fine is a teacher, researcher, and instructional coach. She argues that the key to deep engagement in high school classrooms is "intellectual playfulness." Teachers who offer assignments that are open-ended and projects that involve intellectual risk taking are more likely to have students who are consistently engaged, look forward to class, and work hard when they're there. "Students described their teachers as allies, not as nemeses or task masters," she wrote. "Most notably, the word *boring* was markedly absent from their descriptions of classroom tasks."[2] Mind you, as I said earlier, teaching and learning is a relationship, and it takes effort by the student as well as the teacher. I was talking recently with a group of college students and one of them said, "Some of our professors are really boring. What can we do about that?" I said, "You can't put this all on your teachers. If you're bored, that's something to do with you too. You shouldn't just sit in front of the teacher and think,

'Well, go on, interest me.' It's your education. Get interested and take responsibility."

Dr. Judy Willis is a neurologist who has been a middle school teacher and a teacher of educators. She finds that higher-level thinking, creativity, and "aha" moments are more likely to occur in an atmosphere of "exuberant discovery," where students of all ages retain that kindergarten enthusiasm of embracing each day with the joy of learning.[3] Christopher Emdin is an associate professor at Columbia University's Teacher's College. He talks about "Pentecostal Pedagogy," using the skills that preachers employ to boost student engagement in the classroom:

> That preacher bangs on the pulpit for attention. He drops his voice at a very, very low volume when he wants people to key into him, and those things are the skills that we need for the most engaging teachers. So why does teacher education only give you theory . . . and tell you about standards and tell you about all of these things that have nothing to do with the basic skills, that magic that you need to engage an audience, to engage a student? We could focus on content, and that's fine, and we could focus on theories, and that's fine, but content and theories with the absence of the magic of teaching and learning means nothing."[4]

It's a vivid analogy, and he's right to point to the transcendent possibilities of great teaching. Practiced properly, teaching is an art form, which can inspire students to greater heights of achievement than they thought possible. Indirectly, the analogy with preaching also highlights the personal character of teachers' styles. Like everyone else, some are outgoing, even bombastic entertainers; others are quiet, introverted, and considered.

My English teacher Dr. Bailey was an outstanding educator in his own way, but I can't imagine him speaking in tongues.

Empower

To *empower* is to make someone stronger and more confident. Confidence is a feeling of self-assurance based on an estimation of one's abilities and qualities. There is a difference between self-confidence and what we might call task confidence. Self-confidence is an overall sense of faith in yourself that allows you to meet most situations with a feeling of poise and adequacy. Task confidence is related to particular contexts and comes from having the specific skills to handle them.

I was in a Chinese restaurant recently. In the middle of the evening, the chef pushed a trolley into the room and started kneading a large ball of dough. For ten minutes or so he rolled, folded, and stretched it and eventually formed it into a long tress of perfect noodles. It was a virtuoso performance, carried out with cool assurance and consummate skill. As impressive as he was, it doesn't follow that he'd be equally confident hang gliding, playing the lute, or filling a root canal. Confidence in particular tasks may be limited to them; it doesn't necessarily translate to others or into a general sense of self-confidence either. I know many people who are brilliantly poised in some areas of expertise and shrinking violets in others.

There's a difference between true confidence and false confidence. True confidence is based on a proper estimate of one's abilities; false confidence is based on overestimating them. The chef had true confidence. You could see it in his face as he worked the dough. His calm smile was seasoned by years of practice.

There are various international league tables, which collate data on students' performances on standardized tests, especially in literacy and math. Students from the United States generally register as average on such tables, statistically similar to the United Kingdom and Sweden. In one survey, students were asked how confident they were that they'd done well. The American students ranked number one on that scale—a triumph of false confidence.[5]

We talked in Chapter Two about the need to encourage your children's self-esteem and the dangers of unwarranted praise. Encouragement is important, but compliments without competence can breed false confidence. The way to build true confidence in young people is not to flatter them with superlatives for whatever they do. It is to help them develop the knowledge, skills, and qualities they need to handle the challenges they face.

Great teachers empower students in two ways. They cultivate task confidence by developing students' abilities in their own areas of expertise. They cultivate self-confidence by working together as a learning community to develop students' abilities in all eight competencies. In doing this, they help students acquire the knowledge and skills they need to become independent learners: to experiment, ask questions, and develop their skills in creative and critical thinking.

It's exactly this understanding of the relationship between teaching and learning that underpins the concept of *learning power*. One of the originators of learning power is the educator and author Guy Claxton. He argues that Building Learning Power (BLP) is about helping young people become better learners, both in school and out. It is about cultivating habits and attitudes "that enable young people to face difficulty and uncertainty calmly, confidently and creatively." Students who are more confident of their own learning ability "learn faster and learn better. They concentrate more, think harder and find learning more enjoyable, and they do better in their tests and external examinations."[6]

Expect

Great teachers have high expectations for their students, and it's hard to overestimate the effect that can have on achievement. My writing partner, Lou, was inspired to become a writer, from a standing start, by his ninth-grade English teacher. Lou hadn't considered writing at all; it was just something he did for school assignments, and it came easily to him. This teacher saw something in a piece Lou wrote early in the school year and encouraged him to try his hand at writing short stories and persuasive essays. He also assigned him writing roles on classwide projects. Finding his interest piqued in ways he hadn't expected, Lou would stay late for extra help to work on his writing with this teacher, and he found that he cared more about this work than he had about any other schoolwork before, so much that it didn't feel like work at all. If he'd had a different teacher in ninth grade, Lou might never have discovered his love for writing, and his life might have taken an entirely different course.

Teaching Styles

Teaching and learning is not a mind meld. Teachers don't transfer the contents of their minds into those of their students, like a download. At least not yet. Teaching and learning is a relationship. At the heart of it there are four main elements: the *teacher*, the *student*, the *content*, and the *context*. They all affect each other.

Earlier in the book, I provided a rough classification of parenting styles. Teachers have their own styles too, which have partly to do with how they see their roles and partly with their personalities. There are as many teaching styles as there are teachers, but there are some broad types, which you may recognize. Some years ago, Dr. Anthony Grasha performed an extensive survey of teaching styles. He came up with five main types and offered some thoughts on the pros and cons of each:[7]

- *Expert:* Someone with a high level of subject knowledge who sees teaching as a vehicle for conveying that knowledge to others. Grasha sees an advantage to this type of teacher in sharing mastery of a discipline. The disadvantage is that this level of expertise sometimes prevents the teacher from understanding the challenges that non-experts face in learning this material.

- *Formal authority:* This sort of teacher projects gravitas, is focused on the proper ways to do things, and sets out a firm approach to the curriculum. The advantage to this teaching style is that classroom goals are often focused and clear-cut; everyone knows what the class intends to accomplish. The disadvantage is a tendency toward rigidity, which doesn't work with every student.

- *Personal model:* This teacher tends to offer lots of examples from his or her own life. He or she will show how to accomplish a task and then encourage students to follow those guidelines. The advantage of this style is its hands-on value; the disadvantage is that it's problematic for students who don't learn as effectively with those techniques.

- *Facilitator:* This teaching style concentrates on helping students become independent thinkers by guiding them toward discovery. Facilitators ask lots of questions and serve as a consultant rather than an instructor. Grasha sees an advantage in teachers who use this style to cater to students as individuals but a disadvantage in the time it takes and in the possibility of some students being uncomfortable with the approach.

- *Delegator:* This teacher encourages students to work autonomously, acting as a resource where necessary. Grasha feels this hastens student development as independent learners but warns that many students may not be ready for the level of autonomy a delegator provides.

As is true with parents and parenting styles, most teachers are a combination of these rather than strictly one or the other. Because teachers have their own styles and personalities, some may have a good relationship with your child and some may not. Either way, it's important that your children's teachers connect with them as individuals and help them learn in whatever ways work best.

Students

Your children's attitude to learning is affected by their feelings for their teachers: whether they connect with them personally, like or respect them, want to please them. These feelings can change over time, but whatever they are in the moment is pertinent to how your children work with that teacher. That said, this is a relationship, and teachers' attitudes to your children are affected by your children's attitudes to them. It's in the nature of relationships that different people bring out different aspects of each other. That's why we're just friends with some people and fall in love with others. The same child may be a respectful student with one teacher and a confrontational irritant with another. When you're surprised to hear that your child's in constant trouble with a particular teacher, it may be worth remembering that it usually takes two to tango.

Content

All children have natural aptitudes for some activities and not so much for others. They like some and not others. These talents and preferences have a bearing on how easily they learn in different disciplines and how much they enjoy them. Some have naturally good memories for some sorts of information; others don't and have to work much harder at it. Some have a flair for music or art or physics or dance. A student with a natural feel for something doesn't need the same sort of support as one who flounders. The right teacher may inspire your child to do well in an activity that he or she previously showed no interest in at all. There are many examples of people who discovered a talent and pursued it because a particular teacher inspired and took a special interest in them. Of course, the wrong teacher might turn them off something they have always loved.

Context

How far your child commits to learning is affected by the culture of the school. If his or her peers take a particular activity or teacher seriously, there's a better chance your child will too. If his or her peers disapprove of or ridicule it, your child may pull away rather than fall out of favor with them. As in all relationships, the various elements affect each other, often in unpredictable ways. The mockery of friends may turn your child off a discipline she used to love and look forward to. An unshakeable passion might drive her on to do her best in spite of the teacher or her peers. The complexity of these relationships is what makes teaching such an expert profession.

What Makes a Great Teacher?

How can you tell a great teacher from an average one? To begin with, we expect reasonably that teachers know something that their students don't and that one of their roles is to share that knowledge. My Latin teacher, Mr. Davis, knew a lot more Latin than we did, and his main job was to help us know more of it. Knowing what you're teaching is important for great teaching, but it's not enough. Teachers need to be able to engage, enable, empower, and raise the expectations of their students. These are complex professional skills, which is why all the high-performing school systems—including Finland, Canada, South Korea, Singapore, and Hong Kong—invest so heavily in the selection and training of teachers.

In the United States, many charter schools have waivers that allow them to bring in teachers who might know a lot about what they're teaching but don't have the essential skills to teach it. Some politicians evidently think that having enough subject knowledge is all you need to be a teacher. That's simply not true.

Teach for America (TFA) is a controversial nonprofit that offers a five-week training program for recent college graduates (most of whom do not have degrees in education) and provides them with two-year teaching assignments, mostly in impoverished and under-resourced schools. Some do well and stay in teaching. Many do not and move on to other things, with their résumé suitably enhanced. Inspired by TFA, various other countries have set up similar initiatives to encourage high-scoring graduates to spend some time teaching in schools. They include Teach First in the United Kingdom. The assumption is that the main quality a good teacher needs is good academic qualifications in the subject he or she is teaching. The evidence of experience is that this is not true and never was.

By most criteria, Finland has one of the most successful education systems in the world. Much of its success is due to the expertise of its teachers. Teaching is a respected profession in Finland, and there is intense competition to join it. To do so, applicants have to take a certified teacher education program at a Finnish university, which leads to an advanced research-based degree. They then have to continue their studies a further five or six years before they can teach a class of their own. These programs are so popular among young people in Finland that only one in ten applicants is accepted each year. Because only 10 percent of applicants pass the rigorous admission system, you might assume, as some politicians clearly do, that the answer is simply to recruit new teachers from the top 10 percent of college graduates who apply. It isn't.

Pasi Sahlberg is one of the world's leading experts in the Finnish education system. The idea that Finland recruits the "best and brightest" academically to become teachers is a myth, he says. The candidates who are accepted represent a diverse range of academic achievement, and deliberately so.[8] About a quarter come from the top 20 percent in academic ability and another quarter from the bottom half. This means that about half of the first-year students are "academically average." The University of Helsinki, he says, "could easily pick the best and the brightest of the huge pool of applicants each year, and have all of their new trainee teachers with admirable grades. But they don't do this because they know that teaching potential is hidden more evenly across the range of different people." Young athletes, musicians, and youth leaders, for example, "often have the emerging characteristics of great teachers without having the best academic record."[9] What Finland shows is that rather than tempt those with the highest academic qualifications into teaching, it's better to design initial teacher education to attract people who have a natural passion and aptitude to teach for life. By the way, none of the world's high-performing systems of education encourages fast-track routes into teaching.

Significantly, Teach for America has come to the same conclusion that great teaching is not all about academic qualifications; it's about passion and expertise in helping others to learn. TFA studied its teachers carefully and realized that the teachers who help their students most have some common characteristics:

- They're constantly reinventing their classrooms and evaluating their own progress with the students.
- They work hard at keeping their classrooms inclusive and at engaging parents in what is going on in class.
- They keep a strong level of focus on outcomes.
- They are unusually well prepared both on a daily level and on a yearlong level by working backward from what they hope to accomplish.
- They are relentless, in spite of school and community conditions.[10]

Relentlessness came up in a study by Angela Duckworth, the author of *Grit*. She found that "gritty" teachers were 31 percent more likely *to generate considerable growth* from their students.

She also found that teachers who were satisfied with their lives were much more likely to help the kids they taught.[11] People who love their work tend to be satisfied with their lives and to work with a high level of commitment. This is certainly true of teachers, who invest so much of themselves in their students and in what they teach. That's another characteristic of great teachers. They're passionate about improving their own practice and learning from others. Take Edcamp.

Edcamp provides teachers with the time and space to collaborate and learn together. The first Edcamp was held in Philadelphia in 2010, organized by a group of teachers who were willing to take a risk. Their aim was to provide professional development for educators, built on their own questions, challenges, and passions. The founders spread the word on Twitter and were delighted when a hundred teachers registered and showed up for the first Edcamp. The teachers who took part decided what they wanted to discuss, with the aim of having conversations rather than presentations. The sessions were based on their ideas, showing that teachers want to learn from one another and trust in each other's experience. There are four simple rules that govern what an Edcamp is:

- Edcamp must be free. Teachers who want to learn don't have to raise funds to do it. They can just come to an Edcamp.
- Edcamp is open to anyone. No matter what grade they teach, or what kind of school they are in, Edcamp is for any teacher who cares about kids.
- Edcamp is participant-driven. The people who arrive at an Edcamp decide what will be discussed, so every Edcamp is different and every person who comes can suggest a topic for conversation.

- Edcamp is vendor-free. Unlike large conferences where teachers are bombarded by vendors, Edcamp avoids their presence.

Volunteers, most of them full-time teachers, run every Edcamp. Driven by teachers' passion for their profession, Edcamps have mushroomed around the world. In 2010, there were eight Edcamps. By 2017, there have been close to 1,600 Edcamps in all fifty states and in thirty-three countries around the world. Edcamps range in size from twenty to thirty people to those with over six hundred people attending. The average size is between seventy-five and one hundred.[12]

Home and School

Teaching and learning is a relationship. One of the most important parts of it is between you and the school. Your children are more likely to do well at school if you avoid thinking of school and teachers having sole responsibility for their education. The University of Chicago undertook a detailed seven-year study of the city's elementary schools in low-income urban neighborhoods.[13] The study looked at student achievement and school improvement and the factors that affected them most. Teacher quality was one, as it always is. Another major factor was family involvement. As one—and by no means the only or most important indicator—it found that children in elementary schools with strong family engagement were ten times as likely to improve in math and four times as likely to improve in reading than schools with weak family ties. Why is family, and especially parental involvement, such an advantage to your children's education and to the life of the school more generally?

Motivation and Support

Parents who take an active interest in their children's education can have a big impact on their motivation and achievement. That holds true whatever the families' circumstances and background. When parents talk to their children about school, expect them to do well, help them plan for the future, and make sure that out-of-school activities are constructive, their children generally do better than if their parents seem uninterested. When families and schools work together, children are more likely to go to school regularly, stay on in school longer, like it more, do well, and have higher graduation rates.[14]

Personal Knowledge

You probably know your children better than anyone else. You know more about their individual interests, foibles, strengths, weak spots, moods, backgrounds, and relationships. You don't know everything about them, especially as they grow older and more independent, but you know a lot. Teachers see some aspects of your child; you see many others. Some students struggle in school because they're not understood as individuals. Their particular strengths may not be recognized or provided for. They may have all sorts of interests and accomplishments outside school that their teachers know nothing about, and those teachers might act differently toward them if they did. One of your contributions as a parent is to help teachers gain a fuller picture of who your children are and of their special qualities and capabilities.

The School and the Community

Schools and teachers can face all kinds of challenges with students, including behavioral issues, discipline problems, bullying, drug abuse, violence, emotional stress, and depression. Some of these problems originate in school, and the school may be able to deal with them internally. Some originate in the family, the community, or the wider culture, and students import them into school in their behavior. It may be that you're dealing with them too at home. The closer the relationships between teachers and parents, the more likely it is that these sorts of problems can be properly understood and addressed together.

What about Homework?

There are probably few more vexing issues for you and your children than homework. Some of the mounting stress that young people feel at school comes from the amount of homework they have to do. Some of the stress you feel undoubtedly comes from getting them to do it—or doing it for them. The value of homework is hotly debated by educational professionals. Some see no value in it whatever and argue that it should be eliminated in schools. They include Alfie Kohn, an influential thought leader in education. In his book *The Homework Myth: Why Our Kids Get Too Much of a Bad Thing*,[15] he argues that there is no necessary link between homework and student achievement in school and that the negative effects of homework on students' home and personal lives far outweigh any other benefits that might be claimed for it. Others see a variety of educational and other benefits in homework, and there's a full range of opinion in between.

Let's begin at the beginning. How much homework do

young people typically have these days? What does research and experience say about whether there's any value in it? What can you do as a parent to support your children with the homework they have or, if you think they have too much, to reduce or eliminate it?

How Much?

The amount of homework young people are given varies a lot from school to school and from grade to grade. In some schools and grades, children have no homework at all. In others they may have eighteen hours or more of homework every week. In the United States, the accepted guideline, which is supported by both the National Education Association and the National Parent Teacher Association, is the 10-minute rule: children should have no more than 10 minutes of homework each day for each grade reached. In first grade, children should have 10 minutes of daily homework; in second grade, 20 minutes; and so on to the twelfth grade, when on average they should have 120 minutes of homework each day, which is about 10 hours a week. It doesn't always work out that way.

In 2013, the University of Phoenix College of Education commissioned a survey of how much homework teachers typically give their students.[16] From kindergarten to fifth grade, it was just under 3 hours per week; from sixth to eighth grade, it was 3.2 hours; and from ninth to twelfth grade it was 3.5 hours. There are two points to note. First, these are the amounts given by individual teachers. To estimate the total time children are expected to spend on homework, you need to multiply these hours by the number of teachers they work with. High school students who work with five teachers in different curriculum areas may find themselves with 17.5 hours or more of homework a week, which is the equivalent of a part-time job. The other factor is that these are teachers' estimates of the time that homework should take. The time that individual children spend on it will be more or less than that, according to their abilities and interests. One child may casually dash off a piece of homework in half the time that another will spend laboring through it in a cold sweat.

Do students have more homework these days than previous generations? Given all the variables, it's difficult to say. Some studies suggest they do. In 2007, a study from the National Center for Education Statistics found that on average high school students spent around 7 hours a week on homework.[17] A similar study in 1994 put the average at less than 5 hours a week.[18] Mind you, I was in high school in England in the 1960s and spent a lot more time than that—though maybe that was to do with my own ability. One way of judging this is to look at how much homework your own children are given and compare it to what you had at the same age.

Benefits

There's much debate about the value of homework. Supporters argue that it benefits children, teachers, and parents in several ways:

- *Children* learn to deepen their understanding of specific content; to cover content at their own pace; to become more independent learners; to develop problem-solving and time management skills; and to relate what they learn in school to outside activities.
- *Teachers* can see how well their students understand the lessons; evaluate students' individual progress,

strengths, and weaknesses; and cover more content in class.

- *Parents* can engage practically in their children's education; see firsthand what their children are being taught in school; and understand more clearly how they're getting on—what they find easy and what they struggle with in school.

Dr. Ashley Norris is assistant dean at the University of Phoenix College of Education. Commenting on her university's survey, she says, "Homework helps build confidence, responsibility and problem-solving skills that can set students up for success in high school, college and in the workplace."[19]

That may be so, but many parents find it difficult to help their children with subjects they've not studied themselves for a long time, if at all. Families have busy lives and it can be hard for parents to find time to help with homework alongside everything else they have to cope with. Norris is convinced it's worth the effort, especially, she says, because in many schools, the nature of homework is changing. One influence is the growing popularity of the so-called flipped classroom.

In the stereotypical classroom, the teacher spends time in class presenting material to the students. Their homework consists of assignments based on that material. In the flipped classroom, the teacher provides the students with presentational materials—videos, slides, lecture notes—which the students review at home and then bring questions and ideas to school where they work on them collaboratively with the teacher and other students. As Norris notes, in this approach, homework extends the boundaries of the classroom and reframes how time in school can be used more productively, allowing students to "collaborate on learning, learn from each other, maybe critique [each other's work] and share those experiences."[20]

Even so, many parents and educators are increasingly concerned that homework, whatever form it takes, is a bridge too far in the pressured lives of children and their families. It takes away from essential time for their children to relax and unwind after school, to play, to be young, and to be together as a family. On top of that, the benefits of homework are often asserted, but they're not consistent and they're certainly not guaranteed.

A Mixed Picture

Dr. Harris Cooper is a professor of psychology and neuroscience at Duke University Institute for Brain Sciences. In 2006 he published a detailed analysis of the impact of homework on academic achievement.[21] He concluded that homework does have a positive effect on some aspects of student achievement. He found that the benefits were stronger for secondary students—in grades seven through twelve—than for children in elementary school. Cooper's study suggests various reasons why older students benefit more from homework than younger ones. Younger children, he says, are less able to tune out distractions in their environment. They also have "less effective study habits." It may also be because elementary teachers often assign homework "to help young students develop better time management and study skills, not to immediately affect their achievement in particular subject areas."[22]

Too much homework can be counterproductive for students at all levels. "Even for high school students, overloading them with homework is not associated with higher grades," Cooper said. Overall, the research is consistent with the "10-minute rule" for the optimum amount of homework. The bottom line, Cooper says, is that "all kids should be doing homework, but the amount and type should vary according to their developmental level and home circumstances. Homework for young students should be short, lead to success without much struggle, occasionally involve parents and, when possible, use out-of-school activities that kids enjoy."[23] Even for upper high school students, more than two hours' worth of homework a night was "not associated with higher achievement."[24]

Cooper's team looked at the impact of homework on test scores and other measures of conventional academic achievement. It didn't—because it couldn't—assess the impact of homework across all four purposes of education and all eight competencies, which I discussed earlier. The study did note that homework "is thought to improve study habits, attitudes toward school, self-discipline, inquisitiveness and independent problem solving skills." On the other hand, homework can cause "physical and emotional fatigue, fuel negative attitudes about learning and limit leisure time for children."[25] These side effects are serious for any school that aims to improve young people's achievement and love of learning.

Breaking the Mold

It's partly because of those negative effects that some middle and high schools are reframing homework assignments to make the most of their potential benefits, at home and school. Some elementary schools are reducing or eliminating homework altogether. Maureen Healy is an award-winning author and sought-after advisor on children's emotional well-being. She says that many of the parents of younger children she works with are delighted by these trends, "which remove the nightly nagging of 'Have you done your homework?'"[26] Parents are freer to connect with their child over dinner or other activities without the stress of impending homework. Heidi Maier is school superintendent of Marion County, Florida, which has forty-two thousand students. As Maureen Healy notes, Heidi made national news not only because she banned homework but is replacing it with twenty minutes of reading per night.

Mark Trifilio, principal of Orchard Elementary School in Vermont, has done something similar. In 2016, after consulting with faculty and parents, he decided to eliminate homework on the basis that it had few proven benefits and many drawbacks, except in relation to reading. Better to spend the time doing that and pursuing other interests, he thought. The school agreed on this new policy:

No-Homework Policy: Student's Daily Home Assignment

1. Read just-right books every night—*and have your parents read to you too.*
2. Get outside and play—*that does not mean more screen time.*
3. Eat dinner with your family—*and help out with setting and cleaning up.*
4. Get a good night's sleep.

One year on, he reports that students haven't fallen behind and now they have "time to be creative thinkers at home and follow their passions."[27] As Maureen Healy put it, the subtext of a no-homework policy in elementary schools is: "We trust our teachers, we trust the curriculum, and we trust our students to pay attention as well as learn during the day. No homework for kindergarten through fifth grade doesn't erase learning, but helps students tolerate an often long day better and encourages them to pursue their unique interests after-school."[28]

What to Do?

Take Stock and Take Action

As a parent, what should you do if you're concerned about the amount or the nature of the homework that your children are given? First, you should talk with them about the problems they're having. For example, is overload the problem—having too much homework? Is it about specific areas of study? Does it have to do with support from the school or methods of assessment? When you're clear what the problems are, talk to the school. If the problem relates to specific areas of study, begin by talking to the teachers concerned. If the problem is the overall volume of homework, talk to the principal or, in larger schools, whoever has oversight of the curriculum. Although the school will have guidelines for how much homework teachers should assign, the senior staff may not be aware of the accumulated load for your child in particular.

In those discussions, you could cite the 10-minute rule. If you're still unhappy, you could raise the issue with the school's PTA and cite examples of other schools, including those I mentioned earlier with different approaches to homework. If you accept the homework policy, what can you do to support your children in doing it?

Tips for Managing Homework

Aim to establish some sort of routine to make life easier for them and for you. Ashley Norris makes these suggestions:

- *Resist the urge to do the work for your children:* Homework creates an opportunity for students to learn from their mistakes, so it is important not to overstep. If your child is struggling with a problem, ask questions to help her approach the problem in a different way. Beware of excuses and coping strategies that children use to get out of doing work or to convince others to do the work for them.

- *Do your own homework:* Leverage available resources and look ahead. The key to avoid being overwhelmed with a child's homework is to be prepared. Online resources can help you brush up on concepts you have not studied in a long time. Skim your children's textbooks and look ahead to see where the lessons are going. Ask for an appointment with the child's teacher if you are not confident with the material—the teacher may have some great suggestions.

- *Make a plan:* Avoid the last-minute rush/panic. Create a plan for the week and break up large homework assignments into smaller pieces to avoid being overwhelmed. If your child has a project due at the end of the week, work with him to determine how he is going to get there and how the work can be divided into smaller projects.

- *Create a family calendar:* Create a physical or electronic family calendar that houses all family, school, extracurricular, and work schedules and deadlines. Include smaller deadlines on the way to completion of a larger project or preparation for a test to help children improve their time management skills. Put your own activities on the calendar to show your kids how you manage your time.

- *Set family study time:* Weekly family study time is a good way for parents to connect with children, instill the importance of education, and spend quality time together. Each Monday after children get their assignments for the week, sit down and plan to make it a successful week. Discuss all activities, set deadlines, determine what information is needed, and build in study time. Adults also benefit from time set aside to plan, organize, and learn. While children study, you can pay your bills, read the newspaper, or research your own projects.

- *Tie homework to real-life activities:* Look for opportunities to help children tie learning to real-life experiences. For instance, look at current events to discuss social studies lessons, or research specific jobs to bring science and math concepts to life. Encourage older students to read the newspaper each day for examples of good writing and urge them to research and write their own articles that can be shared with family and friends.

- *Get creative, particularly with young children:* Look for opportunities to expand homework assignments into creative projects. Ask your child to create a digital presentation, build a shadow box, construct an egg drop, or even interview a local leader about a topic. Tying in technology can keep children interested and engaged.

- *Create a calm and supportive environment:* Create an environment that is conducive to studying and learning. Have a quiet space in the house where your child always goes to do homework. The space should be comfortable but should not have access to a television or other distractions. It is also important to keep a routine and determine regular study hours.

As with all such advice, you need to adapt these suggestions to your own circumstances and expectations. The key is to keep in mind the broader principles that should underpin your children's development, including the need for play, relaxation, sleep, family time, good nutrition, and time to explore personal interests. Paying proper attention to all of those isn't a distraction from a sound education: it's the best way to provide one.

A Word of Caution

Being actively involved in your children's education can greatly enhance their progress and achievement. At the same time, parents can be too involved, and the effects of that can be just the reverse. We looked earlier in the book at the problems of over-parenting and especially of parents who go into helicopter mode, "hovering over their child incessantly and swooping down to the rescue when the first hardship occurs."[29]

Some parents try constantly to micromanage their children and whoever comes into contact with them, including their teachers. They call the school about every grade short of an A that their children are given and push the teachers to upgrade them. They try to mitigate any charge of misbehavior against their child and may even threaten to litigate if they think he or she has been treated unfairly. They call other parents to try to enlist them to the cause, or maybe to point out that the children of those parents are the real problem.

Chris Meno of Indiana University recognizes that helicopter parents are usually well intentioned and just want to protect their children from danger or disappointment. In doing that they can do a lot of damage and very little good, for their children, the teachers, or themselves. The children may remain overdependent on their parents and unable to stand up for themselves. Their teachers can become frustrated and feel that their professional authority is being undermined. Other parents are likely to think of helicopter parents as obsessive, hectoring, and plain annoying and to avoid them whenever possible.

Of course, there are times when you or any parents may have legitimate issues to raise with their children's teachers, or even have formal complaints to make against them or the school. We'll look at what you should do in those cases in Chapter Nine. Other than pursuing genuine grievances, your aim should be to have a positive relationship with the teachers, since that's the best way by far to help the relationships between them and your children to be as rewarding as possible.

A school is a learning community, and it has many members. They all matter but the most important for your children's education are their teachers. Your relationships with them can have an important role in enhancing their relationship with your children and in how effectively your children learn as a result. What form should your relationship take with the teachers and with the school as a whole and how can you tell if it's working for you and for them?

CHAPTER EIGHT

Build the Relationship

They say it takes a village to raise children. It certainly does to educate them. I said in the last chapter that teaching and learning is like gardening and that young people learn best in certain conditions. Those conditions are part of a much larger ecosystem in education. It includes you and your family, the communities you're part of, and a host of other people and organizations with responsibilities for what happens in education. As a parent, you are likely to be mainly interested in the education of your own children. You may have wider interests in education too. In either case, there are four ways in which you can influence your children's education and the people responsible for it. You can connect directly with your children's teachers. You can become involved in the life of the school more generally. You can take part in the governance of the school. You can become active in the wider politics of education.

Working with Teachers

As a parent, you're entitled to know what your children are doing in school and how they're getting on and to raise issues that may affect their progress. Typically, there are two ways in which schools keep you in touch: a report card at the end of the semester and parents' evenings.

On the surface, parents' evenings are relaxed opportunities for teachers, parents, and students to compare notes and make plans. In practice, they can be some of the most nerve-racking events of the school year: a succession of short, charged conversations with more left unsaid than said. For some parents, they may be one of the rare occasions they're in the school at all. Bubbling beneath may be all kinds of feelings, not all of which are relaxing. Children's author Allan Ahlberg catches some of them:

> We're waiting in the corridor,
> My dad, my mum and me.
> They're sitting there and talking;
> I'm nervous as can be.
> I wonder what she'll tell 'em.
> I'll say I've got a pain!
> I wish I'd got my spellings right.
> I wish I had a brain.
>
> We're waiting in the corridor,
> My husband, son and me.
> My son just stands there smiling;
> I'm smiling, nervously
> I wonder what she'll tell us.
> I hope it's not all bad.

He's such a good boy, really;
But dozy—like his dad.

We're waiting in the corridor
My wife, my boy and me.
My wife's as cool as cucumber;
I'm nervous as can be.
I hate these parents' evenings.
I feel just like a kid again
Who's gonna get the stick.

I'm waiting in the classroom.
It's nearly time to start.
I wish there was a way to stop
The pounding in my heart.
The parents in the corridor
Are chatting cheerfully;
And now I've got to face them;
And I'm nervous as can be.[1]

One of the reasons why these meetings can be stressful is that they happen so rarely—perhaps two or three times a year—usually when report cards are issued. If there's an impromptu meeting, it's often because there's a problem, which adds to the tension. Apart from brief encounters at the school gates, some parents don't have much more contact with their children's teachers than this.

Report cards are normally a list of grades with short comments, written under pressure by the teachers and read with bated breath by the parents. By the time they sit down to discuss them, the work they're reviewing is probably long over and the moment to do anything about it has passed. It's important for parents and teachers to work together, and the real value is in taking opportunities and dealing with challenges as they come up rather than having a postmortem weeks after the event.

One way to improve collaboration is to have more regular meetings and workshops. Some schools do this, and they can be valuable. You should take part in them if you can and encourage your school to provide them if they don't. Of course, time is limited for everyone, and life is busy. These days there are other ways to collaborate. With the proliferation of mobile technologies, a range of apps now make it possible for teachers, parents, and students to keep step with each other whenever they need to. They include Blackboard Learn, Edmodo, and Fresh Grade, among others.[2]

Fresh Grade allows teachers to post regular, secure updates on how their students are doing in school. Using their smartphones or tablets, they can post images, photos, videos, audio, and written notes to students' digital portfolios, which document their activities and progress throughout the year. Parents can access these materials whenever they choose. They can look at examples of their children's work as it's developing, hear clips of them reading, and see videos of them in activities with other children. They can post comments and questions for teachers to review and they can offer tailored support at home when it's needed.

A parent of a kindergartner, who admitted to "helicopter tendencies," said she felt she was missing out when all she heard about her child's day at school was "It was fun," "It was great," or "Nothing much happened." With the app, she can see the pictures and videos of activities posted by her teacher: "Now, if I ask about a specific math exercise I've seen in a picture, she will tell me all about it. It's a great tool to get us talking." Another parent feels equally enthusiastic: "I feel like I'm being kept in the loop with my son's work and grades. Very easy to use and a nice way to bring up discussions about what he is working on in class."

Some teachers and some students have reservations about this sort of constant, 360-degree documentation. They worry that it's intrusive and can encourage parents to become overly involved in what's going on in school. Like all tools, these apps are neutral in themselves. For unrestrained helicopter parents, these apps could be a turbocharger. The challenge is to learn how to use them responsibly to make education more collaborative and effective for everyone.

Working with teachers to support your own children is the first reason to become more involved in the school. Another is to enhance the life of the school as a whole. As a parent, there are many ways you can do this.

The Life of the School

Richard Gerver, a former head teacher, told me a great story about the mother of one of his students.[3] She was, as Richard put it, "school-phobic," but she was a talented hairdresser and the school felt she could convey valuable skills to the student population. They convinced her to teach the children some of the skills of hairdressing and about hairdressing as a career. The experience exceeded expectations for everyone involved, and her lessons extended far beyond hairstyling. She also helped the students improve their communication skills, "including empathy as a listener to clients which was an incredible thing to watch!" Richard said. "Real literacy, taught by a mum in a real context—one she herself didn't even realize she had!"

Danielle Wood is editor in chief of Education.com. She suggested eight ways in which parents can play a practical role in their children's schools and classrooms:

- Reading to the class or to a group of kids who need more help with reading.
- Helping in one of the activity areas, such as art class or computer lab.
- Offering to tutor or to help out in other ways to help students understand or dig deeper into an exercise.
- Volunteering as a class parent.
- Helping with special interest groups or clubs.
- Sharing your expertise and talking to kids about career opportunities.
- Volunteering at the school library.
- Volunteering in sports programs.[4]

Many parents have specific skills or interests that schools can use. Maybe you have an MBA and can help students develop their entrepreneurial talents. Maybe you have a background in nutrition and you can go into the school a few times a year to enlighten kids about better ways to eat. Maybe you paint or are fascinated with astronomy or know how to run a book club. Take these skills to your school's principal or teachers and see if the school might be open to putting them to use.

Carol Shepard found out that her daughter's elementary school in Georgia had just received laptops to use in class. She thought that this was a great opportunity to show the students how to make a digital film. She pitched the idea to the school and found that one of the teachers was interested in entering a film into the Georgia Movie Academy, a student moviemaking competition. The school jumped at the opportunity to get Shepard's help, and she persuaded other adults to join in.

"We taught the kids how to use morphing software, scratch animation and stop-motion technology to produce Claymation (like *Wallace and Gromit*)," she said. "The kids learned that you couldn't just do something once and expect to master it. We talked about the rule of three in software engineering—by the third time you build something you'll understand what you are building. Our movie took much more work than we had originally planned, but all of the kids arrived an hour or more early for school over a period of multiple weeks to participate in our club and get the work done. By the end of the movie-making process, the kids were starting to shoot new scenes themselves without any adult guidance, and, more importantly, were resolving their own team dynamic conflicts."[5]

The film won the Best Picture award in their category, inspiring the school to grow the program for the future. Shepard was not a professional filmmaker. She had a certain level of expertise in digital filmmaking and wanted to share that expertise with her daughter's school. Her experience shows that you don't have to be a top professional in a field in order to have something valuable to offer. Many schools are understaffed and overly dependent on state and federal standards and may well see your support as a blessing.

Even if you don't feel you have a particular skill to offer, offering whatever time you have can be enormously valuable. Helping with fund-raising, chaperoning events, handing out flyers, or assisting with organizing a function all add to the overall quality of the school experience for the students and others in the school community. Jo Ashline is a former kindergarten teacher, and she knows the invaluable roles parents can play in the vitality of school life. While teachers and administrators are responsible for providing core programs and professional support, she said, school "is much more than just a place where worksheets are distributed and graded." Building a tight-knit community of volunteers who dedicate their time and resources to building a solid foundation of support creates a lasting

impression on staff and students alike. "Planning events, organizing fundraisers, donating time and energy to cleaning up and
beautifying the campus, and using professional and personal
connections to benefit the school takes some serious manpower.
Your child's school is the village and you, my friend, are a vil-
lager, so get to work."[6]

Earlier, I mentioned the University of Chicago study on the
impact of parents on students' achievement in education. The
study also found that collaboration between schools and families is a powerful source of school improvement in general.
When schools build strong partnerships with families and listen
positively to their ideas and concerns, they tend to create more
successful learning environments for everyone.

Close links with parents and the community are one of five
essential supports for school success and transformation. The
others are strong school leadership, the quality of the teachers
and staff, a student-centered learning climate, and strong align-
ment between the school's goals and values and the curriculum.
Parents and community organizations are powerful agents of
change for improved school facilities and staffing and can have a
positive influence on the shape and content of the whole curriculum and on extracurricular provision. Experience shows that
when families and communities bring the right pressure to bear,
school districts are more likely to make positive changes in policy, practice, and resources.

Eric Schaps suggests a simple annual survey that a school
could conduct with its students to determine whether they are
providing a true sense of community. While such a survey would
likely be helpful to any parent in assessing a school, you could do
this yourself simply by speaking with parents as well as the students themselves. It's important to identify whether classrooms
feel like families, whether the students help each other learn,

whether the teachers are sensitive to students' concerns, and whether the school is open to changing rules that the students believe are unfair.

School Governance

Another way to affect the quality of your children's education is by influencing school policy. The most effective route is usually through the school's parent-teacher association. PTAs meet on a regular schedule, provide a direct line to the school's administration, and give parents the opportunity to voice concerns, learn early about proposed changes, and play an active role in whether and how those changes are enacted. PTAs also often have a significant presence in fund-raising, teacher recognition, and supporting extracurricular programs.

The National PTA is America's largest and oldest organization advocating for school improvement. It involves millions of families, educators, and community members. It has set out six national standards for schools to encourage family-school partnerships:

- *Welcoming all families:* Making it clear to parents that they belong as part of the community, that the school is respectful and inclusive of diverse groups, and that events and programs are offered that allow the greatest range and numbers of parents to participate.
- *Communicating effectively:* Keeping parents informed on all of the important issues affecting the school and in ways that take full account of language barriers and welcome feedback.
- *Supporting student success:* Keeping families fully informed—in a timely fashion—of how school is

supporting their children and enabling them to be active participants in their children's learning both in school and at home.

- *Speaking up for every child:* Providing families with a clear understanding of how the school works and showing them how to serve as advocates for their children.

- *Sharing power:* Involving families as full partners in decisions about issues affecting their children both at school and within the community. The aim is for every school to have a broad-based parent organization that offers families and school staff regular opportunities to discuss concerns with each other and with school leaders, public officials, and community leaders.

- *Collaborating with the community:* Connecting the school to the larger community around it. This gives the school greater access to the resources available in the community and gives the entire community a stake in the success of the school.[7]

National PTA president Otha Thornton says that these standards are intended to show that family engagement is not limited to helping children with homework, attending meetings at school, and checking in with teachers. They also include "advocating with local school boards and state and federal government to ensure schools have the resources they need to provide a world-class education to every student."[8]

This only works if your child's school is open to you being involved. I've heard of teachers, schools, and even school systems discouraging parent involvement at any level deeper than participating in a bake sale, but in my experience most schools understand the value of having parents take an active role in the school. To do that, schools need to be active in getting parents involved: organizing parent workshops, holding regular meetings, and building trust among teachers, families, and the wider community.

Edutopia, a nonprofit launched by the George Lucas Educational Foundation, offers ten tips for educators to make their schools more inviting, which parents can also use to guide their interactions with their children's schools:

- *Go where your parents are:* Use social networking sites to keep parents in the loop and encourage interaction.
- *Welcome everyone:* Acknowledge that many families in your community are non-native English speakers, and use technology to help communicate with them.
- *Be there, virtually:* Use Web-based tools to offer virtual windows into the classroom.
- *Smartphones, smart schools:* Use mobile devices to engage families, including group texts and apps.
- *Seize the media moment:* Use current media (the release of a new education-related book or film, for example) as a platform for an open forum on school activities and education reform.
- *Make reading a family affair:* Use programs like Read Across America, First Book, and Experience Corps to promote reading as a family activity.
- *Bring the conversation home:* Flip the parent-teacher conference upside down by having teachers visit student homes.
- *Student-led parent conferences:* Allow students to direct the parent-teacher meeting, presenting some of

their work and exhibiting their strengths, challenges, and goals.

- *Get families moving:* Create school events that encourage exercise and play as a family activity.
- *Build parent partnerships:* Use a range of other strategies, such as starting a parent-based book club or creating assignments that include family interviews, to involve parents in schoolwork.[9]

The Politics of Education

If you want to influence education at an even higher level, there's the school board. School board members come from all walks of life, are usually elected by the general public, and have considerable influence over the policies of the whole school district. In most districts, the superintendent reports to the board; the board allocates the budget, signs off on curriculum, and decides how resources are allocated to the schools. It's a big step up from volunteering for school activities and not something that you should consider without having the time and energy to commit to it. If you do, you could have an enormous influence on education across the community of schools that the board oversees.[10]

If you don't have the time to serve as a member of your local school board, you can still be involved in other ways. Most school boards have open meetings every month during the school year. They report on agenda items and open the room for questions and comments. I've spoken to several parents over the years who never miss a school board meeting and feel their presence gives them an active voice in local school policy. Many school boards also organize focus groups, and you can volunteer to participate in those. A good number regularly organize citizen groups to advise on issues concerning the school community, and you can let the board know of your interest in being part of those too. You can usually find information about school board activities on your school district website.

Moving for Change

Your power to effect change isn't confined to working through the "usual channels." Sometimes those channels don't run in the direction you need to move. In some communities there are serious obstacles to parents engaging with their children's schools. Collective action with other parents and educators can generate a powerful momentum for change.

Tellin' Stories is an initiative of Teaching for Change in Washington, D.C. Allyson Criner Brown, associate director of Teaching for Change, told me that the work of Tellin' Stories began as a student project. "Teaching for Change had been working in schools where there had been a large influx of Central American students into neighborhoods that had primarily been African American strongholds in D.C. Organizationally, our work started by providing resources for teachers to learn about these new students. Who were their families? Where were they coming from?" Teaching for Change had started a project where parents created a felt square involving a story from their culture to include in a large quilt. "The folks who were working on that invited more parents to come and share stories and to make a quilt. They found that was a way to have African American and Latino families come together to learn more about each other."[11]

The Tellin' Stories approach is based on three principles. The first is that not all learning comes from schools or curriculum; parents have valid knowledge to pass along to their children and to others in the school community. The second is that family engagement is an essential part of building a strong school. The third is that community organizing is critical if everyone is going to have a voice. "We recognize that there are inequities in our society and those relate to power," Allyson said. "In schools there are power differentials as well that tie in to race, class, language, and so on. If you are in the group that does not hold power, how do you build power? We believe that community organizing provides the best model for those who do not hold power because of their social groups."[12]

Teaching for Change works to have a parent coordinator in every school. They arrange regular meetings with the principal where the agenda is set not only by the school but by the parents as well. They launch every school year with a welcome-back breakfast for parents where they make them aware of the various resources available to them. Most importantly, they make it clear that parents have a voice in the school community, a voice that is amplified enormously when they work together. It's a spirit driven by the proverb, "If you want to go fast, go alone. If you want to go far, go together."

"A lot of the parents we work with have been discouraged from challenging authority, especially by themselves," Allyson says. "The key for Teaching for Change is to start by building relationships and building community. You have to build relationships with other parents and open a dialogue to find what we have in common in what we want for our children. You can fight the fight alone. If you want support, you need to take the time to build those relationships, to listen to others. When you do, you'll hear something beyond yourself. To shape the school as an institution, we believe it has to be done as a community. We can have one or two people call downtown, and that may get a response, but if we show up with fifty or seventy-five and demand a meeting, that says something greater."[13]

Bruce Monroe Elementary School had an invaluable after-school program that provided homework help and a safe place for young people once classes ended. The program was woefully understaffed, with a wait list that was seventy-five students long. After an e-mail and phone campaign to address the situation, D.C. Public Schools (DCPS) agreed to meet with parents. The large turnout and the passionate presentations from parent speakers led DCPS to add funding for six staff positions to the after-school program, enough to eliminate the wait list. Teaching for Change has had a similar influence on many other initiatives affecting D.C. schools, such as addressing funding, dealing with the challenges of gentrification, and fighting for long overdue funds for schools desperately in need of renovation.

Changing the System

Schools can change. The fact is that they have to change and they are changing. Teaching and learning is a relationship between *students*, *teachers*, *content*, and *context*. All of these are changing and that's why the relationship between them needs to change too. As a parent, you have the power to influence these changes in all the ways we've discussed. As I said in Chapter One, you can work for changes *within the current system*, particularly in your children's own school; you can press for changes *to the system*; or you can educate your children *outside the system*.

Room to Maneuver

There's more room to make changes within the current education system than many people think. Schools operate as they do not because they have to but because they choose to. They don't need to be that way; they can change and many do. Innovative schools everywhere are breaking the mold of convention to meet the best interests of their students, families, and communities. As well as great teachers, what they have in common is visionary leadership. They have principals who are willing to make the changes that are needed to promote the success of all their students, whatever their circumstances and talents. A creative principal with the right powers of leadership can take a failing school and turn it into a hot spot of innovation and inclusion that benefits everyone it touches.

Take Orchard Gardens elementary school in Roxbury, Massachusetts. Ten years ago Orchard Gardens was in the doldrums. By most measures, it was one of the most troubled schools in the state. The school had five principals in its first seven years. Each fall, half the teachers did not return. Test scores were in the bottom 5 percent of all Massachusetts schools. The students were disaffected and unruly and there was a constant threat of violence. Students weren't allowed to carry backpacks to school for fear that they might use them to conceal weapons, and there was an expensive staff of security guards, costing more than $250,000 a year, to make sure they didn't. Remember, this was an *elementary* school.

Principal number six, Andrew Bott, arrived in 2010. People had told him that becoming principal at Orchard Gardens would be a career killer. He knew its reputation as one of the worst-performing schools in Massachusetts and admits that when he arrived it did feel like a prison. He had a radically different solution to its problems, which shocked many observers. He decided to eliminate the security staff altogether and invest the money in arts programs instead.

The school was enlisted as one of eight pilot schools for a new plan created by President Obama's Committee on the Arts and Humanities (PCAH). In the next two years, Bott replaced 80

percent of the teachers and recruited others with special expertise in the arts: teachers who believed in his new vision for the
school. "This was a far better investment," said Bott, than
"spending a quarter of a million dollars on six people to chase a
few kids around who are misbehaving." Together they introduced strong systems to support students as individuals. They
lengthened the school day and started a data-driven approach to
school improvement from monitoring attendance to test scores.
And they focused on reinvigorating the school culture as a
whole. They bought instruments, invited artists to come into
school to work with the children, and ran creative workshops for
the teachers and parents. The arts classes gave the students fresh
enthusiasm for learning, and the walls and corridors were soon
covered with displays of their work, which itself created a more
stimulating environment and sense of ownership by the children. "Kids do well," Bott said, "when you design and build a
school that they want to be in. Having great arts programs and
athletics programs makes school an enjoyable place to be and
that's when you see success."[14]

The school had more than eight hundred students, most of
whom qualified for free or reduced lunches. Half the students
were learning English as a second language, and one in five were
on individual learning plans for special needs. The school's problems were not its students, Bott said. It needed a new approach
to education. Having a broader curriculum, rich in the arts, engaged the whole student and promoted higher levels of achievement across the board.

Students who were struggling in the old system came alive
and graduated with confidence to high school and beyond. For
some people, abandoning security in favor of arts programs
seemed like a crazy idea. Bott knew, and events proved, that it
was a bold innovation rooted in a sound understanding of what

really motivates young people to learn. The transformation is not yet complete, but progress has been considerable. Bott has now moved on from Orchard Gardens, but the school continues to flourish under the leadership of the current principal, Megan Webb.[15]

The transformation of Orchard Gardens didn't depend on any new laws being passed. All it took was a leader with the vision to see beyond the conventional habits of schools to the opportunities to do education differently. The story of Orchard Gardens (and others like it)[16] illustrates an essential truth in education. The problem is not usually the students; it is the system. Change the system in the right ways and many of the problems of poor behavior, low motivation, and disengagement tend to disappear. It can be the system itself that creates the problems.

Changing the Climate

Much of what goes on in schools is the result of habit rather than legislation. It's also true that the pressure of legislation is considerable and tends to reinforce those habits. Attempts to transform individual schools, like Orchard Gardens, are not straightforward, not least because national and state policies and funding restrictions tend to hamper them. The relentless pressure of standardized testing is a key example. Instead of raising standards, it tends to erode the enthusiasm for learning—in students and teachers alike—on which high standards of achievement depend. That's why so many parents and educators are raising their voices against standardized testing and acting together to change the climate in education, which affects them all.

Over the past few years, parents around the world have protested against the negative impact of standardized testing. They have grown so frustrated with the number of high-stakes tests being foisted upon their children that they have taken to a form of civil disobedience to register their protest—they refused to have their children take the test. Parent organizers were so effective in New York that approximately 20 percent of public school students in grades three through eight opted out of state exams in 2015. This made the testing data unreliable, thus defeating the purpose of having the test in the first place. A campaign in Colorado led to most large districts in the state failing to meet the 95 percent participation rate required by No Child Left Behind, sending another powerful message about parent displeasure with the reliance on and the stakes associated with standardized tests.[17]

If you want to be involved on an even broader level, then you can become involved with a statewide or even national advocacy group. These groups actively embrace parent involvement as they address education reform from a variety of perspectives. For example, Parents Across America is an organization started by two education bloggers that has grown into a national organization advocating for public school reform, diversity, and funding equity and against privatization and high-stakes testing.[18] As their name suggests, they build their coalition through parent involvement.

The Center for Education Reform has a different agenda, focused on charter schools and school choice, but they have a number of resources available and ways for parents to become involved.[19] Parent Revolution is a California group that lobbied for the state's controversial "parent trigger" law that allows parents at underperforming schools to trigger changes in the school ranging from removing the administration to turning the school into a charter school.[20] There are many others with positions all along the education reform spectrum. These groups are known as *education reform advocacy organizations*, and an online search of that term will introduce you to a large number of them.

Moving Out

As we saw in Chapter Six, a small but significant number of parents are taking their children out of organized education altogether. Homeschooling and unschooling allow them to develop their own approaches to education, free of the constraints of public policy. As online resources increase and networks evolve to support these options, it's likely that more families will take them. In these and other ways, as parents you do have choices in education. Exercising them may not be easy, but here as everywhere, knowledge and collaboration equals power.

The Rough and the Smooth

We've been looking here at ways in which you can influence the general character of your children's education, in their particular school and in education as a whole, if you choose to get involved in that way. Whatever course you take, all children are individuals and a school or teacher that works well for one child may not for another. The path through education, like the rest of life, rarely runs smoothly. There are always issues to deal with and problems to address. In the best of circumstances, your children may run into trouble at school, or be treated in a way that concerns you. What do you do then, and what are your options?

CHAPTER NINE

Tackle the Problem

Under the best circumstances, your relationships with school would be consistently productive, and you'd feel that everyone there always has your child's best interests in mind. Realistically, there may be more troubling issues along the way, which you may want to address with the school or the district. It's reasonable for you as a parent to do that. You should feel you can question the school on how they are fulfilling their roles and to look for remediation if you think they aren't doing that properly. What do you do then, and what are your options?

We're going to steer clear here of some issues that come up in school. If you and your child are dealing with problems like eating disorders, addiction, or self-harming, there are many excellent resources out there for you, and I recommend you seek them out. You'll need the sort of individualized advice that simply isn't possible here. I'm going to focus on more general issues.

Problems at school range in severity, and your approach to dealing with them needs to be appropriate. They could be relatively small, like your child getting a grade he or she doesn't understand or having trouble with a particular teacher's approach to the class, or they could be more substantial issues like discipline problems, student/teacher battles, or your child being given a diagnosis of learning or behavioral problems that you don't agree with.

When issues like these come up, there's a good chance you'll want to intervene. Many parents struggle with how to do this effectively. You want to make things right for your children while avoiding being a "problem parent." As in global politics, proportional responses to conflicts are usually best. How and if you address your child not being picked for the lead in the school play may be different from how you'd deal with him or her being accused of bullying other students.

Schools can't always accommodate every parent's demands, nor should they; not all parents' demands are reasonable or even good. The website Reddit asked teachers about the "most ridiculous/petty" complaints they'd had to deal with from parents. Here are just a few:

- We had a mom who was mad that we wouldn't let her son be in the class he wanted to be in. He was in grade two, but for the first two or so months of the school year he would go to the kindergarten classroom every day because he liked the toys better. When he was there he would make fun of the younger students and hit them if they were "stupid." When we told the mom what was going on and that we needed her to support the transition she thought we just didn't want her son to be happy at school. We finally got him to go to the correct class but the troubled behavior continued, and so did the mom's ideas that we were just picking on him.

- A parent asked me where our cleaners were from so she could decide whether or not she trusted that they wouldn't steal her daughter's stuff from school. I explained that we didn't use an agency and all the cleaners were employed directly by the school. "No," she clarified, "where are they *from*?" She was quickly invited to leave my office.
- In the school's behavior plan, if the kids don't fall below a certain good behavior level, they get a Friday Lollipop. One child wasn't given a lollipop because he'd spit on another kid, among other stuff. The parents barged into the school in a full rage, screaming and demanding a lollipop for their son.
- A parent forgot to pack his child a lunch. He called the school to tell me I needed to leave the classroom and go across the street to buy the kid a Subway.
- I was almost physically attacked by a father because I gave his child a C in reading.
- I gave one child a D on homework. The parent contacted me to complain that I was picking on him. The parent agreed that most of the child's answers were wrong but said I should have "cut him some slack."
- A parent complained because I played a CD of classical Persian flute music in class. The class was World Languages and Cultures and I played a different CD from around the world every day. The parent thought I was sympathizing with terrorists and should "only teach American stuff."
- I had a parent of a fifth grader who felt that her son wasn't being challenged enough. I ramped up the work and challenge level to a degree I felt he could handle. After the student's grades dropped a tiny

bit, the same parent complained that I was being too tough on her child. Face palm.

- A parent complained that I was speaking too much French in class, which would be legitimate concern if it weren't a high school French class.
- A mother wanted her high school son switched to a different teacher. She claimed that her son was intimidated by my "loud, husky voice" and that's why he wasn't able to pay attention while we read literature passages. He was a 6′2″ football player. I'm 5′7″ and sing soprano.
- I'm reminded of a time one of my parents called to tell me she had decided to homeschool her son. She wanted to know what time each day I would be dropping off his work at HER HOME and when I would come to pick it up to correct it.

Your complaint may be entirely justified, but before you act, try to see things from the school's point of view, as well as your own. Teachers are dealing with many children and families. Remember too that your child may not be the same at school as at home and may well have behaved in that way that you thought was unthinkable—and that overprotecting him or her whatever the circumstances may not always be the best course. Your role isn't always to enforce your views on the school. Even so, you are your child's number one advocate and your voice should be heard.

Fair Expectations

If you do have legitimate concerns, what kind of response should you expect from the school? At the very least, a thoughtful and respectful one. I've known parents, especially ones whose first language is not English, who've told me that the school made them feel they shouldn't interfere at all and made them feel stupid when they did. This is never okay. Here are some guidelines for handling general issues in a proportionate way.

- You should expect the school to be open to your concerns and to offer you a reasonable explanation if they can't fulfill your request. You should expect them to be accessible to you at some point during any school day and to have times either just before or after school when you can meet with them. The school should be willing to discuss anything about your children that might affect their schooling or socialization. For example, if you know your child is struggling with writing, you might ask that the school offer him some extra help or that his teacher spend some one-on-one time with him. If he has genuine difficulties with a certain group of children, it's fair to ask the school to find ways of dealing with that.

- The school should allow you a forum where you can voice your concerns about curriculum, school policies, extracurricular offerings, and more. Schools usually have regular meetings of their parent-teacher organization where such concerns can be expressed. If your children's school doesn't have such meetings, you should ask to discuss this with someone who can make them happen.

- The school should be open to discussing all forms of assessment with you and, where appropriate, your child. This is different, by the way, from negotiating for a higher grade for your child. If you believe a grade received is unfair, it's reasonable to ask for

details about the assessments used to give that grade.
If the data supports the grade, "I still think he de-
serves an A" is not a reasonable argument.

If your child is complaining regularly about a teacher, seems
to be struggling in class, or feels bored or unchallenged, it's important to get a clearer sense from her of why this is happening.
She might be going through something that only tangentially
relates to school, in which case you'll need to deal with the matter in other ways. She might be complaining about school because that's what her friends do. In all likelihood, though, if
your child is expressing a problem, you're perceiving it yourself,
or you've heard something from another school parent, the issue
probably does need your attention. Before you go any further,
the first step is to have a candid conversation with your child to
get her perspective on the issue.

If you think it's warranted, the next step is talking to the
teacher. It's reasonable for you to do this because you know more
about your child than other people do. At the same time, you
need to respect the roles of the teachers, who are often dealing
with many children—not just yours—and are under all kinds of
other pressures as well. You should be firm in your concerns but
also open to the teacher's take on things, as this is more likely to
lead to a positive resolution than if you come in angry, demanding, or intransigent.

If that approach doesn't work, or if you feel that you can't go
to your child's teacher for some reason, it's time to talk to the
principal. If you're going to make this meeting productive, it's
best to keep the principal's perspective in mind. If your child's
teacher seems stretched to the limits handling her teaching
groups, imagine being responsible for the whole school. That's
the principal's role, as well as dealing with the superintendent,

the board of education, and a host of other stakeholders and interested parties.

Michelle Crouch is an award-winning journalist specializing in parenting and health issues. She interviewed principals and former principals across the United States and wrote about "22 Things Your Kid's Principal Won't Tell You."[1] Here are a few that might be helpful:

- "If you want to talk to me about a problem, schedule a morning appointment, when I'm fresh. By the afternoon, I can get pretty frazzled."
- "You're right, that teacher does stink. I'm actually in the process of firing her. Legally, I can't tell you that, though, so that's why I'm sitting here quietly while you complain."
- "My biggest pet peeve? Parents who complain to me before talking to the teacher."
- "Kids are easy. It's the parents who are tough. They're constantly trying to solve their kids' problems for them."

This isn't to say that principals dread meeting with parents: on the contrary, most principals I know are dedicated to the success of their schools and to the well-being of their students and their families. They understand that dealing with the concerns of parents is an essential part of doing their job well. You should just be sure that the situation has sufficient gravity before you make the overture.

When you are in the meeting, have a clear agenda. Tell the principal what the problem is as you see it, what the evidence is, and what outcome you're seeking. Describe any conversations you have had with your child's teacher and have a good argument prepared. This is especially important if you're dealing with something sensitive, such as moving your child to another class or seeking special help for your child from the school.

If talking to the principal doesn't help you, you can talk to the school's PTA. We've discussed the roles of PTAs, so I won't rehash them here, but the board of the PTA usually has a good working relationship with the school's administration and a high level of trust. If you can make your case to them persuasively, they might be more effective than you in advocating for you and your child.

If all of this fails and you still feel the school is wrong—and that can happen—you can lobby the superintendent or the board of education. In this case, you'll want to make your first approach in writing with as much backup as you can provide. This will allow time for the school governor to understand your situation before you meet, which will be especially important if that meeting takes place during one of their regularly scheduled public sessions.

Finally, you could seek the help of outside advocacy groups. For example, if you feel your child needs special attention because of a condition and the school is reluctant to provide it, there are likely to be local or regional organizations that can bring some pressure to bear. The nuclear option is to bring in a lawyer. You should only take that route as a last resort and in full awareness of the potential consequences.

Let's look at three more specific areas that commonly concern parents and how best to approach them with the school: *stress*, *bullying*, and *medication*.

Stress

You'll recall that the percentage of parents who thought their children were stressed was much lower than the percentage of children who feel they are. As we've seen, it isn't always easy for parents to pick up on this. What can the school do to help?

Momentous School is a laboratory school in Dallas, Texas. It provides for students from age three to ten, and alongside their other learning it puts a particular emphasis on their social and emotional health. Michelle Kinder is executive director of Momentous Institute, of which the school is part. The school's program, she says, is "underscored by deep parental engagement, as students thrive when they can be recognized and celebrated both at school and at home." Distinctively, the school teaches the children from age three to understand and control their feelings by learning about their own brains. The institute teaches them that "their amygdala is in charge of their emotions, that their prefrontal cortex helps them make good decisions and that their hippocampus helps them remember. Children learn the basic biology of their emotions so they can feel a greater sense of control in managing them. Once children understand what's going on biologically, when they become upset (amygdala hijack) they can then use breathing and focusing strategies to self-regulate."[2]

As a favorite strategy, the school uses a glitter ball as a model of the brain. "When you shake the ball, glitter swirls around and clouds the water, which is a metaphor for when your brain is flooded with emotion and it's impossible to see clearly and make good decisions." When children take time to breathe and focus their attention on the glitter, it settles and "they are able to see clearly and access the prefrontal cortex to make good decisions. They are always careful to acknowledge that the glitter, or problem, is still there. But when the glitter is settled the children are in charge and can see their way to a solution." The fundamental premise of the program is that "by learning about their brain, self-regulation and understanding of others leads kids to achieve their full potential."[3] The school recognizes that all of our lives are driven by feelings—by the world within us—and that when we learn from the earliest ages to understand and handle our feelings, especially negative ones, we're better able to deal with the situations or problems that give rise to them. There are lessons here for all schools.

If you feel your child is experiencing harmful levels of stress because of school, it's important to talk to the school about it. It may already have programs in place for dealing with this and, if they don't, you're entitled to ask them to come up with a strategy. It's unlikely that your child is the only one who is feeling this way. The school can follow the lead of other schools that are taking seriously their responsibility for managing increased student stress levels. Here are some other examples:[4]

- *Yoga:* In Smithtown High School, New York, gym class offers students four different physical education options: Team or Lifetime Sports, Project Adventure, Personal Fitness, and Yoga.

- *Puppy love:* Pets can be a highly effective form of stress relief, and high schools are now catching on to the benefits of canine therapy for overworked students. At Prospect High School in Mount Prospect, Illinois, the school counseling team includes Junie, an eighteen-month-old golden retriever who acts as a therapy dog to comfort and soothe the students.

- *Transcendental Meditation:* Transcendental Meditation—a form of meditation that involves repeating a mantra for fifteen to twenty minutes per day with the eyes closed—has been shown to decrease psychological stress in students, and many high schools are now offering TM sessions. Schools in San Francisco have experienced significant benefits from introducing a quiet time/Transcendental Meditation program.

- *Nap time:* To boost energy for learning, a short power nap is normally a better answer then reaching for a candy bar or soda. Schools like Lakeside High School in Georgia are helping students boost their energy and cognitive functioning by providing thirty-minute study halls and optional nap times.

- *Wellness rooms:* In Belfast Area High School in Maine, an old language lab has been converted into a wellness room for the entire school community—teachers, students, and administrators—to enjoy. Local alternative health care practitioners offer short massage sessions, Reiki, acupuncture, chiropractic care, and more to ease stress.

- *Recess:* As I mentioned in Chapter Six, some schools are miraculously rediscovering the importance of playtime (recess). To recognize the value of relaxation, social time, and play, some schools are instituting twenty-minute breaks to give their students more downtime between classes. At Chanhassen High School in Minnesota, students enjoy these daily breaks as well as homework-free nights scattered throughout the year to help handle the pressure of potentially overwhelming workloads.

- *Self-esteem conferences:* Struggling with self-esteem and body image issues in high school can add significantly to academic pressures and social stresses. Some schools are providing students with coping resources through classes and conferences on healthy self-esteem and body image. At Union County High School in New Jersey, female students are invited to attend a day of confidence-boosting activities as a part of Happy, Healthy & Whole: A

Conference to Empower Young Women. At British Columbia's G. W. Graham Secondary School, a student-led initiative is inviting young women to celebrate natural beauty by going without hair products and makeup for one week.

- *Mindfulness training:* More and more schools are teaching students mindfulness through meditation, to relax and center them during the school day. One of the best known of these is Mind-Up, an acclaimed program for schools that's focused on social and emotional learning.

Founded by the award-winning actress Goldie Hawn, Mind-Up was designed with a team of neuroscientists and cognitive psychologists and is being practiced successfully in hundreds of schools in North America and Europe. It also includes seven strategies to help parents keep in touch with their children's emotional states:

- *Don't ignore signs that your child is struggling:* A change in behavioral patterns could just be an anomaly, but it could also be an indication that something is roiling up inside your child.
- *Don't trivialize how your child is feeling:* Rather than assuming your child is going through a phase that all kids go through (like "the terrible twos"), check in and make sure that there isn't something specific that's changing your child's outlook and behavior.
- *Be sensitive and attuned, not reactive or parental:* Having an open line of communication with your child is one of the keys to keeping in touch with their emotional health. To get an honest appraisal of

how your children are feeling, you need to avoid reacting defensively to what they have to say.

- *Invite them to spend time with you:* Playing or simply being together can lead to conversation that will clue you in to any troubles your children might be having.
- *If they won't talk to you, help them find a situation they trust:* Sometimes your children won't want to talk to you. If that's the case, it's important that you let them know that you endorse their speaking with *someone.*
- *If they are in real trouble, get them the help they need:* Some parents fail to seek help for their children because they don't want to be perceived by others as having troubled children. If this is you, you need to get over it.
- *Take care of your emotional health:* Your children are more attuned to your own emotional state than you may realize. It's important to check regularly on your own emotional state.

Bullying

One of the most intense sources of stress for children in school is being bullied. Bullying can have devastating effects, including depression and anxiety, physical disorders, and poor performance in school. These effects can be long-lasting, following bullied children long into adulthood. Sometimes they can be fatal.

In 2012, fifteen-year-old Amanda Todd posted a nine-minute video on YouTube. She used flash cards to describe being coerced into taking a topless photo online and how this led to a chilling level of cyberbullying that caused her to move multiple times, resulted in physical and emotional abuse from her peers, and caused her to turn to cutting and substance abuse. The video became an international rallying cry against bullying with more than seventeen million people viewing it. Sadly, this didn't help Amanda, who eventually took her own life.[5]

Around a third of American students say they have been bullied in some way at school. Your child may well be one of them without you being aware of it. Many young people find the experience too painful to talk about, and some even feel they're to blame for what's being done to them and feel guilty. What signs should you look for? The website NoBullying.com offers a number of valuable resources for parents, students, and school personnel. It says that your child might be the target of school bullying if he or she:

- Often has personal items go missing.
- Regularly asks you for extra money or frequently "loses" his or her lunch money.
- Complains frequently of headaches or stomachaches.
- Avoids after-school activities.
- Regularly goes to school early or late.
- Increasingly pretends to be sick in order to avoid going to school.[6]

What is bullying and what can you and the school do about it?

There are two main types of bullying: *direct*, which takes place in the presence of the person being bullied, and *indirect*, which takes place in some other way, such as spreading rumors. There are four main types of direct bullying: *physical*, *verbal*, *relational*, and *damage to property*. The most common are verbal and relational, and most of this happens in middle school. Cyberbullying is rarer than the media sometimes suggest, with about one in ten students in grade six through twelve claiming to have experienced it, though one in two LGBT students have been victims of cyberbullying.[7]

As a parent you can do only so much by yourself to deal with bullying in your children's school. If your child is being bullied, you should contact the school immediately. The school should have an explicit antibullying policy and be diligent about upholding it. It has probably held assemblies with students and evening sessions with parents to address the topic. Simply condemning bullying is rarely enough to stop it. NoBullying.com offers a valuable template for a school antibullying initiative. Noting that bullies are less likely to act out with an authority figure present, they recommend the clear presence of monitors and teachers—who are trained to act accordingly—wherever students gather. It is important that the school have a strong antibullying culture in which students understand the damage bullying causes and begin to self-monitor.

The school's response to bullying needs to be consistent, with clear expectations and consequences. And they need to get their message out to the parent community in an effort to have one constant message sent to all students at all times.[8]

What do you do if your child turns out to be the bully? You might think that's impossible, but about a third of students have admitted to bullying someone at some point.[9] Dr. Mary L. Pulido is executive director of the New York Society for the Prevention of Cruelty to Children. She notes that "bullies come in every shape and size. They are from every ethnic group, race, socioeconomic class, gender, and religion. As a parent, you'll probably be shocked to learn that your child is intentionally causing pain and humiliation to other children."[10]

Upon hearing that your child is bullying others, the first step is to avoid losing your cool. Next, get as much information as you can about the situation and the circumstances, explaining to your child the damage he or she has done, helping your child put himself or herself in the victim's shoes, making it clear that you will not tolerate bullying, and seeking professional help if the situation doesn't improve. She also counsels the importance of setting the right example at home. Young people often bully because their home situations are difficult or because they've seen bullying in their home.[11]

Medication

It's a sad fact of life that more and more children are being medicated to get them through school and to deal with their lives. One of the increasingly common reasons is a diagnosis of ADHD. The term ADHD (attention-deficit/hyperactivity disorder) refers to a range of behavioral characteristics linked to restlessness, inability to concentrate, fidgeting, impulsiveness, and being easily distracted. More and more children—and adults—are being diagnosed with ADHD, and many are being prescribed medications to treat it. There are various controversies surrounding the nature, status, and treatment of ADHD, which you should be aware of as a parent. What are they and what do you do if your child is diagnosed? How can you tell if the diagnosis is well founded, and if it is, should you agree to drug therapy? If not, what are the alternatives?

Hyperactivity is probably as old as humanity. As medical— and especially psychological—research became more systematic in the last century, it came under closer study and went by various names, including *minimal brain dysfunction* and *learning/ behavioral disabilities*. The current conception of ADHD grew out of the work of Dr. Charles Bradley, a psychiatrist practicing in Providence, Rhode Island, in the 1930s. He discovered by accident that a group of children he was treating for behavioral problems, including hyperactivity, responded well to doses of Benzedrine, an amphetamine. In the years that followed, various other doctors and researchers began to identify such behaviors with abnormal brain function and also found that they could be mitigated with drug therapy.

In the United States, the authoritative guide to mental and behavioral disorders is the *Diagnostic and Statistical Manual of Mental Disorders* (DSM), published by the American Psychiatric Association.[12] According to the DSM, ADHD is associated with eighteen general characteristics, or symptoms, nine for inattention and nine for hyperactivity/impulsiveness:

Inattentive symptoms:

- Often fails to pay attention to details or makes careless mistakes.
- Often has difficulty sustaining attention in tasks or play activities.
- Often does not seem to listen when spoken to directly.
- Often does not follow through on instructions and fails to finish tasks.
- Often has difficulty organizing tasks and activities.
- Often reluctant to engage in tasks that require sustained mental effort.
- Often loses things necessary for tasks or activities.
- Often easily distracted by extraneous stimuli.
- Often forgetful in daily activities.

Hyperactive-impulsive symptoms:

- Often fidgets with or taps hands or squirms in seat.
- Often leaves seat in situations when remaining seated is expected.
- Often runs about or climbs in situations where it is inappropriate.
- Often unable to play or engage in leisure activities quietly.
- Often "on the go," acting as if "driven by a motor."
- Often talks excessively.
- Often blurts out answers before questions have been completed.
- Often has difficulty awaiting turn.
- Often interrupts or intrudes on others.

To be diagnosed with ADHD, an individual has to have a minimum of five of these symptoms, in any combination. Specialists in the field say that symptoms typically vary between boys and girls. The condition is normally diagnosed between ages three and seven, and in about a third of cases it continues into adulthood. The diagnosis is based on interviews with a psychiatrist or pediatrician, combined with accounts of the person's behavior by parents, teachers, and others.

Because of these variations, there are widely different estimates of who has ADHD and who doesn't. In the United States, the American Psychological Association estimates that about one in ten children and one in twenty adults have been diagnosed with ADHD. The Centers for Disease Control and Prevention (CDC) puts the figures at twice that. In the United Kingdom, it's estimated that between 3 and 7 percent of children (around 400,000) have ADHD. Although estimates vary, there's no doubt that the numbers of reported cases in the United Kingdom and the United States have risen sharply in the last ten years.

There are two main forms of treatment for ADHD: drug therapy and cognitive-behavioral therapy. The treatment is often a mixture of the two, the form of both depending on how serious the symptoms are thought to be. In the United States, the usual drugs that are prescribed are Ritalin and Adderall.[13]

Controversies

Many psychiatrists, pediatricians, educators, professional organizations, and families have no doubt that ADHD is a real condition and that children and adults who are diagnosed with it respond well to the right treatment. There are well-documented cases of people whose lives and those of their families have been made unmanageable by some of the symptoms of ADHD, and who found essential relief through drug or behavioral therapy. They have no doubt that ADHD is real and are angered by suggestions that it is not. There is a good deal of research and clinical opinion to support their view.

One recent study suggests that there is physical evidence of ADHD: that the developing brains of children with ADHD differ in small but significant ways from those without it.[14] Brain scans showed that five regions of the brain were smaller in people with ADHD and that these differences were more pronounced in children than adults with ADHD. The study suggests that such differences may be temporary and that as the brains of children with ADHD mature, they "catch up" with those without it. The study's authors hope their research will help dispel "widespread misunderstanding of ADHD": for example, that it is a failure of character or parenting rather than a "real disorder."[15] The study's lead author is Dr. Martine Hoogman, a geneticist at Radboud University in the Netherlands. "This research shows," she said, "that there are brain changes involved, just as in other psychiatric disorders, like depression or obsessive-compulsive disorder, and there is no reason to treat ADHD any differently."

Other specialists and families are not convinced that ADHD exists as advertised; or if it does exist, that the methods of diagnosis are reliable; or that the incidence is so high; or that drug treatments are well advised. Others accept that it is a genuine condition but argue that it is wildly overdiagnosed.

Dr. Richard Saul is a practicing behavioral neurologist in New York City and a member of the American Academy of Neurology and the American Academy of Pediatrics. Noting that to qualify for a diagnosis of ADHD, your child only needs to show five of eighteen possible symptoms, he asks how many of us can claim to be entirely free of such symptoms: "We've all had these moments, and in moderate amounts they're a normal part of the human condition." Under these "subjective criteria," he argues, the whole U.S. population could qualify for ADHD.[16]

Most of the symptoms could have different causes, he says. Over the course of his career, he has found more than twenty conditions that produce some of the symptoms of ADHD, each of which requires its own approach to treatment. They include sleep disorders, vision and hearing problems, substance abuse (marijuana and alcohol in particular), iron deficiency, allergies (especially airborne and gluten intolerance), bipolar and major depressive disorder, obsessive-compulsive disorder, and learning disabilities like dyslexia. Anyone with these conditions, he argues, could meet the criteria for ADHD, and stimulants are not the way to treat them.

Some children may be diagnosed with ADHD because they are younger and less mature than others in their class.[17] Another study looked at nearly 400,000 children between ages four and seventeen and found that the percentage diagnosed with ADHD changed significantly depending on their month of birth. Children born in August were more likely to be diagnosed with ADHD than those born in September; they may be wrongly diagnosed because their behavior is being compared to that of children in the same group, who may be up to a year older.

There are concerns about the methods of diagnosis. Since ADHD is called a condition—and not a disease, like malaria or polio, which can be contracted and passed on—the diagnosis is not straightforward or wholly reliable. Identifying genuine cases of ADHD takes care, expertise, and time. I know from my own conversations with parents and specialists in the field that diagnoses are often made quickly and under pressure.

Sometimes there are reasons to doubt the motives of a diagnosis. Some students, parents, or schools hope for a diagnosis because it gives students more time on standardized tests. ADHD drugs are also in demand these days as an aid to more focused study, whether or not the person has any symptoms of ADHD. The pressures of school and testing mean that many young people use stimulants simply to stay awake and complete assignments, and having a positive diagnosis of ADHD is a legal way to get them.

Legal or not, sales of ADHD drugs, especially Ritalin and Adderall, have rocketed in the last ten years or so. In the United Kingdom, almost a million prescriptions a year are written for ADHD medications, almost twice as many as ten years ago. In the United States, sales of ADHD drugs have grown sharply every year from 2010 and are estimated to gross $17.5 billion in 2020, making it one of the top psychopharmaceutical categories on the market.[18] Pharmaceutical companies have invested heavily in these drugs, and they offer plenty of incentives to medical professionals to recommend and prescribe them.

Richard Scheffler is a professor of health, economics, and public policy at the University of California, Berkeley, and coauthor of *The ADHD Explosion*. He says that the explosive growth in drug sales for ADHD is part of a global trend, especially in cultures that put a premium on productivity and high academic achievement. Sales outside the United States, especially in Israel, China, and Saudi Arabia, are increasing twice as fast as in the United States.[19]

Setting aside the status of ADHD as a condition and issues of diagnosis, there are concerns about the largely unpublicized side effects of ADHD drugs. In some users, they can include appetite suppression and weight loss, liver problems, sleep deprivation, anxiety, irritability, depression, and even suicidal thoughts. Less often, they can lead to hallucinations, paranoia, and addiction.

There's evidence that in young children, ADHD drugs may inhibit normal pubertal development. Even more worrying is the rate at which they are being prescribed for infants. In 2016, a report from the CDC found that health care providers had given a diagnosis of ADHD to at least ten thousand children age two or three and then prescribed medications such as Adderall outside American Academy of Pediatrics guidelines.

Dr. Ed Tronick is a professor of developmental and brain sciences at the University of Massachusetts Boston. "I think you simply cannot make anything close to a diagnosis of these types of disorders in children of that age," he said. "There's this very narrow range of what people think the prototype child should look like. Deviations from that lead them to seek out interventions like these. I think it's just nuts."[20]

Bruce D. Perry is a senior fellow at the Child Trauma Academy in Houston and a recognized authority in behavioral disorders. He's concerned that children are labeled with ADHD when they have a range of different physiological problems. He's also cautious about using drugs whose effects aren't fully understood. He argues that behavioral and other treatments—somatic therapies like yoga and motor activities like drumming—can be equally or more effective over time and have none of the adverse effects of drugs. It's also important, he says, to coach and support parents and teachers, who inadvertently may be exacerbating the child's behavioral problems. "You can teach the adults how to regulate themselves," he said, "and how to have realistic expectations of the children, how to give them opportunities that are achievable and coach them through the process of helping children who are struggling. . . . If you can put together a package of those things: keep the adults more mannered, give the children achievable goals, give them opportunities to regulate themselves, then you are going to minimize a huge percentage of the problems that have been labeled as ADHD."[21]

In April 2014, seven leading members of the Centre for ADHD and Neurodevelopmental Disorders Across the Lifetime (CANDAL) at the University of Nottingham in England published a letter repudiating Dr. Perry's views, arguing instead that research does not show that behavioral interventions are equally effective for ADHD and that the evidence for their effectiveness in treating ADHD "has been oversold. . . . Children with ADHD and their families . . . deserve better public understanding of the complex, multifactorial nature of this disabling condition and access to better treatments, not sensationalist and stigmatizing headlines that suggest that these children and young people do not have a 'real' condition."[22]

What Should You Do?

Given these various issues and controversies, what should you do as a parent if your child is suspected of or is diagnosed as having ADHD? Here are some suggestions.

- *Look at the individual:* Even if you are convinced that ADHD is a genuine condition, remember that not everyone who shows some of the symptoms is a genuine case. Look at your child as an individual, not a trend. Some children are naturally more outgoing and boisterous than others; some have a lot of physical energy, while others are naturally quieter and more introspective. Young children especially love to run around and play. Be careful not to pathologize childhood.

- *Consider the context:* See if there are other factors at work: lack of sleep, stress, lack of exercise, or just their age and stage of development. Remember that for many children, school these days is a very sedentary experience. If children are made to sit down all day, doing low-grade clerical work for standardized tests, don't be surprised if they fidget and want to run around. So would you.

- *Get second opinions:* If your child is diagnosed with ADHD, feel free to get a second opinion. Diagnosis in this area is not an exact science; it's not like finding a virus or a broken bone. There are many factors in play and you should be willing to question them if you're not convinced.

- *Explore other options:* Before committing to drug treatment, explore other possibilities. If your children are physically inactive, get them up and moving. If they have trouble concentrating on things they find boring, encourage them in activities they find more stimulating. In Chapter Four, I outlined various ways of promoting greater balance between physical, emotional, cognitive, and spiritual development. Try some of those.

- *Read up:* If you suspect your child has ADHD or any other mental condition for which medication is being recommended, find out as much as you can about it before agreeing, and have your questions answered properly.

- *Remember that it's not all bad:* Some of the symptoms of ADHD may be hard to deal with, but they're not all negative, destructive, or harmful in the long term. Many people didn't fit the mold in school but went on to have successful and fulfilling lives, not in spite of their unorthodox personalities but often because of them.

I said earlier that education is not just a preparation for later life. That's true, but life does go on after high school. What path should your children take then, and how should you guide them?

CHAPTER TEN

Look to the Future

As your children reach their teens, the question of what they'll do after high school (or homeschool) will keep coming up. Some young people know what they want to do next and may have known it for a long time. They've already discovered a talent and a passion (their Element), which they're keen to pursue, and the next steps in doing that may be obvious. Some have no clear idea yet and are open to suggestions. How do you guide them as a parent and on what basis? The answer is not always obvious—and the obvious answer may well be wrong.

The Usual Story

These days, the usual assumption is that young people will be in high school until age eighteen. After high school, they'll begin the transition to independence and earning their own living. That's the theory, anyway. Increasingly, it's taken for granted that this transition involves several years at college. This is a relatively new idea. A couple of generations ago, relatively few people went to college. Most people left school and went straight to work, provided they could find a job. One of the reasons so many people go to college now is that governments recognize that in a high-tech, information-driven world, successful economies need more people educated to higher levels than before. If you look back at Chapter Five, you'll see that I—and many others—have serious doubts about how governments are going about this. The main reason they encourage people to go to college is economic. As a parent you may have a range of other reasons. Here are some of the more common ones:

- *Personal study and fulfillment:* Your child may be interested in a particular field of study and be keen to pursue it for its own sake. It could be anything—pure mathematics, fine arts, astronomy, medieval music—and it may have no obvious link to a particular career. He or she may want to study it for the intrinsic value of doing so.

- *Growth and independence:* You may feel that college will help your children find their feet and learn to take care of themselves in a relatively safe environment before taking on the full responsibilities of adulthood. You may see college like a modern-day finishing school: a time to make new friends and explore interests and lifestyles.

- *Professional requirements:* If your child is set on a particular career, a college qualification may be a basic requirement, as it still is in many professions, such as law and medicine.

- *Status and opportunity:* For some parents, college is a valuable social platform. It's important that their children go to the right college: one that offers opportunities to connect with social networks that will have personal and professional advantages in the medium and long term.

- *Income and security:* Whatever your children's interests and talents, you may assume that a college degree will be the best guarantee of them finding a well-paid job with security and benefits.

- *Just because . . . . :* You may simply assume, as many young people do, that they should go to college because that's just what happens after high school. After all, that's what all the testing and pressure of GPAs and SATs is about. Getting good test results isn't about improving life in high school; it's about impressing the selectors in college. If you don't go to college, what's the point?

Your own reasons for guiding your children to college may be a mixture of all of these, or you may have others depending on your circumstances. Either way it's worth asking whether your expectations of college are well founded and whether college is the best option for your child in particular.

In Chapter Five, we looked at the four main functions of education: *economic*, *social*, *cultural*, and *personal*. It's perfectly reasonable for you to hope that education will enable your child to find work and become financially independent. It's possible a college degree will help, but not inevitable. Studying for a traditional academic degree in a conventional college may be the right thing for some young people, but it's not the best or only direction for everyone. Nor is going to college in the first place. There are equally valuable options in vocational programs or in going straight to work with on-the-job training.

There are two main factors to keep in mind. The first is your children's own talents, interests, and characters and the opportunities that may suit them best as individuals. The second is how the world of work is changing and the general skills and qualifications that are needed these days for young people to make their way in it.

Finding Their Element

Finding your Element can be a tricky thing—so tricky that we dedicated an entire book to the topic.[1] Helping your children find theirs can be even more troublesome. One way to relax about this is to understand that your role isn't to identify your kids' passions for them; it's to create the conditions in which they can find their talents and interests for themselves. Katie Hurley agrees. She is the author of *The Happy Kid Handbook: How to Raise Joyful Children in a Stressful World*. She offers four strategies for helping your children pursue their passions.[2]

- *Know your child's unique interests.* Avoid plugging her into the local soccer program or Chinese class because that's what all of your neighbors are doing. Watch instead (especially when she is playing) for signs of serious interests in particular pursuits.

- *Think outside the box.* Passion is not limited to playing fields and theatrical stages. It can exist in the kitchen, in the workshop, in the woods outside your back door, or in any number of other places. Parents are understandably anxious to offer enrichment to their children, but enrichment doesn't automatically equate with large, organized programs.

- *Nurture optimism.* "Optimistic kids are more willing to take healthy risks, become better problem-
  solvers and experience positive relationships," she
  notes. Since failure is a fact of life and your children
  will certainly have their share of setbacks, help them
  look optimistically at what they do.
- *Avoid judgment.* When you offer a negative judgment of your child's expressed area of interest, you
  run the risk of stealing much of the joy from that
  pursuit. Not only is your child unique and different
  from every other child in the world, he is also unique
  from *you*. If you stomp on his potential passions or
  push him toward a pursuit he doesn't particularly
  like, you're likely to cause him a great deal of internal conflict.

Best-selling author Valerie Frankel had been obsessing over
her teenaged kids' lack of a defining interest until she realized
that this obsession was blinding her to their real interests, which
were hiding in plain sight. In her impatience for her daughters
to find their passions, she realized she had been "throwing out a
million options but not looking for glimmers." Eventually, she
stopped pushing, listened, and looked: "Weeks passed; then,
when cleaning up a stack of Maggie's papers, I noticed that she'd
doodled on every page. Before, I'd criticized this habit as distraction from her schoolwork. This time, I reserved judgment
and appraised." She saw that the doodles were elaborate, detailed
drawings of a monster dog who breathed fire.

"'Fido,' said Maggie when I asked. 'My character. I've been
working on him for a while.' 'Do you like to draw?' I asked.
She was in art class so fast her head is still spinning. Incredibly,
her interest is growing, not dissolving. At a recent school exhibit

of student work, I could plainly see that she had talent as well as passion. Of course, I'm envisioning a fabulous career for her at Pixar."[3]

Well, maybe. Either way, it's never too early (or, as Frankel discovered, too late) to create the conditions in your household that help bring out the best in your children. Let's go back to Thomas Armstrong's definition of *genius*. How do you help your kids give birth to their joy? Like Paul Simon leaving his lover, Armstrong has a list of fifty ways.[4] We can't list all of them here, but here are some interesting suggestions:

- Give your children permission to make mistakes; if they have to do things perfectly, they'll never take the risks necessary to discover and develop a gift.
- Don't pressure them too much to learn; if children are sent to special lessons every day in the hope of developing their gifts, they may become too stressed or exhausted to shine.
- Encourage, but don't push. Keep your own passion for learning alive; your children will be influenced by your example.
- Share your successes as a family. Talk about good things that happened during the day to enhance self-confidence.
- Give your children unstructured time to simply daydream and wonder.
- As they get older, encourage your children to think positively and creatively about their futures.
- Support their visions without directing them into any specific field.
- Encourage them to trust their intuitions and believe in their capabilities.

- Be a liaison between your children's talents and the world around them. Help them find opportunities to discover and develop their talents.

The World of Work

The world of work is changing quickly and will change even more in the years ahead: so too will the challenges that your children face. Many people assume that if their children go to college and take a degree in one of the "safe" disciplines like law, medicine, or accounting, their futures will be secure. In some countries that is still true. In the so-called developed countries like the United States it is not. America has more lawyers per capita than any other country in the world, nearly forty for every ten thousand citizens, and a great many more graduates are not practicing law, either because they do not want to or because there aren't enough jobs to go around. One of the results of this glut of lawyers in the United States is an increasingly tangled web of legislation and litigation. Lawyers, after all, have to do something with their time.

Let me say right away that a college degree is still a well-trodden path to relative financial success. According to a 2014 Pew study, the income gap between college grads and high school grads has never been greater and has widened in a relatively short time.[5] Even so, a college degree is no longer a guarantee of a secure job, or of any job at all.

The Price of Success

According to one estimate, 45 percent of recent college graduates worked in "noncollege jobs." A "college job" is one in which at least 50 percent of the workers in that job indicated that a bachelor's degree or more was necessary. This plays to the Great Recession narrative of college graduates working as taxi drivers and sales clerks, but the authors point out that this isn't an exact number, as a percentage of these people will make the transition to college jobs in the coming years.[6]

The other factors to bear in mind are the mounting costs of college and the rising mountain of student debt. These numbers suggest that the accepted story of school/college/security may not be nearly as rosy for many individuals. For one thing, the cost of college in the United States has skyrocketed—from an average of $18,574 in 2000 to $38,762 in 2015.[7] That's an inflation rate of 209 percent, or 71 percentage points higher than the overall rate of inflation over the same period. Many families can't keep up with this, which has led to the highest levels of student debt we have ever seen—more than $35,000 per borrower in 2015.[8] Our children are entering their adult lives with financial burdens that few of us had to carry.

This scenario—carrying a considerable level of debt while finding oneself underemployed in a field that may offer advancement but doesn't align with your desired degree in any way—is one that bears consideration before you guide your children toward four or more additional years of school. One of the reasons for this problem is that we have so prioritized the need for our children to become doctors or lawyers or to get their MBAs that we've sent them the unconscious message that anything other than that equates to selling themselves short.

Fit for Work?

Meanwhile there is an escalating problem of youth unemployment. In some countries almost 50 percent of young people are not employed or never have been. In the United States the overall rate of youth unemployment is around 10 percent. In some parts of the country, it is almost twice that. Nationwide, about one in seven young people—about six million—are not participating in work, education, or training. They have no role in the economy and no stake in it either. They are sometimes referred to as "the disconnected."[9]

Ironically, millions of jobs are not filled. It's been estimated that by 2020 there will be 95 million such jobs around the world.[10] In 2016 there were 5.5 million unfilled jobs available in the United States.[11] Many of these were in areas of skilled labor, which require specialist on-the-job training but not college.

Bob Morrison of Quadrant Research knows from personal experiences how much of a problem the overemphasis on sending everyone to college can be, even in the field of vocational education: "I see this in my role as president of a large regional school district here in New Jersey. One of the measures of a successful high school is the percentage of students that enroll in college. Schools strive to push all students to go to college because of the impact on school rankings. There has also been a troubling trend in vocational and technical schools (VoTechs). Many of these schools are now becoming elite training schools in STEM with a heavy focus on technology. Many have abandoned the career side of Careers and Technical Education (CTE). We do need more students to look at career pathways outside of the collegiate route, but we also need to take a hard look at the transformation going on in our VoTechs. Now that everyone, including VoTechs, is caught up in this 'move them on to college' mind-set, my worry is that soon we may not have the infrastructure to support the non-college options that so many students need and want."[12]

One of the results is the loss of practical and vocational courses in schools. The loss of these programs and the decline in apprenticeships and other training opportunities has contributed to what has become known as the global skills gap. "Many Americans don't have the skills that those available jobs require," noted Patrick Gillespie, a reporter at CNNMoney. "The skills gap has become a serious problem in the U.S."[13] About a third of job openings in the United States in 2018 will require some kind of noncollege professional training, but only 12 percent of the labor force has any kind of vocational certification.[14] There are exceptions. One of the most significant is the mounting success of Big Picture Learning.

The Big Picture

Big Picture Learning (BPL) was established in Rhode Island in 1995 with the aim of putting students at the center of their own learning. BPL cofounders Dennis Littky and Elliot Washor merged their thirty years of experience as teachers and principals to demonstrate that education and schools can and should be radically different. The first class of Big Picture Learning graduated in 2000 with a 96 percent graduation rate. Today, there are over sixty-five BPL network schools in the United States and many more around the world, including schools in Australia, the Netherlands, Italy, and Canada. Two of the signature features of BPL schools are an emphasis on personalized education and on connecting students learning in school to the wider world of work. BPL students spend considerable time in the community under the supervision of mentors. They're not evaluated solely on the basis of standardized tests but on exhibitions and demonstrations of achievement, on motivation, "and on the habits of mind, hand, and heart, reflecting the real world evaluations and assessments that all of us face in our everyday lives."[15]

Here's the Plan

Big Picture Learning manages personalized education by breaking students into small groups of fifteen students, called an advisory. Each advisory is supported and led by an advisor, a teacher who works closely with the group of students and forms personalized relationships with each member of their group. Students stay in the same advisory for four years, and each student works closely with his or her advisor to personalize their learning by identifying interests and figuring out how they learn best and what motivates them. Parents and families are also actively involved in helping to shape the student's continuation of learning. A major part of this process is the development of a personal Learning Plan.

The Learning Plan is a description of all the work and learning a student has ahead of them for the term. Every student has a Learning Plan Team, which includes the student, parents, advisor, and mentor. It may also include others, such as a special education specialist, additional family member, or staff member. This team works with the student to create the Learning Plan, which is reviewed and updated as the student progresses through the school. Four times a year, students exhibit their work and show what they've learned before a panel.

Making It Work

Because students are encouraged to pursue their own interests and passions, no two students have the same Learning Plan. Most of the plan revolves around the student's Learning Through Internship (LTI) and related project work. It also includes work in seminars, college classes, and extracurricular work. Students pursue LTI opportunities with an adult mentor at a professional work site in a field of their choosing. Each of these LTI opportunities connects students to adults in the community who are doing work in the student's area of interest. By establishing an intern/mentor relationship with an adult who has the same passion, the student has practical opportunities to build relevant skills and knowledge. The student's advisor assists the intern and mentor in developing project work and supports that work through skills development back in school. The result is a student-centered learning experience where students are actively invested in their learning and feel challenged to pursue their interests by a supportive community of educators, professionals, and family members who know them as individuals.

Parents in the Picture

Parents have a unique role in Big Picture Learning schools. They make a choice for their student to attend a Big Picture Learning school. They write an essay as part of the application about why they want their child to attend the school, attend the interview with their child to make sure the school is a good match for the family, and sign an agreement with the school to support their child's learning in many ways. They then attend Learning Plan meetings and exhibitions and whole-school events. In essence, the parent enrolls in the school as well as the child. When families enroll at a Big Picture Learning school, they agree to a partnership with the school, which involves making a commitment to work together in the best interests of the student. These are the commitments.

> *Parents* agree to:
> - Attend all four of their child's exhibitions each year
> - Attend two to four Learning Plan meetings for their child each year
> - Attend at least one whole-school community function (open house, family skills and talent fair, etc.), plus the annual end-of-the-year celebration
> - Keep in regular communication with their child's advisor

- Help with and monitor their child's work at home each day
- Make sure their child gets to school on time each day
- Provide at least ten hours of community service to the school each year (volunteering during the day, serving on the family engagement committee, chaperoning trips, etc.)

Students agree to:
- Be at school on time each day
- Do their work at school each day
- Do their work at home each day
- Respect their classmates and teachers
- Work with a mentor each year as an intern
- Write in their journal three times a week
- Develop a Learning Plan with their Learning Plan Team each quarter
- Exhibit their learning each quarter before a panel

The *school* agrees to:
- Respect each student
- Hold high expectations for each student
- Keep in communication with the family about the student's work
- Develop individualized Learning Plans, write a minimum of four narratives each year for each student, and assist them in the college application/life-planning process
- Help every student exhibit his/her work publicly at least four times per year

Think how many more young people would have a stake in the job market if schools and colleges worked together, with the encouragement of parents, to provide relevant forms of vocational education. Instead, all the pressure is to go to university and get a degree.

This has led to a situation where there are far too many unhappy lawyers and not nearly enough happy construction managers—ironic, considering that the glut in lawyers and the scarcity of construction managers means that in some cases the construction manager can earn more than the lawyer. "For some of my students, a four-year university is by far the best option for them," wrote teacher Jillian Gordon in a piece for *PBS Newshour*. "But this isn't the case for all students, and we need to stop pretending it is. A bachelor's degree is not a piece of paper that says 'You're a success!' just as the lack of one doesn't say 'You're a failure!'"[16]

Fortunately, there are other very strong noncollege options.

Other Options

If your child doesn't go on to college, what are the alternatives? According to the Association for Career and Technical Education, more than nine thousand postsecondary institutions offer technical programs.[17] Some of these can be found in your local community college, while others are available through trade schools, technical institutes, and skill centers.[18]

Another option is an *apprenticeship*. The upside of apprenticeships is that, rather than paying for an education, an apprentice earns money while learning. Mike Taylor didn't discover apprenticeships until after he'd gone to college and built up $75,000 in student loan debt. After college, he pursued a number of job opportunities, such as waiting tables, that didn't pay particularly well. Then he found the apprenticeship program with Plumbers Local 1 in Queens, New York.[19] He's earning enough money now to own a house, and after he's finished with his five-year apprenticeship, he'll be able to make more than $100,000 a year, considerably more than many college graduates or even PhDs.[20]

Other countries have vocational education programs more attuned to the need of the workforce than the United States. In *Creative Schools*, I talked about Finland's notable progress in reforming their education system to the point where it is widely regarded as one of the finest in the world. Finland's high scores compared to the rest of the world in math, science, and language arts have been widely reported. What is less commonly known is that 45 percent of Finnish students choose a technical track rather than an academic track for the equivalent of their high school educations. "It was eye-opening to be in a country where vocational education had high prestige, was well-funded, and included students who could have gone to medical school if that had been their preference."[21] Vocational education is not perceived there as a lesser option. Vocational students are treated with the same level of dignity as students on strictly academic tracks, and vocational institutions are seen as respected learning institutions. This makes a difference in how the students see themselves and in how they perceive the value of following a vocational path.

Austria has a particularly robust vocational educational training (VET) model. All Austrian students attend general schools for the first nine years of their academic lives. After this, they choose to go down the college prep track or the VET track. This is starkly different from the current U.S. model, where most high schools train all of their students on a college track, even if college isn't remotely on the horizon for the student. Eighty percent of Austrian students choose the VET track, with half of those going into skilled labor apprenticeship programs (while they still receive one or two days a week of academic classes) while the other half go to school full-time to learn things like nursing, banking, and accounting. Students in the apprenticeship programs receive a certificate at the end of the program and still have the opportunity to go to college afterward. Austria's youth unemployment rate is half of that in the United States and one-third of the European Union average.[22]

Australia has also built a VET program, one that brings more than 400,000 foreign students to the island continent every year. One of the factors that drives the quality of Australia's VET system is a premium on teaching. All VET teachers need at least five years' experience in their related industry with requirements for regular refreshers. Acknowledging how quickly workplace markets can shift, the Australian system affords students a great deal of flexibility. Nearly 40 percent of Australian students ages fifteen to nineteen are involved in VET programs.[23]

Gabriel Sanchez Zinny is executive director at INET, the Argentine Ministry of Education. He met with Australian VET developers during a symposium in Buenos Aires. "Something that caught my attention was how advanced the debate over educational quality was, and how proud the system participants are about VET. Both the Labor Party, in the left, and the Coalition, in the right, public institutions, foundations, private providers, they all put the student and educational quality in the center of the system."[24]

Wherever your child's skills or interests may lie, there is significant value in making sure that she is aware of whatever vocational program her school might be offering. Assessing a school's approach to teaching practical skills should be an important criterion in your decision about where to send your child.

Entrepreneurship

Another option is to take the entrepreneurial route. Many successful entrepreneurs made their fortunes and changed culture without the benefit of a college degree. Their stories are exceptional, but there are enough people making a living blogging, creating apps, selling crafts online, and marketing their services and products that it's worth considering if this is the right path for your child. Entrepreneurialism isn't for everyone—it takes passion, resilience, vision, grit, and of course a market for whatever it is you're selling—but if your child has these traits and enough of a financial safety net to withstand the possibility of failure, an entrepreneurial path may be the best one.

Donna M. De Carolis is the founding dean of the Charles D. Close School of Entrepreneurship at Drexel University. She thinks we are all entrepreneurs to some degree. "We are all born with the innate ability to survive; and survival involves innovative thinking," she wrote in a piece for *Forbes*. "When we think innovatively and act on that innovation, we are entrepreneurs."[25] Entrepreneurialism may be built into each of us.

Time Out

Maybe college is the exact right thing for your child—but maybe not *right now*. Many kids, especially high-achieving kids, are simply exhausted from all of the stress and pressure of high school, and a couple of months off in the summer isn't nearly enough to allow them to catch their breath. Others feel in their hearts that they want to go to college, but they don't have a clue about what they want to study or where they would like to enroll. In these cases, a gap year might prove valuable.

Gap years are not intended to be yearlong vacations. They

aren't about sleeping until noon and never getting out of your pajamas. At their best, gap years provide teenagers with an opportunity to grow, to connect with the world beyond themselves and their schools, and to gain a level of maturity that they might not reach if they simply go from one academic setting to another. Their value is so considerable that several of the top universities in America, including Harvard and Princeton, have programs in place to encourage them. Studies suggest that teenagers who take a gap year are more polished when they go off to college and that their grades tend to be better than they would have been otherwise.[26]

Gaya Morris took a gap year because she wanted to experience the disciplines she was going to concentrate on before studying them in school. Gaya wound up going to Senegal with a program called Global Citizen Year, spending seven months in the country, volunteering at a local elementary school, attending meetings of a literacy group for women, and organizing an English club for high school students. "On my gap year I discovered many new passions," she wrote. "A passion for elementary school education in the developing world, a passion for teaching children to read, a passion for a sharp, rhythmic language called Wolof, a passion for chopping onions into the palm of my hand and scrubbing clothes in a bucket, in just a few inches of murky water, skin prickly from the soap and the sun. I concluded this year of discovery and challenge so completely excited for college—to open the books and even Microsoft Word, meet new people, and stumble on more unexpected challenges, and pursue new and old passions and interests in an academic context."[27]

Elijah Tucker spent a year traveling by himself in Costa Rica before getting his degree from Bard College. For him, the gap year was about learning how to live independently. "I wanted to go somewhere where I could get lost. Getting lost and being lonely and not speaking the language forced me out of emotional necessity to really get to know myself. I learned how to pray while I was there. I got inside myself and learned how to be really honest with myself." He said he came away with "a fierce appreciation for what college was. It wasn't the first time that I'd had freedom and independence and tried things out. Having that time helped me to hone my focus and vision for what I wanted to do in college."[28]

Addison Voelz was well on her way to following the majority of her classmates to Indiana University, going so far as to sign up for housing on campus. But when she applied for a random roommate and wound up being paired with a friend from high school, she realized that she was on a treadmill and she needed to step off before it was too late. She went to New York, took a tour of the Fashion Institute of Technology, and found a connection there that she hadn't felt before. She spent a year working at a job in the fashion industry and doing two fashion internships. "I knew that this was my time to meet new people, make connections, and network for my future career, and staying in the same circle wouldn't get me any of that," she said. "I was certainly a little scared though, moving to New York and applying to a school that I wasn't sure if I would be accepted to. I began thinking of a Plan B, but I really didn't have one." Fortunately, she didn't need a Plan B, as she was accepted by FIT and embarked on a program to graduate in three years.[29]

As you can see in each of these stories, the students used their gap years to gain a level of insight and experience that they couldn't have gained by going directly to college. If your child is thinking about taking a gap year or if you think a gap year might be beneficial to your child, it's best to plan it properly and with a clear sense of purpose. An increasing number of colleges have gap year programs, so it might make sense for your child to apply to the schools that interest him, even if he wants to take a year before starting, and then seek out the gap year opportunities the school might offer. There are also gap year fairs held across the country that present students with a wide variety of opportunities.[30]

College

This isn't to say that the best path for your child isn't to go to college immediately. Many have done extremely well with their lives following precisely that course. I know dozens of people who describe their college experiences as the best years of their lives, the place where they discovered themselves, and the place where they found the passions that have driven them ever since. All I'm saying is that it isn't the only choice or even the best choice available every time, and that it's important to look at your particular child, to think seriously about her interests and talents (as well as other considerations like her level of maturity and independence), and decide if college is the vehicle that is best going to deliver her to her future.

There are libraries' worth of books available on choosing the right college, so you don't need any of that from me here. It is important to recognize, though, that there are now many other ways of studying for degrees and other college-level qualifications than physically attending a college for four or more years. In the last ten years especially, there has been a proliferation of online courses and colleges, which offer degree-level programs at a fraction of the price of conventional colleges, and considerable flexibility in how and when these programs are taken. The world of online learning is a little like the Wild West at present, with many failed start-ups, false promises, and snake oil vendors in among the legitimate providers of excellent courses and worthwhile qualifications. Here, as in all online transactions, you need to be cautious and use due diligence. But the options are there and they're likely to improve as experience accumulates and systems mature.

The Road Ahead

One of the perils of standardized education is the idea that one size fits all and that life is linear. The truth is that there are many routes to fulfillment. The lives of most people have not followed a standard course. People commonly move in unexpected directions, discover new interests, or take unplanned opportunities. It's important at school not to limit your children's futures by assuming that the sort of education that you had will inevitably be right for them. You may assume that some subjects will necessarily be more useful than others for finding a career. As the world continues to change, that may not be true.

The best you can do is to help your children develop in their different ways and to help them identify the personal talents and interests that engage them most. They will create and live their own lives, as you have done. Care as you must and try as you might, you cannot do that for them.

Notes

CHAPTER ONE: Get Your Bearings

1. She posted the poem on her blog *Motherhood for Slackers* and shared it on Facebook.
2. Peter Gray, "Welcome to the World of Self-Directed Education," Alternatives to School, http://alternativestoschool.com, accessed November 2, 2016.
3. "Learning Less: Public School Teachers Describe a Narrowing Curriculum," Farkas Duffett Research Group, March 2012, http://greatminds.net/maps/documents/reports/cc-learning-less-mar12.pdf.
4. For more on this, see *A Review of State and Regional Arts Education Studies* report prepared for Americans for the Arts by Yael Z. Silk, EdM, and Stacey Mahan, EdM, of Silk Strategic Arts LLC and Robert Morrison of Quadrant Research at http://www.americansforthearts.org/sites/default/files/State_Status_Report_Final.pdf. For further details, see also http://www.quadrantresearch.org/group-list/priorresearch.
5. Anya Kamenetz, *The Test: Why Our Schools Are Obsessed with Standardized Testing—But You Don't Have to Be* (New York: Public Affairs, 2015), p. 5.
6. Ibid., p. 7. For more on the spread and impact of testing, standardization, and privatization on public education, see Diane Ravitch,

Reign of Error: The Hoax of the Privatization Movement and the Danger to America's Public Schools (New York: Vintage Books, 2014).

7. "The Future of Jobs: Employment, Skills and Workforce Strategy for the Fourth Industrial Revolution," World Economic Forum Executive Summary, January 2016, http://www3.weforum.org/docs/WEF_FOJ_Executive_Summary_Jobs.pdf, accessed October 20, 2017.

8. Steven Peters, "Cities Where the Most (and Least) People Graduate High School," 24/7 Wall St., July 18, 2016, http://247wallst.com/special-report/2016/07/18/cities-where-the-most-and-least-people-graduate-high-school, accessed October 30, 2017.

9. Ibid.

10. "Closing the Achievement Gap: Charter School FAQ," PBS, http://www.pbs.org/closingtheachievementgap/faq.html, accessed September 3, 2017.

11. "Average Private School Tuition Cost (2016–2017)," *Private School Review*, September 7, 2016, http://www.privateschoolreview.com/tuition-stats/private-school-cost-by-state. Annual tuition for private high schools in Vermont averages $37,119.

12. John S. Kiernan, "Private Schools vs. Public Schools—Experts Weigh In," WalletHub, July 30, 2016, https://wallethub.com/blog/private-school-vs-public-school/23323.

13. Christopher A. Lubienski and Sarah Theule Lubienski, *The Public School Advantage: Why Public Schools Outperform Private Schools* (Chicago: University of Chicago Press, 2013).

14. I go into this more in *Out of Our Minds: The Power of Being Creative* (Hoboken, NJ: Wiley, 2017).

15. Lily Eskelsen Garcia, personal communication, July 2017.

16. Ibid.

17. Kiernan, "Private Schools vs. Public Schools—Experts Weigh In."

18. From time to time, I'll refer back to *Creative Schools* to support something I say here, which means that you don't have to read that book to make sense of this one. Of course, if you want to read *Creative Schools* as well, I can think of no better way of spending an evening.

CHAPTER TWO: Know Your Role

1. Phillip Cohen, "Family Diversity Is the New Normal for America's Children," Family Inequality, September 4, 2014, https://family inequality.files.wordpress.com/2014/09/family-diversity-new -normal.pdf.

2. Natalie Angier, "The Changing American Family," *New York Times*, November 25, 2013, http://www.nytimes.com/2013/11/26/health /families.html.

3. The world population was growing quickly too, doubling from one to two billion between 1800 and 1930.

4. Even though the family name has passed traditionally through the male line and in noble families, wealth and titles also pass with precedence to male children.

5. The award-winning documentary *India's Daughter* explores the appalling rape and death of twenty-three-year-old Jyoti Singh. Her murder sparked nationwide protests in India partly because it was not unusual. About twenty-five thousand girls and women are raped every year in India, almost all of them by someone they know. At least one thousand women and girls are murdered in so-called honor killings, usually by members of their own families. They may be killed for being in love with the wrong person or even, as in the case of Jyoti Singh, by strangers for being out late in the evening with a male friend. Almost as shocking as the killings is the assumption that they are justified to expiate family shame.

6. Compassion International, "What Is Poverty?" http://www.compas sion.com/poverty/what-is-poverty.htm, accessed September 3, 2017.

7. Virginia Morell, "Why Do Animals Sometimes Kill Their Babies?" *National Geographic*, March 28, 2014, news.nationalgeographic .com/news/2014/03/140328-sloth-bear-zoo-infanticide-chimps -bonobos-animals.

8. Foggy Mommy, "Do Parents Feel Peer Pressure Too?" December 8, 2014, http://www.foggymommy.com/parents-face-peer-pressure.

9. Many people are surprised to hear this and assume that corporal punishment in schools is illegal. It is not. In 1977 the Supreme Court ruled that spanking or paddling children is still lawful where

local districts have not outlawed it. Thirty-one states have abolished corporal punishment in public schools, but it remains widespread or routine in at least nine states, mainly in the South.

10. Storge is not conditional on the personal qualities of the child, though they naturally have more influence on you as the child's personality evolves. Storge is inherent in the parent-child relationship. When your children are young, your love can sometimes feel one-sided and one-way. As you get older together and your respective needs and perspectives change, the balance shifts.

11. I've written elsewhere that my father broke his neck in an industrial accident when he was forty-five years old and was a quadriplegic for the rest of his life.

12. Foggy Mommy, "Do Parents Feel Peer Pressure Too?"

13. Angela Mulholland, "'Super Parent' Pressure Taking Mental Health Toll, Research Shows," CTVNews, September 12, 2014, http://www.ctvnews.ca/lifestyle/super-parent-pressure-taking -mental-health-toll-research-shows-1.2003955.

14. Kendra Cherry, "The 4 Styles of Parenting," About.com Health, October 12, 2014, http://psychology.about.com/od/developmental psychology/a/parenting-style.htm.

15. IU News Room, Indiana University, "'Helicopter Parents' Stir Up Anxiety, Depression," newsinfo.iu.edu/web/page/normal/6073.html, accessed September 27, 2017.

CHAPTER THREE: Know Your Child

1. Macrina Cooper-White, "Nature or Nurture? The Long-Running Debate May Finally Be Settled," Huffington Post, May 29, 2015, http://www.huffingtonpost.com/2015/05/20/nature-nurture -debate-settled_n_7314120.html.

2. Alison Gopnik, Andrew N. Meltzoff, and Patricia K. Kuhl, *The Scientist in the Crib: What Early Learning Tells Us about the Mind* (New York: HarperPerennial, 2001), p. 1.

3. Harvey Karp and Paula Spencer, *The Happiest Toddler on the Block: How to Eliminate Tantrums and Raise a Patient, Respectful and Cooperative One- to Four-Year-Old* (New York: Bantam Books, 2008).

4. Priyanka Pulla, "Why Do Humans Grow Up So Slowly? Blame the Brain," *Science*, August 25, 2014, http://www.sciencemag.org /news/2014/08/why-do-humans-grow-so-slowly-blame-brain.

5. The downside of this slower process of myelination is that human beings are more vulnerable during youth and adolescence to emotional and psychiatric disorders, including depression and schizophrenia, which are also more common in humans.

6. Ethan Remmel, "The Benefits of a Long Childhood," *American Scientist*, May–June 2008, http://www.americanscientist.org /bookshelf/pub/the-benefits-of-a-long-childhood.

7. Saul McLeod, "Jean Piaget," *Simply Psychology*, http://www.simply psychology.org/piaget.html#stages, accessed April 18, 2016.

8. Other theories and models address different aspects of children's development. For example, Erik Erikson argued that there are five stages, each built around a core tension: *trust vs. mistrust* (birth to age one), figuring out whom you can rely on to take care of you; *autonomy vs. shame and doubt* (early childhood), beginning to make simple decisions and gain some control over one's body and environment; *initiative vs. guilt* (preschool years), experimenting with and developing a sense of leadership of taking charge of one's conditions while learning the importance of working with others; *industry vs. inferiority* (ages five through eleven), developing a sense of accomplishment and pride in accomplishment; and *identity vs. confusion* (adolescence), developing a sense of self and independence while learning to live in a social structure.

9. Fritha Keith, "10 Modern Cases of Feral Children," Listverse, March 7, 2008, http://listverse.com/2008/03/07/10-modern-cases -of-feral-children/; Dainius, "Shocking Real Stories of Feral Children Told with Dark Photos," BoredPanda, http://www.bored panda.com/feral-children-wild-animals-photos-julia-fullerton -batten, accessed April 19, 2016.

10. Kitty Stewart and Kerris Cooper, "Does Money Affect Children's Outcomes? A Review of Evidence on Casual Links," UNICEF, November 2013, http://www.unicef.org/socialpolicy/files/CPI_ October_2013.pdf.

11. Lawrence M. Berger, Christina Paxson, and Jane Waldfogel, "Income and Child Development," Science Direct, September 2009,

http://www.sciencedirect.com/science/article/pii/S019074090
9001108.

12. There are also twenty-four known disorders of sexual development (DSDs). Intersex people have XX and XY chromosomes and both testicular and ovarian tissue. Some DSDs are rare: some are as common as twins. In cities like London or New York, an estimated 100,000 people may have DSDs of some sort.

13. "Understanding Gender," Gender Spectrum, https://www.gender spectrum.org/quick-links/understanding-gender.

14. Alice Robb, "How Gender-Specific Toys Can Negatively Impact a Child's Development," *New York Times*, August 12, 2015, http://nytlive.nytimes.com/womenintheworld/2015/08/12/how-gender-specific-toys-can-negatively-impact-a-childs-development.

15. Thomas Armstrong, *Awakening Genius in the Classroom* (Alexandria, VA: Association for Supervision and Curriculum Development, 1998).

16. "The Components of MI," Multiple Intelligences Oasis, http://multipleintelligencesoasis.org/about/the-components-of-mi, accessed April 27, 2016.

17. "Intelligence—Triarchic Theory of Intelligence," StateUniversity .com, http://education.stateuniversity.com/pages/2104/Intelligence -TRIARCHIC-THEORY-INTELLIGENCE.html, accessed April 27, 2016.

CHAPTER FOUR: Raise Them Strong

1. Sharon Jayson, "Teens Feeling Stressed, and Many Not Managing It Well," *USA Today*, February 11, 2014, http://www.usatoday.com/story/news/nation/2014/02/11/stress-teens-psychological/5266739.

2. "Promoting Children's Mental Health," American Academy of Pediatrics, https://www.aap.org/en-us/advocacy-and-policy/federal-advocacy/pages/mentalhealth.aspx, accessed June 2, 2016.

3. Public Relations Staff, "APA Stress Survey: Children Are More Stressed Than Parents Realize," APA Practice Organization, November 23, 2009, http://www.apapracticecentral.org/update/2009/11-23/stress-survey.aspx.

4. We had cell phones before then, but they weren't smart. Most of us didn't even have cell phones until the late 1990s.

5. "The Top 20 Valuable Facebook Statistics—Updated August 2017," Zephoria Digital Marketing, August 1, 2017, https://zephoria.com /top-15-valuable-facebook-statistics.

6. In 2016, video games were estimated to be a $99.6 billion industry, and growing. See Mike Minotti, "Video Games Will Become a $99.6B Industry This Year as Mobile Overtakes Consoles and PCs," Venture Beat, https://venturebeat.com/2016/04/21/video-games -will-become-a-99-6b-industry-this-year-as-mobile-overtakes -consoles-and-pcs.

7. Christopher Bergland, "Social Media Exacerbates Perceived Social Isolation," *Psychology Today*, March 7, 2017, http://www .psychologytoday.com/blog/the-athletes-way/201703/social-media -exacerbates-perceived-social-isolation. The team questioned 1,787 adults ages nineteen to thirty-two about their use of the eleven most popular social media platforms at the time the research was conducted in 2014: Facebook, YouTube, Twitter, Google Plus, Instagram, Snapchat, Reddit, Tumblr, Pinterest, Vine, and Linked-In. See David Hopper, "Brian Primack, University of Pittsburgh— Social Media and Depression," *Academic Minute*, May 18, 2016, https://academicminute.org/2016/05/brian-primack-university-of -pittsburgh-social-media-and-depression/. Participants in the study who visited social media sites fifty-eight or more times per week had three times the risk of isolation of those who visited fewer than nine times per week. The link with isolation was found even after taking account of social and demographic factors that might have influenced the results. Coauthor Elizabeth Miller, professor of pediatrics at the University of Pittsburgh, said: "We do not yet know which came first—the social media use or the perceived social isolation. It's possible that young adults who initially felt socially isolated turned to social media. It could be that their increased use of social media somehow led to feeling isolated from the real world. It also could be a combination of both. But even if the social isolation came first, it did not seem to be alleviated by spending time online, even in purportedly social situations." "Social Media Is Increasing Loneliness among Adults, Say Psychologists," HuffPost United Kingdom,

June 3, 2017, http://www.huffingtonpost.co.uk/entry/social-media -making-adults-feel-lonely-study_uk_58bd26c9e4b05cf0f4016e11.

8. "How Technology Is Changing the Way Children Think and Focus," *Psychology Today*, December 4, 2012, https://www.psychologytoday.com/blog/the-power-prime/201212/how-technology-is -changing-the-way-children-think-and-focus.

9. Cris Rowan, "The Impact of Technology on the Developing Child," Huffington Post, May 29, 2013, http://www.huffingtonpost.com /cris-rowan/technology-children-negative-impact_b_3343245.html.

10. "Childhood Obesity Facts," Centers for Disease Control and Prevention, August 27, 2015, http://www.cdc.gov/healthyschools/obesity /facts.htm.

11. Rowan, "The Impact of Technology on the Developing Child."

12. "Drug Use Hurts Families," National Institute on Drug Abuse, https://easyread.drugabuse.gov/content/drug-use-hurts-families, accessed March 31, 2017.

13. PersilUK, "Free the Kids—Dirt Is Good," YouTube, March 21, 2016, https://www.youtube.com/watch?v=8Q2WnCkBTw0.

14. "The Decline of Walking and Bicycling," Saferoutesinfo.org, http:// guide.saferoutesinfo.org/introduction/the_decline_of_walking _and_bicycling.cfm, accessed August 1, 2016.

15. David Finkelhor, "Trends in Children's Exposure to Violence, 2003 to 2011," *JAMA Pediatrics* 168, no. 6 (2014): 540. Of fifty crime trends studied, there were twenty-seven significant declines and no significant increases between 2003 and 2011. The site Free-Range Kids recently posted the following: Crime is back to the level it was when gas cost 29 cents a gallon and before color TV; pedestrian, bicyclist, and car deaths at lowest rate in decades.

16. Lisa Firestone, PhD, "7 Tips to Raising an Emotionally Healthy Child," *Psychology Today*, November 20, 2012, https://www.psychologytoday.com/blog/compassion-matters/201211/7-tips-raising-emotionally-healthy-child.

17. Victoria Tennant, "The Powerful Impact of Stress," School of Education at Johns Hopkins University, September 2005, http:// archive.education.jhu.edu/PD/newhorizons/strategies/topics /Keeping%20Fit%20for%20Learning/stress.html. She goes on: "High levels of the major stress hormone, cortisol, can depress the

immune system and have even been implicated in the incidences of AIDS, MS, diabetes, cancer, coronary artery disease, Alzheimer's disease, and Parkinson's disease."

18. Melissa Cohen, "Student Guide to Surviving Stress and Anxiety in College & Beyond," LearnPsychology, http://www.learnpsychol ogy.org/student-stress-anxiety-guide, accessed May 12, 2017.

19. "Identifying Signs of Stress in Your Children and Teens," American Psychological Association, http://www.apa.org/helpcenter/stress -children.aspx, accessed November 22, 2016.

20. Matthew Walker, *Why We Sleep: Unlocking the Power of Sleep and Dreams* (New York: Scribner, 2017).

21. Ibid.

22. Arianna Huffington, *The Sleep Revolution: Transforming Your Life One Night at a Time* (New York: Harmony Books, 2016), p. 20.

23. The books by Matthew Walker and Arianna Huffington both have excellent practical guidelines on how to do this, for you and your children. Both are highly recommended. See also http://www .thrive.com.

24. "Report of the Commission on Ending Childhood Obesity," World Health Organization, 2016, http://apps.who.int/iris/bitstream /10665/204176/1/9789241510066_eng.pdf, accessed October 30, 2017.

25. John J. Ratey, *Spark: The Revolutionary New Science of Exercise and the Brain* (New York: Little, Brown, 2008), p. 3.

26. He continues, "They bear names such as insulin-like growth factor (IGF-1) and vascular endothelial growth factor (VEGF), and they provide an unprecedented view of the mind-body connection. There's still much we don't understand about what happens in the microenvironment of the brain, but I think what we do know can change people's lives. And maybe society itself."

27. Ratey, *Spark*, p. 5.

28. "A Conversation with Dr. Alison Gopnik," National Association for the Education of Young Children, http://www.naeyc.org/files/tyc /file/TYC_V3N2_Gopnik.pdf, accessed June 2, 2016.

29. Richard Louv, *Last Child in the Woods: Saving Our Children from Nature-Deficit Disorder* (Chapel Hill, NC: Algonquin, 2005), p. 3.

30. Alan Henry, "Surround Yourself with Nature to Boost Your Productivity," Lifehacker, January 16, 2012, http://lifehacker.com/5876390/surround-yourself-with-nature-to-boost-your-productivity.

31. Tim Smedley, "Swings, Slides and iPads: The Gaming Companies Targeting Kids' Outdoor Play," *The Guardian*, April 11, 2016, http://www.theguardian.com/sustainable-business/2016/apr/11/ipads-playground-gaming-companies-targeting-kids-outdoor-play.

32. Gever Tulley and Julie Spiegler, *50 Dangerous Things (You Should Let Your Children Do)* (New York: New American Library, 2011), p. xv.

33. Angela Lee Duckworth, "Transcript of 'Grit: The Power of Passion and Perseverance,'" TED, April 2014, https://www.ted.com/talks/angela_lee_duckworth_grit_the_power_of_passion_and_perseverance/transcript?language=en.

34. "Six Declines of Modern Youth—Kurt Hahn," *Wilderdom*, August 30, 2004, http://www.wilderdom.com/sixdeclinesofmodernyouth.html.

35. "Four Antidotes to the Declines of Modern Youth—Kurt Hahn," Wilderdom, March 10, 2007, http://www.wilderdom.com/fourantidotes.html.

36. "Philosophy," Outward Bound International, http://www.outwardbound.net/about-us/philosophy, accessed August 3, 2016.

CHAPTER FIVE: Understand What School Is For

1. For details, see Mark Muro, "Manufacturing Jobs Aren't Coming Back," *MIT Technology Review*, November 18, 2016, https://www.technologyreview.com/s/602869/manufacturing-jobs-arent-coming-back.

2. Youth and children together—that is, everyone age twenty-four and younger—account for nearly 40 percent of the world's population.

3. Mark Phillips, "Why We Need Vocational Education," *Washington Post*, June 5, 2012, https://www.washingtonpost.com/blogs/answer-sheet/post/why-we-need-vocational-education/2012/06/04/gJQA8jHbEV_blog.html.

4. They include: the Hammer Museum at UCLA, Skirball Cultural Center, L.A. Central Library and Readers of Homer, Project 51's Play the River initiative, the Chinese American Museum, the California African American Museum, the GRAMMY Museum, and UCLA Art and Global Health Center.

5. In addition to artworxLA Level 1 workshops at his school for three years, he participated in eleven-week art residencies at Art Center College of Design and Street Poets (Level 2). Through the artworxLA scholarship program (Level 3), he completed the GRAMMY Museum's weeklong GRAMMY Summer Sessions program in 2014, and in the summer of 2015, he explored sculpture and crafts-building at UCLA.

6. U.S. colleges normally look for the following: math, three to four years (algebra, geometry, calculus); English, four years (composition, literature, speech); social sciences, three to four years (history, sociology, psychology, political science, geography, economics); science, three years (biology, chemistry, physics, Earth science).

7. Grace Fleming, "What Are Core Academic Classes?" ThoughtCo, March 11, 2016, https://www.thoughtco.com/what-are-core-academic-classes-1857192.

8. For a detailed look at creativity and how it works, see my book *Out of Our Minds: The Power of Being Creative* (Hoboken, NJ: Wiley, 2017).

9. There is a growing interest in and literature about critical thinking. For a good starting point, see Edward M. Glaser, *An Experiment in the Development of Critical Thinking* (New York: Teacher's College, Columbia University, 1941).

10. Ken Robinson with Lou Aronica, *Finding Your Element: How to Discover Your Talents and Passions and Transform Your Life* (New York: Viking, 2014).

11. Martin Seligman, *Flourish: A Visionary New Understanding of Happiness and Well-Being* (New York: Free Press, 2011).

12. Ibid.

13. Tom Rath, *Well Being: The Five Essential Elements* (New York: Gallup Press, 2011). Kindle, loc. 60–65/1997.

14. Ibid., Kindle, loc. 78/1997.

15. Ibid., Kindle, loc. 138/1997.

16. Sonja Lyubomirsky, *The How of Happiness* (New York: Penguin, 2008), p. 21.

17. Ibid.

18. Matthieu Ricard, *Happiness: A Guide to Developing Life's Most Important Skill* (New York: Little, Brown, 2007), p. 7.

CHAPTER SIX: Choose the Right School

1. For some practical examples, see *Creative Schools* and especially the examples of Grange Elementary School in England and Room 13 in Scotland.

2. See, for example, *Arts Eduaction Data Project, California Executive Summary Report*, Quadrant Research, October 2016, http://www .createca.dreamhosters.com/wp-content/uploads/2016/09/California -Data-Project-Executive-Summary-Report1.pdf.

3. My talk, "Do Schools Kill Creativity?," has since been viewed online over forty-seven million times in 150 countries and is the most viewed talk in the history of TED. Clearly the message resonates. Although I mention the arts, the talk is not specifically about them: it's about education as a whole and the need for more creative approaches to teaching and learning in all disciplines. The response to the talk confirmed that people in many fields—including the arts, science, technology, math, public life, and business—are just as concerned that public policies have been taking education down the wrong path and that it's essential, for the sake of our children and our communities, that we change course. If you're interested, the video of the full talk is on YouTube: https://www.youtube.com/watch?v=5oNrxHX5GKU.

4. In the United Kingdom, *mathematics* is shortened to the plural *maths*, not the singular *math*, as in the United States. Go figure, as they say.

5. Charlotte Svendler Nielsen and Stephanie Burridge, *Dance Education around the World: Perspectives on Dance, Young People and Change* (New York: Routledge, 2015).

6. According to a two-year evaluation of the program in New York City by Rob Horowitz, associate director of the Center for Arts Education Research at Columbia University's Teachers' College. For more on this and on Dancing Classrooms, see Audrey Cleo Yap, "Learning Empathy through Dance," *The Atlantic*, January 22, 2016, https:// www.theatlantic.com/education/archive/2016/01/learning-empathy -through-dance/426498/. Dancing Classrooms was also featured in the 2005 documentary *Mad Hot Ballroom*.

7. "Dancing Principals Special Edition—Toni Walker, Lehigh Elementary, Lee County, FL," Dancing Classrooms, April 25, 2014, http://www.dancingclassrooms.org/principalspotlight.

8. "Dancing Principals—Antwan Allen, St. Mark the Evangelist School, Harlem, NY," Dancing Classrooms, February 19, 2013, http://www.dancingclassrooms.org/principalspotlight.

9. "Principal Spotlight," Dancing Classrooms, http://www.dancing classrooms.org/principalspotlight.

10. John J. Ratey, *Spark: The Revolutionary New Science of Exercise and the Brain* (New York: Little, Brown, 2013), p. 8.

11. As Ratey notes, Naperville 203 is a demographically advantaged school district: "83 percent white, with only 2.6 percent in the low income range, compared with 40 percent in that range for Illinois as a whole. Its two high schools boast a 97 percent graduation rate. And the town's major employers are science-centric companies such as Argonne, Fermilab, and Lucent Technologies, which suggests that the parents of many Naperville kids are highly educated. The deck—in terms of both environment and genetics—is stacked in Naperville's favor."

12. Ratey, *Spark*, p. 15.

13. Ibid.

14. Ibid., p. 22.

15. *A Review of State and Regional Arts Education Studies* report prepared for Americans for the Arts by Yael Z. Silk, EdM, and Stacey Mahan, EdM, of Silk Strategic Arts LLC and Robert Morrison of Quadrant Research, May 2015, http://www.americansforthearts.org/sites/default/files/State_Status_Report_Final.pdf. For further details, see http://www.quadrantresearch.org/group-list/priorresearch.

16. Maryellen Weimer, PhD, "Five Things Students Can Learn through Group Work," Magna: Faculty Focus, March 15, 2017, https://www.facultyfocus.com/articles/teaching-professor-blog/five-things-students-can-learn-through-group-work.

17. Lilian G. Katz, "The Benefits of Mixed-Age Grouping," *ERIC Digests* (May 1995): 1–6, http://files.eric.ed.gov/fulltext/ED382411.pdf.

18. There are several examples in *Creative Schools*. A quick Internet search will show many more.

19. "Eric Schaps," Aspen Institute, https://www.aspeninstitute.org/our-people/eric-schaps, accessed October 31, 2016.

20. Eric Schaps, "Creating a School Community," *Educational Leadership* 60, no. 6 (March 2003): 31–33, http://www.ascd.org/publications

/educational-leadership/mar03/vol60/num06/Creating-a-School
-Community.aspx.

21. For more information, see http://www.educationrevolution.org.

22. Jerry Mintz, *School's Over: How to Have Freedom and Democracy in Education* (Roslyn Heights, NY: Alternative Education Resource Organization, 2017).

23. For more on this movement, see the Institute for Democratic Education at http://www.democratic.co.il/en/local-municipalities.

24. If you're considering homeschooling, *Parents* magazine has a useful resource guide at http://www.parents.com/kids/education/home -schooling/best-homeschooling-resources-online.

25. Bridget Bentz Sizer, "Unschooling 101," PBS, http://www.pbs.org /parents/education/homeschooling/unschooling-101, accessed December 8, 2016.

26. Some states make it much tougher to unschool than others. If you're thinking about this for your child, you'll want to check for any local guidelines and restrictions.

27. Earl Stevens, "What Is Unschooling?," The Natural Child Project, http://www.naturalchild.org/guest/earl_stevens.html, accessed December 8, 2016.

28. Luba Vangelova, "How Do Unschoolers Turn Out?" MindShift, September 2, 2014, https://ww2.kqed.org/mindshift/2014/09/02 /how-do-unschoolers-turn-out. The public television and radio station KQED has compiled a list of homeschooling and unschooling resources at https://ww2.kqed.org/mindshift/2014/06/17/guide-to -the-best-homeschooling-and-unschooling-resources.

29. Ken Robinson with Lou Aronica, *Creative Schools: The Grassroots Revolution That's Transforming Education* (New York: Penguin, 2015), p. 254.

30. For more information, see "What Is Steiner Education?" at http:// www.steinerwaldorf.org/steiner-education/what-is-steiner-education.

31. For more information, see http://www.summerhillschool.co.uk /about.php.

CHAPTER SEVEN: Go to the Source

1. Alistair Smith, *High Performers: The Secrets of Successful Schools* (Carmarthen, Wales: Crown, 2011).

2. Sarah M. Fine, "A Slow Revolution: Toward a Theory of Intellectual Playfulness in High School Classrooms," *Harvard Educational Review* 84, no. 1 (2014): 1–23.

3. Judy Willis, *Research-Based Strategies to Ignite Student Learning: Insights from a Neurologist and Classroom Teacher* (Alexandria, VA: Association for Supervision and Curriculum Development, 2006).

4. Christopher Emdin, "Transcript of 'Teach Teachers How to Create Magic,'" TED, October 2013, http://www.ted.com/talks/christopher _emdin_teach_teachers_how_to_create_magic/transcript? language=en. He is the founder of Science Genius B.A.T.T.L.E.S. (Bring Attention to Transforming Teaching, Learning and Engagement in Science), which shows how to bring the tools of hip-hop into classrooms.

5. William Kremer, "Does Confidence Really Breed Success?" *BBC News*, January 4, 2013, http://www.bbc.com/news/magazine-2075 6247, accessed October 30, 2017.

6. "Overview," Building Learning Power, https://www.buildinglearn ingpower.com/about/, accessed June 20, 2017.

7. Anthony F. Grasha, "A Matter of Style: The Teacher as Expert, Formal Authority, Personal Model, Facilitator, and Delegator," *College Teaching* 42, no. 4 (1994): 143, http://www.jstor.org/stable/2755 8675?origin=JSTOR-pdf.

8. Pasi Sahlberg, "Q: What Makes Finnish Teachers So Special? A: It's Not Brains," *The Guardian*, March 31, 2015, https://www.theguard ian.com/education/2015/mar/31/finnish-teachers-special-train-teach.

9. Ibid.

10. Amanda Ripley, "What Makes a Great Teacher," *The Atlantic*, January–February 2010, http://www.theatlantic.com/magazine/ar chive/2010/01/what-makes-a-great-teacher/307841.

11. Ibid.

12. Edcamp's success at empowering educators has been recognized by numerous organizations, including the U.S. Department of Education, the Association for Supervision and Curriculum Development (ASCD), TED Talks, and the Bill and Melinda Gates Foundation. More importantly, it has resonated and found a great following among its core constituency: educators dedicated to improving their practice, the field, and student learning. For more information, see http://www.edcamp.org.

13. Anthony S. Bryk, Penny Bender Sebring, Elaine Allensworth, Stuart Luppescu, and John Q. Easton, "Organizing Schools for Improvement: Lessons from Chicago," Urban Education Institute, University of Chicago, January 2010, https://consortium.uchicago .edu/publications/organizing-schools-improvement-lessons-chicago.

14. Anne T. Henderson, Karen L. Mapp, and Amy Averett, *A New Wave of Evidence: The Impact of School, Family, and Community Connections on Student Achievement* (Austin, TX: National Center for Family and Community Connections with Schools, 2002).

15. Alfie Kohn, *The Homework Myth: Why Our Kids Get Too Much of a Bad Thing* (Cambridge, MA: Da Capo Press, 2008).

16. The online survey of more than one thousand full-time K–12 teachers in the United States was conducted on behalf of University of Phoenix College of Education by Harris Poll. See http://www .phoenix.edu/news/releases/2014/02/survey-reveals-how -much-homework-k-12-students-are-assigned-why-teachers -deem-it-beneficial.html.

17. National Center for Education Statistics, "Table 35: Average Hours Spent on Homework per Week and Percentage of 9th- through 12th- Grade Students Who Did Homework outside of School and Whose Parents Checked That Homework Was Done, by Frequency of Doing Homework and Race/Ethnicity: 2007," http://nces.ed.gov/pubs 2012/2012026/tables/table_35.asp, accessed September 6, 2017.

18. National Center for Education Statistics, "NAEP 1994 Trends in Academic Progress," November 1996, https://nces.ed.gov/nations reportcard//pdf/main1994/97095a.pdf.

19. University of Phoenix, "Homework Anxiety: Survey Reveals How Much Homework K-12 Students Are Assigned and Why Teachers Deem It Beneficial," news release, February 25, 2014, http://www .phoenix.edu/news/releases/2014/02/survey-reveals-how-much -homework-k-12-students-are-assigned-why-teachers -deem-it-beneficial.html.

20. Allie Bidwell, "Students Spend More Time on Homework but Teachers Say It's Worth It," *U.S. News & World Report*, February 27, 2014, https://www.usnews.com/news/articles/2014/02/27/students -spend-more-time-on-homework-but-teachers-say-its-worth-it.

21. Harris Cooper, Jorgianne Civey Robinson, and Erika A. Patall, "Does Homework Improve Academic Achievement? A Synthesis of

Research, 1987–2003," *Review of Educational Research* 76 no. 1 (2006): 1–62.

22. Duke Today, "Duke Study: Homework Helps Students Succeed in School, as Long as There Isn't Too Much," news release, March 7, 2006, https://today.duke.edu/2006/03/homework.html.

23. Cooper acknowledges many limitations in current research on homework. For example, little research has been done on whether race, socioeconomic status, or ability level affects the importance of homework in students' achievement.

24. Duke Today, "Duke Study."

25. Katie Reilly, "Is Homework Good for Kids? Here's what the Research Says," *Time*, August 30, 2016, http://time.com/4466390/homework-debate-research.

26. Maureen Healy, "New Trend: No Homework for Elementary Students," *Psychology Today*, August 1, 2017, https://www.psychologytoday.com/blog/creative-development/201708/new-trend-no-homework-elementary-students.

27. Valerie Strauss, "What Happened When One School Banned Homework—And Asked Kids to Read and Play Instead," *Washington Post*, February 26, 2017, https://www.washingtonpost.com/news/answer-sheet/wp/2017/02/26/what-happened-when-one-school-banned-homework-and-asked-kids-to-read-and-play-instead/?utm%5fterm=.bce0129859e4.

28. Healy, "New Trend: No Homework for Elementary Students."

29. Patrick F. Bassett, "When Parents and Schools Align," *Independent School*, Winter 2009, http://www.nais.org/Magazines-Newsletters/ISMagazine/Pages/When-Parents-and-Schools-Align.aspx.

CHAPTER EIGHT: Build the Relationship

1. Allan Ahlberg, *Collected Poems* (London: Puffin, 2008).

2. You can learn more about Blackboard Learn at http://www.blackboard.com/learning-management-system/blackboard-learn.aspx. Information about Edmodo can be found at https://www.edmodo.com. For more about Fresh Grade, go to https://www.freshgrade.com.

3. Richard's work was featured in *The Element*. He is now an author, speaker, and advisor in education and corporate development. See http://www.richardgerver.com.

4. Lisa Capretto, "38 Easy Ways to Get Involved in the Classroom," Oprah.com, June 18, 2010, http://www.oprah.com/relationships /38-Ways-for-Parents-to-Get-Involved-in-the-Classroom -Back-to-School.

5. Marian Wilde, "Real-Life Stories about Improving Schools," Great Schools, April 2, 2015, http://www.greatschools.org/gk/articles /improving-schools.

6. Jo Ashline, "5 Reasons You Should Volunteer at Your Child's School," *Orange County Register*, October 15, 2012, http://www .ocregister.com/articles/child-374635-reasons-volunteer.html.

7. "National Standards for Family-School Partnerships: E-Learning Course Notes," PTA.org, September 2014, http://www2.pta.org /NewNationalStandards/story_content/external_files/National %20Standards%20Course%20Notes%20(v1.0).pdf.

8. Otha Thornton, "Families: An Essential Ingredient for Student Success and Excellent Schools," Huffington Post, April 29, 2014, http:// www.huffingtonpost.com/otha-thornton/families-an-essential-ing_b_5232446.html.

9. "Home-to-School Connections Guide," Edutopia, http://www .edutopia.org/home-to-school-connections-resource-guide, accessed September 3, 2017.

10. If you think this is something you might want to do, you can learn more about how to run for school board in your state by going to https://www.nsba.org/services/state-association-services.

11. Allyson Criner Brown, personal communication, October 5, 2016.

12. Ibid.

13. Ibid.

14. For more on this and related initiatives, see President's Committee on the Arts and Humanities, 2015, *Turnaround Arts, Summary of Key Findings,* https://pcah.gov/sites/default/files/Turnaround%20 Arts%20phase%201%20Final%20Evaluation_Summary.pdf.

15. For more on Orchard Gardens, see http://orchardgardensk8.org /about/a-message-from-principal-megan-webb/. See also http://www .huffingtonpost.com/2013/05/02/orchard-gardens-andrew-bott _n_3202426.html.

16. For many others, see *Creative Schools*.

17. Valerie Strauss, "Concrete Victories Won by the Anti-Testing Movement (So Far)," *Washington Post*, November 17, 2015, https://www.washingtonpost.com/news/answer-sheet/wp/2015/11/17/concrete-victories-won-by-the-anti-testing-movement-so-far.

18. "What We Believe," Parents Across America, July 5, 2016, http://parentsacrossamerica.org/what-we-believe-2.

19. "Advocacy," Center for Education Reform, https://www.edreform.com/issues/choice-charter-schools/advocacy, accessed November 29, 2016.

20. "School Transformation," Parent Revolution, http://parentrevolution.org/school-transformation, accessed November 29, 2016.

CHAPTER NINE: Tackle the Problem

1. Michelle Crouch, "22 Things Your Kid's Principal Won't Tell You," *Reader's Digest*, http://www.rd.com/advice/parenting/13-things-your-kids-principal-wont-tell-you, accessed September 13, 2016.

2. "Services," Momentous School, Momentous Institute, http://momentousinstitute.org/services/momentous-school.

3. Ibid.

4. Carolyn Gregoire, "School Stress: 8 Awesome Ways High Schools Are Helping Students Unplug & Recharge," Huffington Post, March 4, 2013, http://www.huffingtonpost.com/2013/03/04/school-stress-8-awesome-w_n_2806869.html.

5. "The Unforgettable Amanda Todd Story," NoBullying.com, May 19, 2017, https://nobullying.com/amanda-todd-story.

6. "School Bullying," NoBullying.com, October 13, 2016, https://nobullying.com/school-bullying.

7. "Facts about Bullying," StopBullying.gov, October 14, 2014, https://www.stopbullying.gov/news/media/facts/#listing.

8. "Designing Effective Bullying Prevention Response," NoBullying.com, December 22, 2015, https://nobullying.com/designing-effective-bullying-prevention-response.

9. "Facts about Bullying," StopBullying.gov.

10. Mary L. Pulido, Ph.D, "My Child Is the Bully: Tips for Parents," Huffington Post, April 19, 2012, http://www.huffingtonpost.com/mary-l-pulido-phd/bullying_b_1435791.html.

11. Ibid.

12. The first version (DSM-1) was published in 1952, and it's been revised periodically since then. The first two editions didn't include ADHD as a recognized condition. DSM-2 was published in 1968 and referred to *hyperkinetic reaction of childhood*. It wasn't until DSM-3 in 1980 that the term *attention-deficit disorder* (ADD) first appeared. Subsequent editions, including the most recent, DSM-5, went on to use the term *ADHD*.

13. Ritalin acts by stimulating the central nervous system and increasing the concentration of dopamine in the brain. It was approved by the U.S. Food and Drug Administration as a treatment for hyperactivity in the mid-1950s. Adderall is an amphetamine, similar to Benzedrine, and has been available as a brand since 1996.

14. Martine Hoogman et al., "Subcortical Brain Volume Differences in Participants with Attention Deficit Hyperactivity Disorder in Children and Adults: A Cross-Sectional Mega-Analysis," *The Lancet* 4, no. 4 (April 2017): 310–319, http://www.thelancet.com/pdfs/journals/lanpsy/PIIS2215-0366(17)30049-4.pdf. A team of neuroscientists analyzed brain scans of more than 3,200 people between ages four and sixty-three (with a median age of fourteen). They measured total brain volume as well as the volume of seven brain regions thought to be linked to ADHD. Roughly half of the participants had a diagnosis of ADHD.

15. "Myth #1: ADHD Is Not a Real Disorder," CHADD, http://www.chadd.org/understanding-adhd/about-adhd/myths-and-misunderstandings.aspx#myth1, accessed September 3, 2017.

16. Richard Saul, "ADHD Does Not Exist, Writes Dr. Richard Saul," *Time*, March 14, 2014, http://time.com/25370/doctor-adhd-does-not-exist.

17. Whereas just 2.8 percent of boys born in September have the condition, the figure jumps to 4.5 percent in August, rising steadily over the school year. For girls it rose from 0.7 percent to 1.2 percent. The authors conclude that relative age may play a role in being diagnosed with ADHD and receiving medication among children and adolescents. They recognize that the issue is not as simple as assuming that age always influences ADHD symptoms, "as we do see a significant number of adults presenting to psychiatric services for the first time with symptoms of ADHD. . . . Our findings

emphasize the importance of considering the age of a child within a grade when diagnosing ADHD." Sarah Knapton, "ADHD Is Vastly Overdiagnosed and Many Children Are Just Immature, Say Scientists," *The Telegraph*, March 10, 2016, http://www.telegraph .co.uk/news/science/science-news/12189369/ADHD-is-vastly -overdiagnosed-and-many-children-are-just-immature-say -scientists.html.

18. Report by market research firm IBIS World: https://www.ibis world.com/industry-trends/specialized-market-research-reports /life-sciences/prescription-drugs/adhd-medication-manufacturing .html.

19. See Luke Whelan, "Sales of ADHD Meds Are Skyrocketing. Here's Why," *Mother Jones*, February 24, 2015, http://www.motherjones .com/environment/2015/02/hyperactive-growth-adhd-medication -sales/; see also Stephen P. Hinshaw and Richard M. Scheffler, *The ADHD Explosion: Myths, Medication, Money, and Today's Push for Performance* (New York: Oxford University Press, 2014).

20. Alan Schwarz, "Still in a Crib, Yet Being Given Antipsychotics," *New York Times*, December 10, 2015, https://www.nytimes.com /2015/12/11/us/psychiatric-drugs-are-being-prescribed-to-infants .html?_r=0; Alan Schwarz, "Thousands of Toddlers Are Medicated for A.D.H.D., Report Finds, Raising Worries," *New York Times*, May 16, 2014, http://www.nytimes.com/2014/05/17/us/among -experts-scrutiny-of-attention-disorder-diagnoses-in-2-and-3-year -olds.html.

21. Daniel Boffey, "Children's Hyperactivity 'Is Not a Real Disease,' Says US Expert," *The Guardian*, March 30, 2014, https://www.the guardian.com/society/2014/mar/30/children-hyperactivity-not -real-disease-neuroscientist-adhd.

22. "The Reality of ADHD—CANDAL Researchers," IMH Blog (Nottingham), April 14, 2014, https://imhblog.wordpress.com/2014 /04/14/the-reality-of-adhd-candal-researchers.

CHAPTER TEN: Look to the Future

1. Ken Robinson with Lou Aronica, *Finding Your Element: How to Discover Your Talents and Passions and Transform Your Life* (New York: Viking, 2013).

2. Susan Newman, PhD, "How to Support and Nurture Your Child's Passions," *Psychology Today*, October 20, 2015, https://www.psychologytoday.com/blog/singletons/201510/how-support-and-nurture-your-childs-passions.

3. Valerie Frankel, "Help Your Kid Find Her Passion," *Good Housekeeping*, October 11, 2011, http://www.goodhousekeeping.com/life/parenting/tips/a18330/nurture-your-childs-interests.

4. Thomas Armstrong, PhD, "50 Ways to Bring Out Your Child's Best," American Institute for Learning and Human Development, http://www.institute4learning.com/articles/50_ways.php, accessed April 28, 2016.

5. The income gap is more than $17,500 a year in full-time salary for those aged between twenty-five and thirty-two. For early boomers in 1979, the gap was $9,690 (all dollars are adjusted). Danielle Kurtzleben, "Study: Income Gap Between Young College and High School Grads Widens," *U.S. News & World Report*, February 11, 2014, http://www.usnews.com/news/articles/2014/02/11/study-income-gap-between-young-college-and-high-school-grads-widens.

6. Jaison R. Abel and Richard Deitz, "Working as a Barista after College Is Not as Common as You Might Think," *Liberty Street Economics*, January 11, 2016, http://libertystreeteconomics.newyorkfed.org/2016/01/working-as-a-barista-after-college-is-not-as-common-as-you-might-think.html#.VpPCi_k4Fph.

7. Travis Mitchell, "Chart: See 20 Years of Tuition Growth at National Universities," *U.S. News & World Report*, July 29, 2015, http://www.usnews.com/education/best-colleges/paying-for-college/articles/2015/07/29/chart-see-20-years-of-tuition-growth-at-national-universities.

8. Jeffrey Sparshott, "Congratulations, Class of 2015. You're the Most Indebted Ever (for Now)," *Wall Street Journal*, May 8, 2015, http://blogs.wsj.com/economics/2015/05/08/congratulations-class-of-2015-youre-the-most-indebted-ever-for-now.

9. See *One in Seven*, a report of the Measure of America Project of the Social Sciences Research Council, http://www.measureofamerica.org. According to the report, "Of the twenty-five largest metropolitan areas, Boston and Minneapolis–St. Paul perform the best, with fewer than one in ten young people disconnected from

the worlds of school and work. In Phoenix, nearly one in five is disconnected. African Americans have the highest rate of youth disconnection, at 22.5 percent. In Pittsburgh, Seattle, Detroit, and Phoenix more than one in four African American young people are disconnected. Latinos have the second-highest national youth disconnection rate, at 18.5 percent. In Boston, New York, and Phoenix, more than one in five Latino young people are disconnected."

10. "A Multilateral Approach to Bridging the Global Skills Gap," *Cornell HR Review*, May 8, 2015, http://www.cornellhrreview.org/a -multilateral-approach-to-bridging-the-global-skills-gap.

11. "Table A. Job Openings, Hires, and Total Separations by Industry, Seasonally Adjusted," U.S. Bureau of Labor Statistics, November 8, 2016, http://www.bls.gov/news.release/jolts.a.htm.

12. Bob Morrison, personal correspondence, July 2017.

13. Patrick Gillespie, "America Has Near Record 5.6 Million Job Openings," CNNMoney, February 9, 2016, http://money.cnn .com/2016/02/09/news/economy/america-5-6-million-record-job -openings.

14. "Report: Vocational Training Misses Mark in Many Countries," *U.S. News & World Report*, November 18, 2014, http://www.us news.com/news/articles/2014/11/18/report-vocational-training -misses-mark-in-many-countries.

15. "Our Story," Big Picture Learning, http://www.bigpicture.org /apps/pages/index.jsp?uREC_ID=389353&type=d&pREC_ID =882353, accessed September 14, 2017.

16. Jillian Gordon, "Why I'm Telling Some of My Students Not to Go to College," *PBS Newshour*, PBS, April 15, 2015, http://www.pbs .org/newshour/updates/im-telling-students-go-college.

17. "Frequently Asked Questions," Association for Career & Technical Education, https://www.acteonline.org/general.aspx?id=2733#many _cte, accessed December 1, 2016.

18. An extensive listing of trade schools is available at http://www.rwm .org, and the Department of Consumer Affairs lists the Bureau for Private Postsecondary Education's Approved Institutions at http:// www.bppe.ca.gov/schools/approved_schools.shtml.

19. The program started him at $28 an hour and then moved him up to $42 an hour once he gained the requisite skills. Apprenticeships are

often highly competitive and can be difficult to locate. The U.S. Department of Labor has an apprenticeship finder available at https://www.careeronestop.org/toolkit/training/find-apprentice ships.aspx.

20. Patrick Gillespie, "The $100,000 Job: Be an Apprentice and Bridge the Jobs Skills Gap," CNNMoney, October 2, 2015, http://money .cnn.com/2015/10/01/news/economy/america-job-skills-gap -apprentice/?iid=EL.

21. Mark Phillips, "Why Should We Care about Vocational Education?" Edutopia, May 29, 2012, https://www.edutopia.org/blog /vocational-education-benefits-mark-phillips.

22. Tom Duesterberg, "Austria's Successful Model for Vocational Education: Lessons for the US," *Aspen Institute*, October 1, 2013, https://www.aspeninstitute.org/blog-posts/austria-s-successful -model-vocational-education-lessons-us.

23. "Vocational Education and Training (VET)," Australian Bureau of Statistics, May 24, 2012, http://www.abs.gov.au/ausstats/abs@ .nsf/Lookup/by%20Subject/1301.0~2012~Main%20Features ~Vocational%20education%20and%20training%20(VET)~106.

24. Gabriel Sanchez Zinny, "Vocational Education and Training: The Australian Model," Huffington Post, June 28, 2016, http://www .huffingtonpost.com/gabriel-sanchez-zinny/vocational-education -and-_b_10587444.html.

25. Donna M. De Carolis, "We Are All Entrepreneurs: It's a Mindset, Not a Business Model," *Forbes*, January 9, 2014, http://www.forbes .com/sites/forbeswomanfiles/2014/01/09/we-are-all-entrepreneurs -its-a-mindset-not-a-business-model/#7d90bcc4cd16.

26. "Gap Year Data & Benefits," American Gap Association, 2015, http://americangap.org/data-benefits.php.

27. "The Princeton Gap Year Network: Our Stories," Princeton University, https://gapyear.princeton.edu/blurbs, accessed December 2, 2016.

28. Weezie Yancey-Siegel, "Taking a Gap Year to Get Ahead: 4 Alumni Share Their Stories," InformED, November 18, 2016, http://www .opencolleges.edu.au/informed/alternative-education/taking-a -gap-year-to-get-ahead-4-alums-share-their-stories.

29. Alex Gladu, "Taking a Gap Year before College: 3 Collegiette Success Stories," Her Campus, June 12, 2013, http://www.her

campus.com/high-school/taking-gap-year-college-3-collegiette
-success-stories?page=2.

30. You can learn about these at https://usagapyearfairs.org/programs.
The American Gap Association (http://www.americangap.org) can
also be a valuable resource for learning more about gap years.

Index